Hardt

THE AN

by RALPH STEPHENSON

$2.95/£1.10

WATKINS INSTITUTE

In the same series, produced by THE TANTIVY PRESS and edited by Peter Cowie:

THE MARX BROTHERS Their World of Comedy by Allen Eyles

FRENCH CINEMA SINCE 1946 (Vol. 1: The Great Tradition)
  (Vol. 2: The Personal Style) by Roy Armes

BUSTER KEATON by J. P. Lebel

THE ANIMATED FILM by Ralph Stephenson

HITCHCOCK'S FILMS by Robin Wood

HORROR IN THE CINEMA by Ivan Butler

THE CINEMA OF JOSEPH LOSEY by James Leahy

SUSPENSE IN THE CINEMA by Gordon Gow

THE CINEMA OF ALAIN RESNAIS by Roy Armes

4 GREAT COMEDIANS Chaplin, Lloyd,
  Keaton, Langdon by Donald W. McCaffrey

EARLY AMERICAN CINEMA by Anthony Slide

GRIFFITH & THE RISE OF HOLLYWOOD by Paul O'Dell

HOLLYWOOD IN THE TWENTIES by David Robinson

HOLLYWOOD IN THE THIRTIES by John Baxter

HOLLYWOOD IN THE FORTIES by Charles Higham and Joel Greenberg

HOLLYWOOD IN THE FIFTIES by Gordon Gow

HOLLYWOOD IN THE SIXTIES by John Baxter

HOLLYWOOD TODAY by Allen Eyles and Pat Billings

RELIGION IN THE CINEMA by Ivan Butler

THE CINEMA OF FRITZ LANG by Paul M. Jensen

THE CINEMA OF JOHN FRANKENHEIMER by Gerald Pratley

SCIENCE FICTION IN THE CINEMA by John Baxter

THE CINEMA OF ROMAN POLANSKI by Ivan Butler

THE CINEMA OF FRANCOIS TRUFFAUT by Graham Petrie

THE CINEMA OF CARL DREYER by Tom Milne

THE CINEMA OF OTTO PREMINGER by Gerald Pratley

THE CINEMA OF JOSEF VON STERNBERG by John Baxter

USTINOV IN FOCUS by Tony Thomas

THE CINEMA OF JOHN FORD by John Baxter

THE CINEMA OF LUIS BUNUEL by Freddy Buache

THE ANIMATED FILM

by Ralph Stephenson

THE INTERNATIONAL FILM GUIDE SERIES
THE TANTIVY PRESS, LONDON
A. S. BARNES & CO., NEW YORK

WATKINS INSTITUTE
LIBRARY

Author's Notes

This history is based generally on an earlier work, *Animation in the Cinema* (Zwemmer/Barnes, 1967) and much of the material is the same. However, the history has been brought up to date and extensively revised, new material has been added throughout, and the sections on computer animation, abstract animation and the influence of comics are fresh additions. While my opinions and viewpoint remain mostly the same, I have taken the opportunity in a few cases to revise them in the light of further knowledge or reassessment of the facts.

I should like to express my gratitude to those authors whose work I have consulted, to film-makers who have helped with information and stills, to Raymond Maillet of the Annecy and Grenoble Festivals and to the Information Department of the British Film Institute. In particular the assistance of the last-named has been invaluable.

R.S.

Cover designed by Amy Myers

FIRST PUBLISHED 1973

Copyright © Ralph Stephenson 1967, 1973
(Parts of this work appeared in *Animation in the Cinema,* by Ralph Stephenson, in 1967)
Library of Congress Catalogue Card Number: 72-178:
ISBN 0-498-01202-6 (U.S.)
SBN 90073059 5 (UK)

Printed in the United States of America

Contents

LABYRINTH, by Jan Lenica.

Picture on half title page is from FRITZ THE CAT

1. Animation, Characteristics and Definition

Animated films are usually considered a branch of the "live" cinema. But the connection between the two is rather a matter of historical accident than any necessary identity of structure.

The invention of the cinema took place gradually throughout the Nineteenth century, and the date of the first live picture-show is usually taken as December, 1895, when the Lumière brothers opened their cinema in the Boulevard des Capucines in Paris. Two adventitious features of this development are significant here. First it happened that the development of photography occurred over the same period, slightly preceding the recording of movement: the first black-and-white photo was produced in 1839, the first colour photo in 1861 and the first roll-film camera in 1888. Secondly, most of those connected with the invention of the cinema (Plateau, Muybridge, Marey, the Lumières, Edison) were scientists, for whom the cinema was a means of research, a way of spreading information, a living newspaper, a mirror of reality. Thus there was at the outset a purely coincidental combination of recorded movement with photographic realism.

The history of animation throws an interesting light on the invention and development of the cinema as a whole. As it does equally on the general relationship between hand-made and machine-made artistic products. A feature of the Nineteenth and Twentieth centuries has been the way in which society has come to terms with the machine. Here we are concerned with the artistic field, and a development of opinion which began by condemning machine-made products as ugly and inferior, and has finished by accepting as normal not only television and hi-fi but psychedelic designs and computer music.

What C. P. Snow has called the two cultures—the scientist, and engineer on the one hand, the painter, the poet, the pianist on the other—began with the Industrial Revolution and the withdrawal of the aesthete from the dirt and brutality of early industry. It did not exist in the time of Leonardo da Vinci or Roger Bacon or even Pepys and Evelyn who were diarists and musicians as well as being businessmen and scientists. If the illusion of movement had been invented earlier or later, there might have been an alliance between graphic art and the apparatus of kinema, which would have led to something different from the movie industry which actually evolved. For animation, unlike live-action film-making, has its roots in graphic or plastic art, since its images have been hand-made, their composition, their colour and their movement being created and controlled by the artist. It is because photography dominated the cinema that animated film-making has become tied to it, both in its technical processes of realisation and in its means of presentation in cinemas and on television.

When men first learned to show moving pictures, the pictures they showed were hand-drawn—simple, gaily-coloured clowns and columbines, dogs and hoops and sambos. It was simple art created by humble artists. The Rossettis, the Burne-Jones's, the Watts's and Whistlers had no part in it, and were no more likely than the Grand Academicians to meddle with the mere *mechanical*—a trick, a scientist's toy, beneath the dignity of a serious artist. In any case many of them were living in a romantic, pastoral past where there were no machines or factories or ugly towns. Thus the animated picture was left to the scientific dabblers, the men who made discoveries, often men on a lonely quest, eccentrics and out of the social swim. Consequently the early beginnings of animation were easily swept aside and forgotten when, at the end of the century, the movie cameras reached the point of capturing the movement of the world about us and flashing it on the screen. The artists were not interested in animation, the inventors themselves saw the cinema as a scientific tool of analysis and report in which hand-drawn pictures had no part, and the showmen were concerned with what could be most easily and cheaply put on the screen.

★　　★　　★

There were other reasons why live film-making went leaping ahead —its realism, its ease and its abundance. The ability to present the real world undoubtedly impressed audiences, and even carried over into the fictional world of drama and romance, making these seem more authentic. The abundant ease of live-action is of course simply a particular case of machine production which holds good generally. When a camera had been invented which took pictures automatically, there was no limit to the number of pictures which could be produced. Live-action film-making is largely an art of selection. A director can afford to shoot a scene several times, pick out the best one, and put the rest in the dustbin. For a documentary he can take ten hours of film, edit it down to one hour and throw away nine hours of unwanted material. Although the graphic artist may use trial and error especially in the early stages of his work, no such conspicuous waste is possible with hand animation. Again a photograph can as easily produce a detailed as a simple image—a charging herd of buffalo, a busy street comes as easily as a blank wall. Thus neither the breadth of canvas nor the length of live movies present problems of sheer labour. By contrast hand-made cartoons or puppet films have been slow, difficult and laborious in the making. Profusion of material is only possible with large man-power or over a long period, and a feature-length cartoon has always been a major undertaking. This profusion of the machine can have great advantages. In manufacturing it has transformed material existence, but in art the machine cannot itself ensure quality, as the miles of rubbishy movies testify. But the machine does not debar quality and it means, if there is a discriminating audience, that the best can be made widely available. Also more and bigger pictures can bring a qualitative difference, not merely an increase in quantity, as movies like *Intolerance, Storm over Asia, Gone with the Wind* or *La terra trema,* testify. It is significant that now after seventy years of development animation is turning to computers and other mechanical aids that may eventually ease the burden of its hand methods. But this is a long way ahead, and we must go back to the beginning.

★ ★ ★

The first moving toys of the century, Horner's zoetrope and Plateau's phenakistoscope, used paper strips,[1] hand drawn and coloured, of clowns juggling, birds flying, children skipping, tumblers tumbling. They were miniature, two-second cartoons. Following them, there was one inventor, Emile Reynaud, who tried to develop hand-made animation to the limit. Reynaud invented the praxinoscope, a refinement of the zoetrope using mirrors set at an angle to separate the frames, instead of slits. From this he developed a miniature theatre and then by 1888 a public show, a Théâtre Optique, in which he presented colour cartoons, ten and fifteen minutes in length. Unfortunately Reynaud's enterprise ended in failure, all interest was concentrated on the photographed image, and nothing like Reynaud's pictures existed in the cinema until Disney's colour cartoons of the Thirties.

The camera is now universally used in making every animated film and while its use (together with photographic film which can be cut and joined freely) puts at the disposal of the animated film-maker a tool of marvellous flexibility, and while photography is an invariable part of the process of animation, it is not (as with live action) its very heart and essence, but is merely a convenient means of copying and showing what is made by hand. The animator is not working as is the live-action film–maker with "bits of reality."

It follows that in cartoons the typical photographic techniques which,

---

[1] Each strip would contain a dozen frames showing successive stages of the movement and when spun in the machine (the zoetrope had a drum that revolved, the phenakistoscope a disc that rotated) and viewed through separate slits, the eye saw movement on the same principle as on a cinema screen.

Emile Reynaud's Praxinoscope Theatre

in live-action, form the basis of "the art of the film" have not got the same meaning for cartoons. Close-ups, long-shots, camera-angles, tracking shots, panning—these do not form the cartoonist's basic stock-in-trade.[2] Even the central artistic feature of the live-action film—cutting—has not got the same primary significance. Cartoons often do have "shots," and "cuts" between the shots, but only to the extent that a cartoon simulates real live-action. The cuts (or other transitions such as fades, wipes, iris-in-and-out) are simply drawn into the film, an imitation of the techniques of live-action photography. After all to achieve a cut a cartoonist simply puts a completely different drawing in front of the camera instead of a slightly different one.

More effective than cuts, because essentially related to cartoon technique, will be purely graphic methods of linking the story. For instance in a Czech cartoon, *Parasite* by Vladimir Lehky, the action takes place within boxes drawn on the screen, and for successive sequences the little quarreling figures jump or climb or drop down from one box to another across the intervening dark spaces. Again an Italian cartoon, *La Linea No 3,* in which the characters are drawn from a single continuous line, has only the remotest reference to reality, yet is completely successful in graphic terms.

Cartoons in telling a story have to go from one place or one time to another, but these switches are most effectively achieved by conventions of graphic art, not of camera photography. For a change of place cartoon characters may simply stay where they are on the screen and the background change round them. For a change of time their clothes may alter in style, their face grow wrinkled, without their even moving. The background or the characters themselves may change colour to indicate an emotional state. Significantly this is a technique which is highly effective in a colour cartoon because it is natural to the medium of painting, but rather ineffective (although it has been tried by tinting the filmstock) in photography. Another Italian cartoon, *Alpha Omega,* is an excellent example of graphic methods of scene changing.

In many cartoons, for example Dunning's *The Wardrobe* or Teru Murakami's *The Insects,* the film ends with the central character running further and further away into the distance until he finally disappears. The same kind of ending is not uncommon in live-action films in which the camera gradually draws backwards away from the scene as the film moves to a close. However, in cartoons it is the graphic artist's use of perspective by drawing his figures successively smaller and

---

[2] An animation camera has command of various movements and it may be economical and convenient to use them—but nevertheless they are not the fundamental heart of the technique as they are for live-action films.

smaller, which is involved and very properly the effect is quite different from the back-tracking shot which ends a live-action film.

The relative ineffectiveness of, for instance, Disney's multiple plane camera technique[3] is explicable because it is a technique of photography and thus not appropriate for an art of drawing or painting. In fact the range and power which are available to the cartoon by means of its painting, drawing (brush, charcoal, pen, pencil, pastel), or collage techniques, are so great that camera techniques in comparison with them are both feeble and unnecessary.

The position is not quite the same so far as animated puppet films are concerned, or animated films using real objects: match-boxes, buttons and thread, plasticine, or eggs, to name but a few of the things which have been "animated." Here in a three-dimensional world there is room for camera movements and in Jiri Trnka's puppet films, for instance *Archangel Gabriel and Mother Goose,* there is effective use of tracking shots. However even here there are limiting factors. In the case of puppets and usually of animated objects also, we are dealing with a miniature world and camera movement or angles cannot have the same sweep or effectiveness as in a real world. Even in the skilled hands of Trnka there may be something a little ridiculous about an upward angle shot of a tiny marionette, whereas a similar shot in a live-action film will succeed perfectly in giving the desired effect of dominance and power. In some cases because of the small scale of the marionettes it may be difficult, perhaps impossible, to achieve particular angles or camera movements with normal-sized apparatus even shooting on 16mm film. In general in puppet films downward angles tend to be easier and more effective. In the case of objects, small things seem to lend themselves more readily for animation, perhaps because they are more easily manipulated, perhaps because they combine more readily to create a plausible, imaginary world of their own, a world in which

"Her whip of cricket's bone, the lash, of film,
Her waggoner a small grey coated gnat,
Not half so big as a round little worm . . .
Pricked from the lazy finger of a maid;
Her chariot is an empty hazel-nut . . ."

[3] The cels on which different parts of the scene are drawn are photographed with gaps between them instead of superimposed, thus giving an illusion of depth to the finished product.

Animators opposite: Disney, Grimault, Lenica, Borowczyk (top row); Richard Williams with Chuck Jones, and Raoul Servais (centre); McLaren, Vukotić, Halas (bottom row)

Again in many cases camera movements are of less relevance because the objects used are flat or almost flat and relief, except the imaginary relief created by graphic perspective, plays little part. In Norman McLaren's *Rythmetic* queer numerals cut out of paper move and change. There have been several animated films using flat cardboard-like figures in recent years, such as Laguionie's *La Demoiselle et le violoncelliste* and they are very effective. Generally there are many films using drawn or cut-out shapes which themselves do not change their form but combine together or change position to form according to the context an infinite variety of meanings—a famous example is *Once upon a Time* by Lenica and Borowczyk. The use of flat objects like leaves, pieces of cloth, or envelopes, minimises the role of camera movements and angles and the same applies to the silhouette film developed by Lotte Reiniger.

★   ★   ★

There is another type of animation which uses live-action photography in the sense that the individual shots are of real people and real locations. Perhaps the best term for this technique is "pixillation," descriptive of the way the characters jerk and jump about as if they were pixillated or bewitched. It can be achieved in two different ways. First the film-maker can treat his live actors as though they were puppets, posing them in successive positions and taking single photographs on successive frames which when run together will form a recognisable action. This is the method by which Norman McLaren is said to have made *Neighbours*. The technical difficulties inherent in the procedure seem appalling, and it is to be doubted whether anyone but McLaren, who seems to go on with each film to a different and more difficult technique, would have tackled it.

An alternative technique is to take live-action shots and, from the exposed film, select single frames, editing these single frames together and discarding the intervening film so that the finished product is in effect made up of a series of jump-cuts. This not only avoids the difficulty of posing and re-posing actors, but offers greater flexibility at the editing stage. Examples are Arcady's *Ondomane* and a hilarious Yugoslav film *Justice* made by Ante Bajaja in 1962, which used other camera tricks in addition to jump-cuts. In these films the camera has a greater part to play, but they are still very different from live action.

WHAT IS AN ANIMATED FILM?

This brings us to the question of definition and to some difficulties. The following is a definition which has been accepted by animators

From LA DEMOISELLE ET LE VIOLONCELLISTE

themselves: *an animated film is one that is created frame-by-frame.*
This is clear enough when dealing with the conventional cartoon in
which thousands of different drawings or different positions of a drawing are set up and shot frame-by-frame with a special animation camera.
It is clear enough with puppet films or films made using inanimate
objects. But it hardly applies to the second type of pixillated film described above. This is not shot frame-by-frame but by ordinary live
action photography, and then extreme methods of editing are used.
And yet on the screen it may be indistinguishable from the first pixillation technique described, in which a strict frame-by-frame method is
used.

There is another type of film on the border between animation and
live action. That is a film like Colin Low's *City of Gold* or Arthur
Lipsett's *Very Nice Very Nice* made entirely of still photographs. The
team of Ray and Charles Eames have made many films of this type:
House, Death Day etc. A recent British example is *The Arp Statue*
(Alan Sekers). A division of opinion exists among animators themselves, and some would admit these films. Others hold that animated
films must create movement which did not exist in nature, and in these
films there is no real appearance of *movement*. The still pictures remain
still, the camera merely flicks from one to another. In any case it seems

clear they have not been created frame-by-frame but each photograph is shot, if only for a second, by live action. Consequently films from still photographs, paintings and the like, even though they may cut rapidly and continuously from one picture to another, have been excluded from this book. Films on art, about painting or sculpture, which cut from one part of a picture to another or explore the canvas by camera movements; these are a related *genre* even more obviously different from animation, and more clearly belonging within the field of live-action. Halas and Batchelor's *The Axe and the Lamp* which gradually covers Bruegel's painting of common proverbs, is a case in point.

Another technique which may seem akin to animation is frozen action in which a live character is held still on the screen for a longer or shorter period. *The Duel* (director Janusz Majewski), a Polish film showing athletes putting the shot, uses it almost continuously, and it is fashionable nowadays both in shorts and features. The effect is achieved by copying a single frame again and again in the final print so that the same image is repeated and held on the screen when the film is projected. Again it is simply ordinary live-action photography given a special effect in the process of editing and not true animation. A film like Carson Davidson's *Help! My Snowman's Burning Down* is full of surrealistic transitions achieved by trick photography, but although the camera may be stopped at a particular frame to achieve some of these results, it is not true frame-by-frame photography.

One is tempted to suggest an alternative definition drawing the line between, on the one hand, films using materials which the film-maker as an artist creates himself expressly for the film; and on the other hand films which, in one way or another, work with photographs of already existing material. Such a definition would accord with the point made at the beginning of the chapter that animation became entangled with and dependent on photography by an historical accident, but there would still be anomalies. The artificially created sets of the feature film belong to live action. Also the film-maker can create an animated film just as much by selection and arrangement of already existing material (thread, wool, stones, beads, shells, buttons etc.) as by drawing, painting, or manipulation of marionettes.

The frame-by-frame distinction has the virtue of drawing attention to the painstaking technical requirements of animation. The other definition, that of stressing the aesthetic difference between animation and live action. In animation the film-maker has almost absolute control over his material. In the live-action film there *is* selection and arrangement otherwise it would not be an art. But in the animated film the artist is more completely freed from the world of reality, limited only by the medium in which he draws, paints, or models, by the structure of the work itself, and by his own imagination.

ANIMATION TECHNIQUE

This book is not intended to show its readers how to make animated films, but how to look at them with more discernment. Nevertheless something should be said about production techniques. Knowing a little about the back-breaking work necessary to take Bugs Bunny through one of his amazing evolutions, while it may not alter our opinion of the drawing or the story's artistic merits, will lead to a fuller appreciation of the animator's economic problems. These problems are by no means irrelevant to the artistic view, since they may encourage stereotyped, repetitive work, make new, individual cartoons more difficult, and, by raising costs of production, force animated shorts out of the entertainment or creative field into advertising.

★　　★　　★

To make his drawings move, a cartoonist ideally has to produce twenty-four different drawings for every second of screen-time, corresponding to the twenty-four pictures (or frames) per second of the sound movie camera and projector. A ten-minute cartoon thus needs 14,400 different drawings. When one compares this with the output of even the most prolific painter or illustrator the sheer burden of drawing becomes apparent. There are various means of economising. By using layers of transparent celluloid, and by painting or drawing different parts of the scene on different layers, backgrounds or characters which are stationary can be used again and again, and only the part actually moving at the time (lips, fingers, eyes etc.) need be re-drawn. Again an arm on a separate cel can be moved by tilting the cel instead of re-drawing. A second means of economy, possible with slower movements, is to repeat the same drawing for two (even three) frames. This is equivalent to projection at twelve frames a second, intervals are adjusted to correspond, and the eye accepts movement as normal or nearly normal. In more recent cartoons less realistic movement is accepted. As John Halas says, "Now we can get away with four drawings a second whereas once twenty-four were necessary."

The third way of lightening the labour of drawing involved in the cartoon is by simplifying the style. The patient composition of the painter in oils or water colour, the intricate traceries of the pen-and-ink artist or the etcher, the careful building up of subtle colour effects, are outside the range of the cartoonist. Simple line, clear, readily-grasped colour effects, are what the animated artist must go for. The

17

economy of drawing dictated by the conditions of production may seem a handicap. The cartoon will never emulate the wealth of detail which enriches the picture galleries of the world. But when we come to the conditions of viewing, the cartoon's simplicity is an advantage. If the moving cartoon were as complex as the static painting the viewer would never be able to grasp it. A clear, quickly-understandable composition is essential.

As a further compensation the added dimension of movement gives the cartoon an advantage which static art has been reaching out for over the centuries. Even the simplest drawing can be made interesting when things start moving. The composition of the cartoon lies not only in the arrangement of lines and masses in each individual picture, but in the relationship of one picture with the next—contrast or harmony will exist between picture and picture, as well as within the individual image. Thus the cartoon, though lacking some of the possibilities of painting, nevertheless has a richness of its own which offers infinite possibilities and presents a serious artistic challenge to the film-maker.

A fourth method of meeting the demands of the cartoon medium is by organisation and division of labour. Carl Fallberg writes in *The American Cinematographer:* "Assembly-line methods are essential. It is technically possible for one person to do everything from the first preliminary story sketches to photographing the finished drawings on film, but there is such an infinitude of detail involved that the number of hands doing the work simply must be multiplied."

In every animated film-studio of any size the work is divided up and different people specialise in particular jobs. In a small studio the workers will know each other's jobs, there may be interchange of work or at any rate a rewarding feeling of group effort and mutual appreciation of each other's skills. In the large studios it may be more like a factory process. There are individual variations in different studios but the general procedure is as follows. Before the animation drawing is started there are several preparatory stages—story-board, work-book, layout, model sheets, sound track charts, dope sheets. The *story-board* is the same as for any film: a series of small sketches with enough description to enable the plot of the film to be followed. The *work-book* is a much more detailed, almost photo-by-photo analysis without drawings, describing the action in words and giving dialogue or other sound to accompany each action; it is a kind of film script. *Layout* and *model sheets* are preliminary drawings to determine the type and relative size of the characters and the style of the film. The *soundtrack charts* show the music, bar by bar, related to the visuals, and the *dope-sheets* or camera exposure charts, schedule in more detail each single exposure. The film is then fully planned and the actual film-making begins.

The following now set to work: the background artist, the key animator, the in-betweeners, the inker, the painter, the checker, the cameraman, and the film editor. The *key-animator* draws the key positions of each movement, the *in-betweeners* copy his work, varying it slightly to provide the necessary movement between one position and another. Then the *inker* blocks in the outline on the celluloid sheet and the *painter* or *opaquer* fills it in with the correct colour. *Checkers* ensure that the cels are properly lined up and matched and in the correct sequence for the cameraman who photographs the drawings. An animation camera and its rostrum are especially designed to photograph drawings or models or objects, photo-by-photo, frame-by-frame. One sequence or scene of the film will be completed at a time and viewed. Finally, the various sequences will be assembled by the editor and the completed film is ready for viewing.

Fallberg goes on to say that standardisation is a necessary element in cartoon production, that conformity of methods and systematised procedure are absolutely essential in all phases of production from the initial story idea right through to the finished print. He also contends that an assembly line "isn't as uninspirational as it might sound. All it amounts to is organised disciplined thinking." There are dangers in this view and drawbacks as well as advantages in rigid studio organisation. It is not just a question of consistency within a single work of art, but of carrying on from one cartoon to another in a fixed pattern, or of imposing the manager's or businessman's view on that of the artist. It all depends on circumstances, but individuality and allowing free play to the individual imagination are just as important in animation as in any artistic field. There is a danger in any rigid system that the individual artist will be lost in a crowd of checkers, in-betweeners, opaquers and the rest.

★　　★　　★

This question—who is the artist responsible, who is the author of a cartoon film?—deserves further consideration. It is far from straightforward in the case of a live-action film though here the convention that it is the director who is the artist responsible, generally works reasonably well. It is more difficult in the case of cartoons, the result of a closer combination of talents than the live-action film. Many cartoons are made in large studio factories, full of talented draughtsmen who are experts at reproducing the appearance of, even the flavour of, other people's work. Van Meegeren was celebrated for his forgeries, because he imitated Vermeer so skilfully that his pictures were more like Vermeer than Vermeer's own pictures. Any cartoon artist would take this as being all in a day's work. In the film-cartoon world not only are comic strips and characters taken over from newspaper and magazine cartoonists, but once a character is established different artists and even different studios can turn out films indistinguishable from one another. As an example of this the first Popeye film was taken from a comic-strip character invented by the cartoonist Segar, and animated by Max Fleischer in 1933. In the Forties and Fifties although Paramount remained the production company several different directors made Popeye films (for instance I. Sparber, *Popeye's Mirthday,* 1953). In 1961 a *Popeye* series was made in England by Halas and Batchelor. Gene Deitch in charge of a team working in Prague turns out *Tom and Jerry* cartoons which have little to do with their originators Hanna and Barbera except that they are produced by M-G-M. And he has made a *Popeye* series too.

In writing about cartoons this creates a practical difficulty and in many cases it will only be possible to say that a cartoon is made by a certain studio. Ideally the director should be *an* artist, even if he is not *the* artist who originated the drawing. Otherwise there will be less *rapport* between the two main film-makers than between live director and cameraman who both need only a flair for composition. In smaller studios the personality of one man usually inspires the work and the resulting films have true individuality. Some larger studios, for example Zagreb Films, may work in several styles and ascribe the authorship quite clearly. Again, in a film like *Peter Pan* there are dozens and dozens of names on the credits but the film is exactly like any other Disney film—and, though the result may be full of invention and smooth as custard, there is a loss of individuality.

★   ★   ★

Puppet films have to cope with the same laborious technique as cartoons and for a ten-minute puppet film the little dolls ideally have to be posed 14,400 times. Again elaborate studio routines have been built up. Here is a description of a puppet film being made.

"Around the big table on which the model set has been built, stand the operators who look like surgeon's assistants. They are dressed in white smocks, and hold mysterious wands in their hands. A film puppet can hop, skip or jump, can move its lips, talk, smile, weep. You can see the love-light in its eyes. All this is achieved by minute and exact calculations and almost inhuman patience. Nine seconds of screen time may require a whole day's work. The operators use thin metal

Jiri Trnka with one of his puppets

sticks, fine brushes, little geometrical measuring instruments, wads of cotton, tubes of colour, bowls of water. One paints a smile, one measures a movement, one alters a leaf, a flower, one puts tears into an eye. As the doll speaks his mouth is moved, letter by letter. It may take four hours for a short phrase 'good morning grand-pa.' The unit working on the film are bound by rigid conventions—there must be no negligence, lack of liaison or technical slips."

There are puppet factories in the East, as there are cartoon factories in the West, and the keenest imitators of the commercial American methods in art as in industry have been Russia and Communist China. And in the East as in the West production by assembly-line methods in which organisation becomes more important than inspiration, has led to stereotyped and boring puppet films. To sum up one may say that these methods are acceptable so long as they are kept subordinate to the individual artistic imagination and used merely as convenient tools. It is when the organisation begins to be thought of as important in itself or as a substitute for thought and feeling, that the work will suffer.

The development of lighter, more-easily-handled film equipment has made live-action easier and cheaper for the non-professional team, for the experimental or *avant-garde* film-maker; and there has been some carry-over into the field of animation. Again there is more widespread interest and readiness to tackle the work of animation. For film festivals, film societies, art centres, art cinemas and bodies like ASIFA (the International Association of Animation Film-makers) have all helped to spread an appreciation and knowledge of animation. One way or another it seems that more and more personal cartoons are being made at the present time either by one or two people working alone or by small groups or small studios. Unfortunately few of these films are shown in public cinemas or on television.

Relevant to the question of authorship and the role of the individual in animation is the relationship which has existed between cinema cartoons and the comics (or the funnies) in newspapers and children's magazines. The tie-up between newspaper strips and cinema cartoons can be compared with that between novels and feature films. Like novels, comics are one-man, literary/graphic creations in which the individual can work alone and allow his fantasy free play. As in the case of the novel, the literary/graphic comic strip with its ready-made reputation and established following, has been taken over and adapted for the cinema. The history of comics is not the subject of this book, but it is closely related, so titles for further reading are included in the bibliography and early comics are briefly mentioned in the next chapter.

★   ★   ★

It has been stressed already that, although animated films are shot on celluloid and shown in cinemas, they are closer to the graphic and plastic arts than they are to live-action film-making. An animated film-maker should be basically a graphic artist or a sculptor. The best cartoonist will be one who is an artist, who has both an artist's vision and the sureness of an artist in his line and composition. It may seem that formal artistic ability is no longer highly regarded in the art world nowadays; *academic* is a term of reproach, and the cartoonist, like the painter or illustrator, may choose to conceal his technical mastery under a dry astringent style; or cultivate distortion; or harden his line to evoke the ugliness of the modern mechanical world. But nevertheless formal proficiency, professionalism, provided it has been assimilated

22

and absorbed into the spontaneity of a personal style will make a fundamental difference to the work of a cartoon film-maker.

The drawn or modelled animated film is potentially heir to the whole traditional heritage of the visual arts in a sense that is not true of the photographed film, a new phenomenon of the Twentieth century. However both the cartoon and the puppet film have gone only a very little way towards realising their limitless possibilities, and of the thousands of cartoons made, by far the greatest number remain at the level of children's comics.

In recent times more and more graphic artists and more and more art colleges, have begun to take an interest in film-making. But it is a pity that in most cases their interest has been confined to live film-making. While any accession of talent is welcome, live-action is a field that has already been more cultivated than animation. And if we can look to anyone to support, develop and experiment with, the animated picture, surely it should be to the graphic artist, who starts with a special advantage, and who can now look beyond old territories to fresh but related fields, fields that ultimately should offer him the possibility of communicating with new and wider audiences.

2. Early Animation to the Twenties

The beginnings of animation go back to prehistoric times. At the 1962 Annecy Festival a French research worker, Madame Prudhommeau, showed one of the least polished yet one of the most interesting films ever made: one sequence, for instance, was built up from photographs of separate cave drawings of a bison taken on the spot and subsequently put together on a strip of film. It showed the bison running along, then falling into a pit, the cave-man's method of trapping his prey. The cave man artist had accurately drawn successive positions of movement so that when put together they formed a moving picture —one created thousands of years ago. By the same technique successive drawings of an acrobat on a Greek vase showed the figure doing a somersault. These ancient artists were able to analyse movement and draw it; all they lacked in order to reproduce it on the screen was the apparatus of film and projector.

When the cinema was being invented it was the graphic artist's work which first came alive. Almost the first movements on a screen were those of the silhouette puppets of China, Java and Turkey, imported to Europe as *ombres chinoises,* and, superficially, their black and white shapes resemble and might seem closely related to the *chiaroscuro* of the photograph. Nevertheless there is a fundamental difference between the two images, the one is a hand-made picture, the other, although subject to artistic control, a chemical reproduction.

★ ★ ★

The heir to *ombres chinoises* is not live-image photography but **Lotte Reiniger's** charming silhouette films created by scissors, black paper, and frame-by-frame filming. In them tiny figures in a fretwork landscape shuttle across the screen to courtly music. Lotte Reiniger produced her first films in Germany in the Twenties and Thirties: *The Flying Coffer, Cinderella, Carmen, Papageno, The Little Chimney Sweep,* and in 1926 made the second feature cartoon, a sixty-five-minute silhouette film, *Prince Achmed,* based on the *Arabian Nights.* In the mid-Thirties she emigrated to England to escape the Nazi *régime* and has made several more films mostly for television. The sharp outline and simple composition of these pictures suit the small screen, and in the late Fifties she made two silhouette movies in colour—*La Belle Hélène* and *The Seraglio*—for the BBC. It is significant of the contrast between the animated picture's rich resources and the meagre extent of their exploitation, that this effective *genre,* the silhouette film, has been fully cultivated by one artist only, though there are isolated early examples (Samuel Armstrong's *Mr. Asquith and the Clown,* England, 1911, and G. Petit's *Le Premier Cirque,* 1922) and one or two more recent pictures. However rich Lotte Reiniger's style, one cannot believe that this method of animation has been fully developed or all its possibilities explored.

★   ★   ★

In the early development of moving images, more important than *ombres chinoises* were the coloured strip cartoons of the zoetrope ("life-wheel") the phenakistoscope ("deceit-look") and praxinoscope ("action-look"). The phenakistoscope, invented in 1832 by the Belgian Professor, Plateau, was a revolving disc with slits at the edge and figures drawn on it which came to life when viewed in a mirror through the slits with the disc revolving. The zoetrope was a revolving drum with slits, through which the spectator looked at a strip with successive drawings fitted inside the drum, and it was invented in 1834 by W. G. Horner, a watchmaker of Bristol. The praxinoscope, invented later in the century by Professor Emile Reynaud, also used a series of drawings on a strip, but animated them more successfully by means of mirrors set at an angle. The pictures on these paper strips were in frames (about the same size as the present 35mm cinema film) drawn and coloured by hand, and were limited to simple movements, but they used a variety of styles and showed ingenuity and wit. One of the most striking, a black-boy juggling with his own head, is used today as a badge by the Annecy Animated Film Festival.

The fullest development of this early hand animation was carried out by **Emile Reynaud.** Reynaud is said to have made the first praxinoscope out of an empty biscuit-tin merely to amuse the son of his housekeeper, but later in its larger, more elaborate form it absorbed all his hopes and energies. In 1882 he combined the principle of the praxinoscope with a projector and by 1888 had developed longer films with the pictures painted on strips of celluloid. For public performance he used back projection (the apparatus being concealed behind the screen) and he accompanied the films by special music, and ingeniously contrived sound effects. In 1892 he opened his *Théâtre Optique* in the Musée Grévin in Paris and between that date and the turn of the century half a million people attended the performances. Programmes included a ten-minute circus film, *A Clown and His Dogs,* and a love story with characters from the harlequinade called *Poor Pierrot,* which lasted for fifteen minutes.

Reynaud's work was overtaken by the cinema proper. He was unable to adapt or develop his apparatus further and unable to compete with the Lumière brothers, the ingenious Georges Méliès or the many show-men in America, France and England who began to develop live-action film. In 1910, depressed at his lack of success, he threw much of his apparatus and film into the Seine and died in 1918 in a sanatorium. C. W. Ceram in *Archaeology of the Cinema,* while admitting the curious charm of Reynaud's films, thought him "a mediocre draughts-man . . . hardly an artist" . . . However . . . André Martin talks of "the clear and modest inspiration of Emile Reynaud" and Georges Sadoul thought his work "spirited, perfect and lasting."

Whatever his absolute merits as a pure artist, there is no doubt about his place in the history of animation. He not only invented a technique, he originated a new art and was the first to develop the ani-mated film (indeed the cinema if by *cinema* we mean movement, not photography) into a spectacle.

★   ★   ★

Reynaud's work finished in a dead end. The future lay with the Lumière brothers, Edison, and their imitators, and after the turn of the century moving images, even in animated films, involved photog-raphy.[1] Though the film might originally derive from painting, or drawing, or arrangements of puppets or objects, these would have to be recorded on a strip of film in order to be projected.

Henceforward the animated film was tied to the photograph, became part of the cinema proper, and was subject in many ways to the in-fluence of the live-action film. The hand-made moving image for in-stance, lost its colour, and did not regain it until the general introduction of colour in movie photography in the Thirties. It also lost its sound, and like the live-action film, was silent until 1927. The construction of cartoons in "shots" built into "sequences" and using drawn close-ups, long-shots or camera angles copied features of live-action with little meaning in the cartoon field.

Between Reynaud's work and other pre-cinema there was in fact a clean break, and the present techniques were invented again from the beginning, in the early years of the century. About 1906 **Stuart Blackton** discovered the trick of "one turn one picture" and applied it to a pixillated film, *The Haunted Hotel,* in which the furniture and props jumped about the screen as if by magic. He applied the same technique to drawings in a film called *Humorous Phases of Funny Faces* and another, *The Magic Fountain Pen.* The first of these is said to have been shown in April 1906, the second in 1909, though the

---

[1] The latest means of recording movement on electronic or magnetic tape can still be regarded as *photography* in its literal meaning of "light-writing" since the beginning of the process and the final product still depend on variations in light.

earlier date has been ascribed to it also. *The Magic Fountain Pen* issued by Vitagraph shows a man and a woman being drawn facing each other, then their faces change until they are a couple of beaky birds. At about the same time in England, British distributors released *The Hand of the Artist* in which a hand is seen drawing a coster and his girl who then come to life and dance a cake-walk. It was by **Walter Booth,** a conjurer turned trick film-maker who also made *Comedy Cartoons* (1907), *The Sorcerer's Scissors* and *Prehistoric Man* (1908). One of the earliest animated films using objects was *The Bewitched Matches* issued in 1913 by American Standard Films and made in the U.S. by Emile Cohl. There is an introduction in live-action in which three giggling Gibson-girls are having their fortunes told by a witch. Papa comes home and send the witch away while the guilty girls cover him with attention and bring his pipe and matches. But the witch has cast her spell on the matches! Before our eyes they make patterns, whirl in circles, form pictures of a cottage, a man, a dog. Papa crouches in horror and finishes by throwing them into the fire where they explode.

There was early animation of a sort in a number of countries. Segundo de Chomon, a Spaniard, made *The Electric Hotel* in 1905. In England, besides Walter Booth, there was Samuel Armstrong (*The Clown and the Donkey,* 1910), Harry Furniss (*War Cartoons,* 1914), George Ernest Studdy (*Studdvis War Studies,* 1914), Lancelot Speed, Dudley Buxton, Anson Dyer, Tom Webster (*History of a German Recruit,* 1917) and others. In Italy there was Arnaldo Ginna—*Song of Spring* and *The Rainbow,* 1912. In Sweden **Victor Bergdahl** who also worked with Winsor McCay in America—*Captain Grog's Balloon Trip* and *Mr. Sphere, Mr. Spindleshanks and Little Miss Needle,* 1916. In Poland, Feliks Kuczkowski; in Germany Julius Pinschewer (*The Bottle,* 1912) and Otto Herman (*How Plimps and Plumps Tricked the Detective*—they tricked him by disappearing into a bag and behind a sapling); in Russia and France, Ladislas Starevitch; and in France, O'Galop (Marius Rossillon) who made *Le Circuit d'alcool* and *Le Taudis doit être vaincu,* both in 1912. A successor of Cohl in France was Lortak (Robert Collard) who made cartoons alone and in collaboration in the Twenties. His pictures feature an eccentric inventor, Professor Mecano or Mechanicas. Many of them are undated but it is unlikely Lortak started before 1920. The majority of these animators were newspaper cartoonists trying their hand out in a new medium, and, except for Emile Cohl, the number of movies they made was small.[2] Although the artistic side was stronger in Europe, it was only

[2] But see Chapter Six and the reference to Lortak as the most prolific French animator.

in the States that regular cartoon production was put on an organised basis and the economic vitality of both "the funnies" and "the movies" put America ahead in the teens and the Twenties and even attracted artists from other countries.

★   ★   ★

Thus right from the beginning there was interchange between the world of newspaper comics and that of cinema cartoons. In its modern form the comic slightly pre-dated the cinema, the first English comic being *Ally Sloper's Half-Holiday* dating from 1884. In 1890 came two of Alfred Harmsworth's papers, *Comic Cuts* and *Chips,* whose heroes were two tramps, Weary Willie and Tired Tim. The first American comic-strip drawn by James Swinnerton with animal characters, appeared in the "San Francisco Examiner" in 1892. The first popular character in America was the Yellow Kid, who appeared in the "New York World" in 1896, and later in the "New York Journal."

Comics developed differently in England and America. In England they remained separate weekly papers confined to a juvenile and adolescent readership. In America they came out weekly (or more often) as a supplement, or even an integral part of a daily paper. Thus in America they reached a far wider public which included adults as well as children, and achieved a very different status. Also since cartoon strips would be sold through a syndicate to many different papers, the characters in the funnies were well known all over the country. Thus conditions were more favourable for the animator who could present on the screen a character already widely popular with the whole of the family. Furthermore American cinema had the drive and organisation to sustain a steady flow of pictures. In England none of the characters from children's comics—the Bruin Boys, Tiger Tim, Billy Bunter and the rest—ever appeared in the cinema.

The pattern of borrowing from the comics differed widely. Sometimes only the characters were transferred, sometimes the same artist worked in both media. Some characters were more popular in the cinema than as a strip (*Popeye the Sailor* and *Felix the Cat*) some the other way about. George Herriman's *Krazy Kat* was supreme in the world of the funnies but did not transfer very successfully to the screen. *Koko the Clown* originated in the cinema and remained there. *Betty Boop* went from the cinema to the newspaper world. Few if any of the strip heroes—Prince Valiant, Tarzan, Superman, Captain America, Thor—have been brought to life on the screen, presumably because heroic action, science fiction, horror and adventure, can be more forcefully portrayed by real actors. The comics have drawn freely on live film actors—Charlie Chaplin, Chester Conklin, Harold Lloyd. And so to a lesser extent have cinema cartoons. A recent creation, *Peanuts,* has been popular in both media. Some newspaper strips, e.g. those of Jules Feiffer, depend more on the wordy captions than on the drawing, and such material is clearly less adaptable to the screen. In later periods the cartoon movie has drawn also on painters and illustrators for its material, for instance UPA's *Madeleine* from Bemelman's paintings, *Unicorn in the Garden* from Thurber's drawing, and Halas and Batchelor's series based on Gerald Hoffnung's caricatures of odd musicians and their even odder instruments.

The earliest cartoonist to set the pattern of transferring a character from a comic strip was **Winsor McCay** who drew *Little Nemo* for the "New York Herald." The hero was McCay's son and his *Adventures in Slumberland* including a voyage in a mysterious air-ship had a distinct science fiction flavour. McCay's first movie was not *Little Nemo* but *Gertie the Dinosaur* which appeared in 1909. The style is delicate line drawing against a plain background, and seen today the picture has considerable charm. McCay was also a vaudeville performer and the cartoon was designed to fit in with his act. A highlight was when Gertie seemed to take an apple from McCay's hand and eat it. *Little Nemo* appeared in 1911, other films being *Jersey Skeeters* (1916) and *The Sinking of the Lusitania* (1918). The last was a long film and the first feature cartoon to be made.[3]

The first American cartoon units were formed between 1909 and 1920. They developed very early the specialisation and division of labour and regular production techniques, which Disney was to intensify. Whether they used the actual characters or not, American comic-strips gave them ideas to develop and a drawing tradition suitable for the cartoon medium. The Mack Sennett comedies also spilled over into the animated field, and provided another source of gags. The influence of live cinema can be seen in the custom of introducing film stars more or less caricatured, into cartoon films. They were popular with the audience who were tickled to see in the cartoon a star who might be playing in the "big picture," and they formed a point of contrast with the "real" world of live-action, which heightened the effect of the crazy antics shown in the cartoons. The most developed was Disney's *Mother Goose Goes to Hollywood* (1939), in which film stars appear as nursery-rhyme characters, Katharine Hepburn as Little Bo-Peep, Greta Garbo, Edward G. Robinson, Spencer Tracy and

---

[3] But see Chapter Ten. *The War and Momi's Dream* (1916) may have been of feature length, which would give it pride of place.

Charles Laughton. There was also a Disney parody of Mae West in *Who Killed Cock Robin?* (1935) and recently there has been George Dunning's cartoon featuring the Beatles.

A few cartoon movies were made from the strip *Bringing Up Father* by George McManus. The characters were Maggie, the culture-hungry, nagging wife, and her elegant daughter, amusingly at loggerheads with Jiggs, her long-suffering husband, the universal recalcitrant male, always deserting the drawing-room and sneaking off for a beer with the boys. The French cartoonist, Emile Cohl, worked for some time with McManus in America, and the character *Baby Snookums* (1912–1914) was their joint creation. *Colonel Heeza Liar* made in the early Twenties by **John Randolph Bray** and Shamus Culhane was a lampoon on the ex-president, Teddy Roosevelt. Bray is said to have introduced drawing on cels in 1914 but the technique has also been attributed to Earl Hurd in 1915. Another early cartoon creation was the pair, *Mutt and Jeff,* animated by Bud Fisher in 1916. In 1916 also Walter Lantz launched his career with the *Katzenjammer Kids.* An animator who started in 1917 was Isidore Klein. He worked on *The Katzenjammer Kids, Mutt and Jeff* and *Krazy Kat,* then later at Paramount "Famous Studios" on *Popeye, Barney Google, Casper the Friendly Ghost* and *Little Lulu,* going on from there to Terrytoons, Columbia and the Disney Studios.

★　　★　　★

Max Fleischer began to make cartoons in the early Twenties, his first character being *Koko the Clown* who came out of an ink bottle to play tricks in the real world of live action. *Bubbles,* an early Koko film made in 1922, is full of gags. Koko is blowing bubbles, then the bubble blows him up. He gets his head stuck in a bubble, the first space-man. A cat comes out of the pipe. Then other characters. They enter the bubble; when it bursts, they disappear. Koko gets his head stuck in the pipe. There is a contest between him and Fleischer to see who can blow the biggest bubble. Fleischer's bubble finally fills the room, but Koko runs away and disappears into a car radiator. Finally he is put back into the inkwell. Another of Fleischer's early creations was the first and only cartoon vamp, Betty Boop. For a long time she had difficulty with the censor, for (rather oddly) censorship of cartoons seems generally to have been stricter than of live cinema. In the Thirties Claribel Cow was not allowed to show her bare udder, but had to wear a skirt! Fleischer went on to a career only second to that of Disney and deserves fuller mention in the next chapter.

These were human characters, but cartoon animals proved popular early on, in particular *Krazy Cat* and *Felix the Cat.* George Herriman,

BETTY BOOP, the cartoon vamp

the creator of Krazy Kat, was the most eccentric and individual of comic-strip artists, and the most highly praised by later critics. In almost every cartoon the aggressive Ignatz Mouse hurls a brick at Krazy Kat, who bears no malice but suffers patiently. Punishment is meted out, if at all, by Offissa Pup, a kind of canine policeman. One wonders why the attempt to transfer Krazy Kat to the movies was only moderately successful, and why, despite the enormous reputation of the comic strip, the early films seem to have been virtually forgotten. Perhaps they were too idiosyncratic for audiences of the time and no opportunity for reassessment has since occurred. The earliest Krazy Kat movies on record are *Krazy Kat Bugologist* and *Krazy Kat and Ignatz Mouse* made in 1916 by George Herriman, Leon Searl and Frank Moser. Eleven pictures were made in 1916–1917 by the International Film Service, in 1926 and 1927 seven Krazy Kat cartoons were made by the Winkler Picture Corporation and finally in 1936 to

1939, six pictures (including *Krazy's News-Reel* and *Krazy's Magic*) by Charles Mintz for Columbia.

More successful in the cinema was *Felix the Cat,* the creation of the Australian, **Pat Sullivan.** The character was said to have been taken from Kipling's "the cat who walked by himself," and the style from the comic artist, Marriner. Sullivan was born in 1888 and emigrated to America where from 1914 he was a newspaper cartoonist, and is said to have continued the work of Winsor McCay. It is not certain exactly when Felix made his bow or whether he appeared first in a comic strip. Sullivan's first film work is said to have been an animated title showing an elephant bursting into a nursery and upsetting alphabet blocks which spelled out *Metro Pictures Present.* If this is so it would be the first use of animation credits, antedating Saul Bass and Company by some forty years. Felix movies first appear in the Congress Copyright record between 1925 and 1928 (though it is always possible they were made earlier and copyrighting was delayed) when nearly eighty titles are recorded. Certainly round about this time *Felix the Cat* had an enormous vogue in the cinema and, helped by the song "Felix kept on walking . . . kept on walking still," achieved a world reputation, for a short time rivalling that of Mickey Mouse.

These cartoons were based on a rapid succession of tricks, transformations, association of ideas, visual puns. Krazy Kat has someone wind up his tail and turns into an aeroplane. Felix wanting to travel as a stowaway turns into a bag, his tail for the handle. A mosquito shoots stings at him like darts; he seizes one and they fence together. Baffled and perplexed Felix uses two question marks that grow over his head as skates to escape across the ice. A man running loses his hat but it stays in the air and he dashes back for it. Krazy Kat stuns his opponents with an exclamation mark that comes out of his astonished brain. In an early Popeye film we see the outline of a flat-iron in Popeye's muscles, and the faint shape of an imaginary flight of steps up which Olive Oyl walks in her sleep. Fallen off a high building, Mutt "swims" back through the air with a huge effort. They were uncomplicated fun, mostly without the social implications of *Life with Father,* without the never-ending, extreme violence of the post-Hitler era. At the same time in the pre-occupation with the visual possibilities of the cartoon they were true to the medium in a way that was lost sight of in the Disney era and until the UPA revolution: the work of UPA can, from one point of view, be seen as a return to the logic of a world that was not a real world but one of pen-and-ink.

★　　★　　★

Although he founded no school, perhaps the most important of the early cartoonists was **Emile Cohl.** Cohl was born in Paris in 1857 and was first apprenticed to a jeweller, but he sketched all his fellow workers and later during his military service all those in his regiment. In 1878 he became a pupil of André Gill, a famous cartoonist, and before long Cohl's work appeared in all the leading French papers. In 1885 he also became a fashionable photographer. By 1884 he was well enough known to be included in a series *"Men of Today."* However, it is because of his films that his name will be remembered. His first cartoon film was *Fantasmagorie* shown in August 1908, his second *Le Cauchemar du Fantoche* produced in the same year. Between 1908 and 1918 he made nearly two hundred cartoons, over fifty of them in the States where he worked just before the First World War. *Transfiguration, Don Quixote, The Little Faust, Metamorphoses, Castro in New York, Round the World in 80 Minutes, Flambeau the Lost Dog,* are a few of the better known. Like his friend and fellow artist Méliès, Emile Cohl was ruined by the war. He made no more films after 1918 and died in poverty in the Thirties.

Cohl had a fertile imagination, and a sharp sense of the comic. His skill as a caricaturist of living persons could hardly be transferred to his film cartoons, because he worked alone and his drawings of movement had to be reduced to the simplest of lines. But his little figures are full of expression and intensely alive. Sometimes he drew in black on white, sometimes in white on black but always effectively, always individually, with a sure sense for the medium. The pace of his films never flags and they are packed with the fantastic invention appropriate to the cartoon world. Fantoche pushing his umbrella right through an aggressive military gent then politely apologising as if he had merely bumped his arm, a hen that laid an alarm-clock, a man who flew by flapping his coat tails, an obelisk that cried, a house that turned into a man. His gags today are as fresh as when he made them.

He was also the first to develop a consistent character, Fantoche, the prototype of all the later "little men" of the cartoon world. This figure of *everyman* crops up again and again in human or animal guise, and seems a necessary myth of our modern amorphous, democratic society. He is "the little feller," the tramp, the ordinary, anonymous, defeated but undefeatable man-in-the-street, so successfully characterised in the flesh by Charlie Chaplin.

★   ★   ★

These early cartoons nowadays have a period charm. They seem to belong to a world that has passed away, no doubt a world that never existed, an innocent world without automation, without social or economic problems, without violence, hatred or inequality, almost without sex. The hero triumphs over his enemies by light-hearted tricks, he meets life with a sublime naivety which is invariably justified.

So far as the realisation of these ideas is concerned there were individual variations in style, but generically speaking artists of this period are alike. There was a strong tradition of comic drawing born of magazines like *Punch* and its counterparts in France and America, waiting to be taken over, adapted and made to move. It was typically line drawing and eminently suitable for the black-and-white cartoon.

There was no dialogue (*Gertie the Dinosaur* with its provision for a live narrator was an exception) and no captions. The plot explained itself visually, and if occasionally there was need for something more, a balloon would appear either from the character's head with *idea* or *thinks* in it, or from his mouth with the necessary words. In this respect the modern animated film has not changed very greatly from the primitive early work and remains very much a visual art. But the age of innocence has gone.

3. Disney and His Contemporaries

It must be rare that an art has been dominated by one man in the way Disney has dominated the cartoon. To many people in the Thirties, a golden age of the cartoon, a period when the masses' weekly entertainment meant the movies and no movie programme was complete without its *Mickey Mouse*—to many people then and since, the cartoon has simply meant Walt Disney's work. This is all the more so since with the gradual disappearance of the short cartoon from cinema programmes Disney has been able to rationalise his production to meet the new conditions.

Not only have his characters been used as badges, designs or decorations in every branch of life from fighting planes to fancy toilet-soap and children's sand-buckets, but he has diverted his film production into the field of live-action, both nature films and fictional features. At the same time his past work remains as a vast fund of capital on which his studio can draw indefinitely at will, reviving his feature cartoons on holiday occasions with suitable publicity, both in cinemas and on television, and one way and another perpetually keeping his name before a world public.

★　　★　　★

Walt Disney was born in Chicago in 1901 of an Irish-Canadian family, one of five children. His father worked in the country and the town, drifting about, never very successful. Disney had a hard childhood and received most protection and support from his elder brother, Roy. He became an ambulance driver in the war and after it, worked as a commercial artist in Kansas City. There he met **Ub Iwerks** who was to become a life-long collaborator. From all accounts it was Iwerks who had the talent for drawing and for cartoon technique, Disney who had the organising ability, the determination to succeed and the flair for knowing what the public wanted. In 1930 a distributor, Pat Powers, persuaded Iwerks to leave Disney and he produced a series, *Flip the Frog* which was only moderately successful. Iwerks later rejoined the Disney studio and has remained there since, but as an employee, not as the partner and friend he was in the early days.

Disney's first cartoons were made working for the Kansas City Film Ad Company, one-minute, black-and-white commercials, using cut-out paper puppets with jointed limbs. He produced a satiric newsreel called Laugh-O-Gram for a local theatre, then using the same name started his own company. Laugh-O-Gram made seven animated

The first Disney sound film, SKELETON DANCE

fairy-tales, *Tommy Tucker's Tooth* (teaching dental hygiene) and a series *Alice in Cartoonland* which combined a local child model in live-action with cartoon characters. In 1923 the firm went bankrupt and Disney, with Iwerks and his brother Roy, moved to Los Angeles where he made a new start, reviving *Alice* and in 1927 originating *Oswald the Rabbit* with the collaboration of a distributor Charles Mintz, and George Winkler. The *Alice* films were relatively unsuccessful and seen today the girl star has neither charm nor vivacity, while the cartoon work is undistinguished. Further at the end of his contract, Disney lost *Oswald* to Mintz, since the rabbit was copyrighted in Mintz's name —a mistake Disney never made again. Undeterred by his setbacks he thought up a new character—Mickey Mouse.

The first two Mickey Mouse pictures, *Plane Crazy* and *Gallopin' Gaucho,* were silent, but *Steamboat Willie* had dialogue and music exactly fitted to the action, and released in 1928, was an immediate success. Disney was now established, and from then on his story is one of a small businessman striving to expand, living frugally himself, putting all his profits back into the business, a good salesman and manager, looking always to the future. In film-making Disney depended on others for drawing, his major contribution being as story-editor, but he was by nature a perfectionist and the finish and consistently high workmanship of his movies were due to his persistence and drive. They were due also to his willingness to spend money. Right up to the Sixties Disney continued to risk what he had already made on fresh investment at an ever higher level. A lot of his work was barely profitable in the short run, and he owed his millions to a few bonanzas (*Three Little Pigs, Snow White and the Seven Dwarfs, Cinderella, Mary Poppins*) and increasingly in later years, to re-issues.

★   ★   ★

One of the factors in Disney's success was his progressive outlook in the technical field. Although for a long time it was Ub Iwerks who provided much of the expertise, again it was Disney who found the money and gave the go-ahead. First in the colour field with *Flowers and Trees* (1932), Disney was able to negotiate a special agreement with Technicolor for processing his films. He was first to use a story-board in planning a picture. The multiplane camera was only one among many innovations he sponsored in animation work, innovations affecting both equipment and studio organisation. Later on he brought a number of improvements to the work of nature photography. Every new advance was of course well publicised and accompanied by a flourish of trumpets. Though some were gimmicks, colour and sound did transform the cartoon. His *Skeleton Dance* made in 1929 is not only one of the first sound movies, but also a classic example of frame-by-frame synchronisation between the music and the movements of the drawing. This exact split-second co-ordination was possible only with the cartoon, and the meticulous timing achieved is a compensation for the infinitely laborious technique which had to be used. Today in live-action very close co-ordination of sound and image is still called "Mickey Mousing." Animated films are, in more senses than one, jewels. They are gem-like in their miniature scale, gem-like in the infinite care and patience that must go into their "cutting" and "setting," gem-like in the fact that this very fineness of work gives scope for brilliant or subtle effects. It follows too that this is an art for the craftsman whose work can stand any scrutiny. The amateur may reveal new techniques, break outworn traditions, obtain fresh effects; but if his work is to stand comparison with the professional, he must match him in skill and persistence.

To return to Disney. The two further factors in his success were his stories and his characters. Disney's shorts had carefully structured plots, sometimes very neat. They were not simply a string of violent gags, in the style of later American cartoons originated by Tex Avery. Disney in fact was presenting the world of the average American, preaching a moral, giving a message of optimism, of success. He has been compared more than once with La Fontaine. There is a reassuring, homely, honest-Joe quality about his shorts founded on resemblances between the animal and the human world. The stories end happily, the characters are essentially good fellows, violence is not too extreme, and cruelty and tragedy are excluded.[2] There may be nursery vulgarity, babies' bottoms are permissible, but real sex is taboo. Any satire is more than gentle, and the setting is generally the reality of everyday life.

Just as important were the characters, broadly drawn human types in animal disguise, with whom an audience could feel at ease. Mickey, the first and foremost, was an endearing innocent with a squeaky voice (for years the voice of Walt Disney) and an eternal optimist. More mischievous and violent in the early pictures, he mellowed as the years went by and became a universal favourite. In 1929 in *Karnival Kid* he was joined by Minnie. In *The Grocery Boy* (1932), and *Playful Pluto* (1934), they were joined by a loose-jointed, flop-eared dog, a hound with an inextinguishable zest for life and very little brain. He was an ideal subject for animation and provided some of the most hilarious, most brilliant animation sequences in Disney's work. Donald Duck was established in *Mickey's Circus* 1936, a dignified member of the community, taking life seriously, flying into a rage when things went wrong, and doomed to suffer one setback after another. Goofy, another hound with buck teeth, completed the *ménage*.

To go with these homely plots and characters was a "literary" style, based not on the graphic nature of the medium, but on a cartoon reproduction of reality, following loosely traditional story-book illustration and using much of the idiom of live cinema in its story-telling methods. As a cartoon it was not an exact copy of reality, but it was a world of limited make-believe in which characters moved, events happened and things existed, as in a real world, not as in a world of pencil and paper, paint and brush or one of marionettes. There was

---

2) There are potentially cruel and dangerous characters in Disney's longer films. There is a case of *Snow White* having been given an X certificate and I have known children terrified by *Pinocchio*. Perhaps what frightens them are situations in which the child hero or heroine is in danger of being ill-treated, and they identify very strongly with these characters. Possibly, though adults dislike the unmotivated violence of the Tex Avery school, children find it more acceptable on a slap-stick level.

not the notion that "anything . . . was possible" that had existed with Felix the Cat, but had progressively disappeared as Disney's success grew. This imitation world was presented with supreme technical competence, and the various factors were blended to comfort and soothe the audience (especially an audience habituated to the diet) and to give it something easy and undemanding, even though the result might finally be false in its banal optimism and in its "naturalising" of the cartoon medium.

★   ★   ★

Although Mickey and Donald remained supreme, the *Silly Symphonies* introduced other characters, noteworthy among them being *The Three Little Pigs* (1933), *The Farmyard Symphony,* and *Music Land* (a contest between jazz and classical music). In 1937 came the first of Disney's features, *Snow White and the Seven Dwarfs.* The huge success of Disney's first feature and changes in the pattern of cinema exhibition making short films less profitable, combined to influence Disney and gradually turn his work from shorts to features. In 1940 *Pinocchio* followed and then *Fantasia. Fantasia* was made on a tide of success and perhaps Disney's bid to be considered a serious as well as a comic artist. If so, it was a failure, for despite its richness the work was a hotch-potch without real unity and some of the episodes were vulgar and tasteless. Perhaps the best were a Mickey Mouse story to the music of Dukas's "Sorcerer's Apprentice," a delicate scene of lanterns at night to the music of "Ave Maria," and a series of moving abstract patterns to Bach's music, though the last was not original, deriving from the abstract films of Fischinger and Pfeniger in Germany and Switzerland, as well as the work of a number of Russians: Avraamov, Jankovski, Voinov, and Cholpo, who had studied the problems of drawn sound and of images derived from sound. There was also some brilliant animation in the "Nutcracker Suite" sequence; but a section to Stravinskys' "Rite of Spring" showing the struggles of prehistoric monsters, drew this comment from the composer: "The musical performance . . . is execrable. I will say nothing about the visual complement as I do not wish to criticise an unresisting imbecility."

After *Fantasia,* came, in 1942, *The Reluctant Dragon,* and *Dumbo,* an ugly-duckling story of a little elephant with big ears, one of Disney's most successful films. There is an amusing dream sequence (a typical Disney euphemism, for it should have been a drunk sequence) in which Dumbo keeps seeing pink elephants. Later came *The Three Caballeros* and *Bambi,* the story of a fawn. Then came a series of features adapting more children's stories: *Ichabod and Mr. Toad (The*

Wind in the Willows) (1949), *Cinderella* (1950), *Alice in Wonderland* (1951), *Peter Pan* (1953), *The Sleeping Beauty* (1958), *The Jungle Book* (1967), and *The Aristocats* (1970). If one compares the cartoons with the original illustrations, it is apparent that Disney has assimilated them all to the uniform "Disney style," a style now ridden with *clichés* of its own creating, a style become so deadly familiar as to be completely insipid. There were also feature cartoons based on original stories or adaptations of less familiar material such as *Lady and the Tramp* (1955), and *101 Dalmatians* (1960).

In 1953 Disney, possibly spurred by the success of UPA, broke new ground in two films shown at the Cannes Festival, *Melody* and *Toot Whistle Plunk and Boom*, **Ward Kimball** being the director of the films and responsible for their different style. *Melody* was a 3-dimensional seven-ages-of-man cartoon with surrealist figures and objects. *Toot Whistle Plunk and Boom* was a potted history of music, a departure from Disney's other films and more in the style of UPA. However the films were not an unqualified success with the critics, who thought Disney had misunderstood the revolution which had occurred, and the experiment was not repeated.

★   ★   ★

After 1950 Disney turned increasingly to live-action. There are the nature films: *Jungle Cat, Perri, Seal Island* (1948), *Beaver Valley* (1950), *The Living Desert, The Olympic Elk*. It is interesting to see how Disney carried over into these nature films the cosy, nursery anthropomorphism of his cartoons. The photography of wild animals was superb, something that had never been done better. But accompanying it was a "humanising" commentary: "Soon Bobby beaver will be married to Bella and then oh my, what happy times they'll have taking their family for a picnic in the woods." In some films (e.g. *Jungle Cat*) the commentary was in doggerel verse: "He always could outwit that cat, and here's a living proof of that." For some people these sentimental commentaries spoil the films, but mass audiences conditioned to the Disney philosophy readily accept them, and they have been widely popular. Then there have been adventure films: *Treasure Island, Robin Hood, Rob Roy, 20,000 Leagues under the Sea* and so on—good, plain, uncomplicated adaptations, suitable for children of all ages. Disney also made several light comedies: *The Shaggy Dog* (1959), *The Absentminded Professor, Lieutenant Robinson Crusoe, RN*. Probably in terms of screen time the Disney studio has produced more live action than it has animation. Another enormous success was the mixture of live-action and animation in *Mary Poppins* (1965), the story of a magical nanny, delightfully played by Julie Andrews. So well-established by now was the studio, that the death of Disney himself in 1966 does not seem to have been a major setback to production. As well as live cinema, cartoons have gone on and even widened in scope. *It's Hard to Be a Bird,* director Ward Kimball, had excellent notices, and *The Aristocats,* a splendid story of colourful feline personalities in high and low life, borrowing something from the style of the cartoonist Ronald Searle, was as good as if not better than, any of the previous animation features. *Winnie the Pooh and the Blustery Day* 1968, from A. A. Milne's characters, caught the spirit of the original better than earlier adaptations. Only *Bedknobs and Broomsticks* (1971), another mixture of live-action and cartoon, failed to repeat the success of *Mary Poppins.*

★   ★   ★

Though strictly they are outside the scope of this book, a brief word should be said about the amusement resorts, since they have a bearing on any assessment of Disney's achievement. They are by no means footnotes or postscripts to his career. From the very start model railways, mechanical marvels and the creation of a childhood dream world, attracted Disney. It was only latterly he had the millions necessary to realise these dreams on the perfectionist scale he required. *Disneyland* in California opened in 1955 and with extensive TV coverage, was an immediate success. A ski resort at Mineral King combined entertainment with recreation. Largest and most ambitious of all, the *Disneyworld* in Florida only recently opened, covers 27,000 acres and includes besides an Amusement Park to end all amusement parks, a model community called EPCOT—Experimental Prototype Community of Tomorrow. It has been suggested that Disney himself regarded his amusement worlds as greater achievements than his cartoons, which he had left behind long ago, and in which anyway he played largely an organisational role. Richard Schickel, Disney's most perceptive biographer, puts this point of view: "It is culturally blind not to see that Disney was a forceful and, in his special way, imaginative worker in . . . the American business tradition. The only fitting honour to be paid him is to associate him firmly with it, and not with some artistic tradition that was fundamentally alien to him." At the same time the best of Disney's animation work will last because of its high spirits, its cheerful optimism, its deeply human qualities. If he was not a great artist, he was certainly a great popular entertainer and made a permanent contribution to modern folk lore.

All through the Thirties, Disney had rivals, and all the major film companies had their cartoon division, supplying suitable "product" to go with the rest of the programme. It is impossible to give more than a brief indication of the films produced and for the most part their quality would hardly justify it. They were programme fillers designed to provide light relief for a programme that itself was light entertainment. In many cases they are the work of anonymous artists working in the Disney tradition, borrowing ideas and styles and not aiming at anything personal or original, although they produced some characters that achieved wide popularity.

The brief summary here refers primarily to the Thirties but many of the characters live on in the present, in the cinema or on television, with different artists and possibly different studios. They are a part of modern folk lore and as such not tied to their creator.

Columbia produced *Scrappy Cartoons* (*The Gold Getters, Happy Butterfly, The Gloom Chasers*) and also *Krazy Kat Cartoons,* the second generation of the Krazy Kat of the early years of animation: *Goofy Gondola, Hot Cha Melody, The Bird Man. Colour Rhapsodies* included *Babes at Sea, Shoemaker and the Elves, Make Believe Review*. **Charles B. Mintz** was the head of the studio with a staff of about two hundred.

Twentieth Century-Fox distributed the very average cartoons of Education Pictures Production, also Terrytoons whose studio with a staff of a hundred was in New York under the direction of Paul Terry. **Paul Terry** had started as a graphic artist in 1913 with a comic strip character called *Little Herman*. In the First World War he worked on animated films showing surgical operations, and afterwards a series *Aesop's Fables* as well as several Mutt and Jeff cartoons. His company, Audio Cinema, failed in 1928 and it was then that he joined 20th Century. Some Terrytoon characters were *Mighty Mouse* (a heroic mouse, a take-off of Superman), *Heckel and Jeckel* and *Farmer Alfalfa* (or *Farmer Gray*). Later, in the Fifties, the Terrytoons studios were to produce some excellent cartoons including Al Kouzel's *The Juggler of Notre Dame* and Pintoff's *Flebus,* when Gene Deitch was supervising director and CBS had taken over from Paul Terry. Kouzel's film, taken from R. O. Blechman's drawings, showed tiny figures lost in the depth of a CinemaScope screen. Apart from these exceptional productions, Terrytoons are closer in style to UPA than are other commercial studios for instance in their *Clint Clobber* series. Universal took over *Oswald the Rabbit,* which between 1926 and 1928 had been produced by Disney, and was then made by **Walter Lantz.** *Do A Good Deed, Hill Billies,* and *Two Little Lambs,* were some of the titles. Other Universal characters were *Winchester the Tortoise, Andy Panda,* the little black boy *Eight Ball,* and a miniature faun, *Peterkin.* In the Californian studio a hundred artists produced ten cartoons a year under Walter Lantz.

In Hollywood, Vitaphone (Warner Brothers) produced *Looney Tunes,* whose star was *Bosko,* a loquacious little Negro, created by Harman and Ising. Another series, *Merrie Melodies,* included *Mr. and Mrs. Is The Name* (Ben Clopton and Isidor Carlton), *Buddy's Theatre* and *Buddy of The Legion.* Leon Schlesinger and then Edward Selzer were in charge of production, about thirty cartoons a year. *Bugs Bunny* was created in 1938–39 as was *Porky Pig* (the first character to speak with the voice of the celebrated Mel Blanc), but they did not reach their full popularity until after the war. They were later joined at Warners by *Daffy,* a black duck, and *Beaky,* a vulture.

RKO for some time distributed Disney's films but had another

Below: Pintoff's little man, FLEBUS

series *Rainbow Parade* and in 1934 produced three cartoons from O. Soglow's *Little King* which were quite successful.

M-G-M made some good clown cartoons, for instance *The Lost Chick*. There was also a series *Happy Harmonies* (*Hey Hey Fever!* and *When the Cat's Away*). Production was directed by Fred C. Quimby, but Rudolf Ising and Hugh Harman started in this studio as also did Tex Avery, William Hanna and Joseph Barbera.

Ub Iwerks has already been mentioned in the section on Disney, and most of his cartoon work has been for the Disney Studio. *Flip the Frog* and *Little Negro,* his own creations working for Pat Powers, and distributed by M-G-M, had a comparatively modest career, lacking perhaps the apt story line which helped to sell Disney's short cartoons.

POPEYE THE SAILOR

Paramount had a series, *Colour Classics,* which included *The Elephant Never Forgets* and *Song of the Birds.* However, their most important films were those of Max Fleischer which they distributed up to 1942. Max Fleischer was the only cartoonist who in the Thirties rivalled Disney in popularity. Lo Duca reports the results of a popularity poll in 1938 in which American children voted Popeye the Sailor into first place in preference to Mickey Mouse. One wonders whether the preference shown for the violence of the growling Popeye over the gentle Mickey with his small voice, may not have influenced the nature of subsequent American cartoons.

Fleischer was born in Austria in 1885 but came to America as an infant. He drew cartoons for the "Brooklyn Daily Eagle," earning two dollars a week, then for "Popular Science Monthly." During the first world war he made instructional cartoons for the army and afterwards created *Koko the Clown* and *Betty Boop.* There was a studio in Florida directed by Dave Fleischer, Max's brother, with four hundred employees. Dave claimed in 1929 to have patented a system for drawing sound direct on the film and also a cartoon cine-meter to facilitate split second synchronisation.

The first Popeye film was made in 1933 and was taken from the comic-strip character created by the cartoonist Segar. Popeye's girl was Olive Oyl, his opposite and foil, thin where he was muscular, squeaky instead of gruff, timid when he was bold, refined instead of rough. Other characters were Wimpey, a neighbour friend, and Sweetpea, a tough baby. Most of the films followed a common pattern. Popeye would come up against his bitter enemy, Bluto, a huge barrel of a man with a fierce black beard; Bluto had all the advantages;

44

stronger, better placed, he would violently bash Popeye about until he was hardly alive, or else he would kidnap Olive Oyl, ill-treat her, threaten her with nameless outrages. Then at the crisis of the film Popeye would somehow, from somewhere, produce a can of spinach, prominently labelled so there could be no mistake—SPINACH. Immediately the tide would turn, Popeye invincible, from whatever impossible position, would triumph: push back railway-engines, move mountains, drink up rivers, carry ocean liners, fight tigers, and even treat the world itself like a flabby punching-ball. As for Bluto he would be punched, pummelled, flattened, banged, stretched, poked, blown up, and utterly routed. Popeye fasting was a wizened little sailor with tattooed arms and a croaking voice; with spinach inside he was a combination of Hercules, Samson, Goliath, and the Atomic Bomb. Fleischer is said to have had a financial agreement with the American Spinach Canning Syndicate, but it is doubtful how many children were converted to spinach because of seeing the films. There is no doubt that thousands of them were converted to Popeye and clamoured for another helping.

★   ★   ★

In 1936 Fleischer made a medium length Popeye film, *Popeye the Sailor Meets Sinbad the Sailor,* one of the best of the series. Sinbad was a close cousin to Popeye, alike but different. The contrast was a novelty, the likeness was reassuring. Popeye's old enemy Bluto appeared in new guise and there were all the wonders and monsters of the Arabian Nights into the bargain. Then in 1939, apparently spurred by the success of Disney's *Snow White,* the Fleischers dropped Popeye to produce a full-length cartoon from Swift's *Gulliver's Travels.* The film covered only the first part of Swift's book, Gulliver's voyage to Lilliput, the plot (the war between King Little of Lilliput and King Bombo of Blefusen) was simplified and several new characters introduced: Princess Glory, Prince David, Towncrier Gabby, a trio of spies, Sneak, Snoop and Snitch, and a carrier pigeon, Twinkletoes. *Gulliver's Travels* was quite amusing, the comic characters more successful than the straight leads, but it was not Popeye. Fleischer's next long film *Mr. Bug Goes to Town,* released in England as *Hoppity Goes to Town,* with insect characters, was a flop. Fleischer never succeeded in going beyond his established characters as Disney did. The failure of *Mr. Bug* meant that Fleischer was unable to break out of short cartoons and though Paramount continued to make Popeye films it was on a reduced scale.

Fleischer's difficulties freed Disney of one rival, though there still remained the growing competiton of the new Tex Avery school at Warners and M-G-M. About the same time another new group was to break away and set up in rivalry—UPA. A new influence also, more powerful than even the biggest film giants was about to come on the scene—television. These developments deserve a new chapter.

The Tex Avery school of violence: TOM AND JERRY

4. Postwar America: UPA, Avery and Avant-Garde

Throughout the Thirties the Disney Studio steadily grew in out-put and man-power, far surpassing in size, equipment and efficiency, any other animation studio in the world. It was the biggest and the best. But in some ways it was a restrictive organisation for the graphic artists who worked there. Disney himself, as time went on, became more and more the businessman, the manager, concerned with script conferences, audience reaction, box-office, output, man-hours, dead-lines. After the war his corporation had over three thousand em-ployees, a gross income of ten million dollars a year, and there were thirty conferences a week. Walt was disposed to express a hostile atti-tude to art at this time. "I dream that one of my pictures ended up in an art house (he said) and I wake up shaking." Or, "we're selling corn and I like corn." The organisation he had built up from nothing was his pride and joy, and though this emotional involvement had brought him success, it led him to take a personal, paternalistic interest in details which left little room for others' personal tastes. In the long run anyone who worked above the purely routine level had to be an extension of his personality. In this way control was far tighter than at the Canadian National Film Board where McLaren has collaborated with and encouraged other animators without dominating. The same applied to John Grierson in his relations with British documentary directors at the Empire Marketing Board and the GPO Unit. These bodies did not need perhaps the same toughness as Disney's studio, working without protection in the commercial field, but they have produced more varied, individual creative work.

In 1940 Disney's studio moved into new, expensive premises where working conditions were both more impersonal and more controlled. At the same time due to temporary financial difficulties there were wage cuts and lay-offs. There were other grievances: for many years the only film credit had been to Disney himself, then when credits were given on some of the feature pictures, so many names were briefly shown that any individual name was lost in the crowd; there were personal jealousies too, due to differences in conditions, put down to the boss's favouritism. One way and another matters came to a head in a series of disputes in the summer of 1941 which lasted nine weeks and temporarily closed the studio.

Disney who, apart from taking the whole thing too personally, was suffering from overwork, was persuaded to go on holiday, and the strike was settled in his absence. Later, however, there were dismissals and resignations. To some extent the dispute can be seen not as concerned with hours and wages, but as the reaction of highly individual artists seeking more freedom of expression. It was a number of these (Stephen Bosustow, Bill Hurtz, Pete Burness, John Hubley, Bob Cannon) who after leaving Disney formed UPA—United Productions of America. UPA was a much looser group than Disney, allowing more individual work, producing cartoons in a wide variety of styles, giving the artist his head. It is interesting to note that UPA, either because it lacked the same discipline or because its artists were more independently minded, showed a strong tendency to disintegrate. By 1955 it had lost several of its original members, among them those with the strongest personal styles. In the long run, UPA settled down to producing cartoons in a few styles which by then had become routine, and given the progress which had been made were not significantly more original than those of Disney. This is only to say that for any artist there is a temptation to repeat what has been successful, inspiration sometimes flags, and any new style becomes less exciting as it becomes more familiar. The UPA breakaway was undoubtedly a rejuvenating, fertilising influence whose value can hardly be overestimated. Even its offshoots, though they may have weakened UPA itself, established important creative artists in the animation field: Gene Deitch, Bill Sturm, Pintoff, Hubley. The diversification of UPA also encouraged further diversification and made it easier for later *avant-garde* experimental work by Carmen D'Avino, Robert Breer, Ed Emshwiller, and Teru Murakami. In art, value is not necessarily related to size of output, and a single work may be a landmark. *Unicorn in the Garden, The Juggler of Notre Dame, Munro, Flat Hatting,* or the first *Mr. Magoo,* the first *Gerald McBoing Boing,* the first *Flebus*—any one of these is of more significance than the three-hundred-and-fifty-sixth *Mickey Mouse.*

★　　★　　★

Not only did UPA encourage individual and different work. It marked a general change in style which pointed the way to what has become almost a new approach to the cartoon, not only in America but all over the world. The trend can be described as moving away from realism, but towards greater economy and towards a more appropriate use of the cartoon medium. Disney's figures are far from absolute realism: his mouse, his duck, his dog are not real animals, his human characters are not real people. Nevertheless the drawing of his characters and the way they move are based on reality. His methods,

UPA's most popular character: DESTINATION MAGOO

that is the standard, commercial cartoon methods, currently involve the use of a rotascope, an instrument which reproduces real movement so it can be copied (with modification if necessary) in a cartoon. The characters have, more or less, the curves of nature and their movements are smooth and life-like. Disney's backgrounds are in the realistic, reproduction-of-nature tradition, carefully drawn, in bright but natural colours.

By contrast, in the typical modern cartoon the background may simply be non-existent or it may be a bit of brightly-patterned wallpaper. The figures may be made of sticks or lines; or cut out of cardboard with jointed arms; or made up from unjoined roughly-torn scraps of paper (for head, body, arms etc.). The movements may be jerky, unrealistic, or even a series of static shots. The new style can be seen too as a movement away from the romantic to a tougher, truer confrontation of life—the cynicism, the sophistication, the depth of adult attitudes are not ruled out.

UPA started this. Here is a comparison of the two styles by a British animator, John Smith: "In Disney's cartoon films . . . the rich, even sugary colouring and bulbous forms are matched by movements that resemble a bladder of water moving floppily and sensuously. The sentimentality of mood is matched with cute, coy, easy movement and sadism, by excessive distortion and squashing. UPA artists favour simplicity of form and simplicity of movement, the essence without the frills. Acid colours and sharp forms are matched by movement the way cane, glass, wire would move, springy, whippy, staccato. The wit and cynicism of these cartoons is acted out in slapstick of a high but *blasé* kind." What John Smith does not say is that UPA created a different kind of world. In UPA cartoons light fittings hang from nothing, a staircase appears in the void, a door is put on the screen just as one of the characters comes through it. This sort of surrealism was not only witty, it was entirely appropriate to the medium.

THE WORK OF UPA

The founder of UPA was **Stephen Bosustow,** a six foot young Canadian. He won an art prize at the age of eleven and began his "animated" career as painter in a small company, then worked with Ub Iwerks on *Flip the Frog* (1932), with Walter Lantz (1934), and spent seven years with Disney. After leaving Disney he became a production illustrator for Hughes Aircraft and while there was commissioned to make a film on industrial safety, *Sparks and Chips Get the Blitz.* A cartoon made in 1944 for Roosevelt's last presidential campaign, *Hell Bent for Election* (director Chuck Jones), was seen by ten million people, and made his name. In 1945 he started UPA with a staff of six. By 1948 it had grown to 175, they had studios at Burbank, California, and their films were being distributed by Columbia. Bosustow as producer and head of the studio gave up directing after *Swab Your Choppers* (1947).

Ragtime Bear, the first Magoo picture, was directed in 1949 by John Hubley who had made *Robin Hoodlum* and *The Magic Fluke,* and was to make *Fuddy Duddy Buddy,* another Magoo picture, and *Rooty Toot Toot,* a version of Frankie and Johnny, in 1952. Magoo was the most popular of UPA characters and **Pete Burness** the most prolific director, turning out several Magoo pictures a year, for example *Captains Outrageous* (1952), *Magoo Goes Skiing* (1954), *Stage Door Magoo* and *When Magoo Flew* (1955). A bad-tempered, short-sighted, middle-aged fuss-pot, Magoo lived dangerously, getting involved in one misunderstanding after another: playing tennis with a walrus, fighting a duel with a mirror, mistaking striped curtains for a convict suit, a boxing-ring for a dance floor, a bear for a golf-caddie. His appearance, bulbous nose, red face and croaking voice, were a tribute to the comedian, W. C. Fields.

In 1951 **Bob Cannon** directed *Gerald McBoing Boing,* a film about a little boy who made noises like a jew's harp whenever he tried to talk. This too became a popular series, with surrealism on the soundtrack as well as in the images. *Gerald on Planet Moo* (1955) shows Gerald travelling in a spacecraft to a new planet where the inhabitants think his strange noises are the language of Planet Earth. Another character, *Christopher Crumpet,* was introduced by Cannon in 1952, a little boy with impossible demands, who got so cross when his father could not give him what he wanted that he kept turning into a chicken.

There were two outstanding UPA films based on graphic artist's work, Bob Cannon's *Madeline,* the story of a little girl's adventures on the continent from Ludwig Bemelman's paintings, and *Unicorn in the Garden* (Bill Hurtz, 1953) which brilliantly transferred Thurber's sex-satire and line-drawing to the screen in a surrealist style. When the

Another UPA stalwart: Gerald McBoing Boing

man wants to buttonhole his wife upstairs in her bedroom his arm simply grows long enough to reach her. In 1953 Ted Parmelee made two more-serious films, *The Tell-Tale Heart* (Poe's story) and *The Emperor's New Clothes* (Hans Andersen) in a fantastic decorative style. *The Tell-Tale Heart*, Poe's story of a murderer betrayed by the heart-beats of a man he has buried under the floor boards, was one of the first examples of the cartoon being used to express the horrific and macabre.

Gene Deitch, another UPA director, made *Howdy Doody and His Magic Hat* in 1952, then in 1957 after he had become supervising director of Terrytoons, two outstanding cartoons, *Flebus* from an Ernest Pintoff story and *The Juggler of Notre Dame*, a cartoon he worked on with Al Kouzel. *The Juggler of Notre Dame* animated the drawings of the well-known cartoonist R. O. Blechman, shaky line-drawing reduced to the ultimate economy of expression. The tiny figures set in the huge CinemaScope screen were something new in cartoon design. Deitch in *Munro* also brought to life the work of another celebrated cartoonist, Jules Feiffer. Since 1960 Deitch has moved to Prague, directing and producing cartoons for the American market: *Tom and Jerry, Popeye, Krazy Kat, Nudnik.*

★   ★   ★

The most individual of UPA's artists, and the most important individual cartoonist working in the States, is **John Hubley.** He started with Disney, working on *Snow White, Pinocchio, Fantasia, Bambi* and *Dumbo.* Then he worked for UPA until the Fifties and made some of their best early cartoons, but his style was too rich to be contained permanently within the sharp economy of the UPA image, and he finally formed his own company, *Storyboard,* his first independent film being *Adventures of an Asterisk* (1956). He is a fine artist with an unmistakable trade-mark although from film to film his style has developed and matured. Again one of his films, *Harlem Wednesday,* is taken from the Negro portraits of the American painter, Gregorio Prestopino. Hubley's early work for UPA and the first Storyboard films, *Moonbird* and *The Tender Trap,* are light-hearted, gentle, romantic. His later work (*Children of the Sun, Of Stars and Men, The Hole, The Hat*) is more serious, even didactic. Hubley's whole outlook is one of confident optimism, there is nothing tortured or tragic in any of his films. He is very much a family man, his wife Faith Hubley has collaborated in much of his work, and in *Of Stars and Men* and *Moonbird* he used the voices of his own children to good effect.

In *Moonbird* we follow two charming, crazy kids who burble about in a moonshine landscape to lure the great, gaunt moonbird with scat-

John Hubley's OF STARS AND MEN

tered sweets, most of which they eat themselves. The composition is
loose brush-strokes, the colours moonlit blues and greens, and everything is translucent and fluid as moonlight itself. *Of Stars and Men* is
a cartoon history of the Universe. Hubley takes us back to geological
ages at the beginning of the world, works through the stages of evolution, and wonders about the future. It is an astonishing achievement,
conventional in ideas, but original in approach and often very beautiful
in its pictorial effects. In some ways it is reminiscent of Hendrick Van
Loon's *History of Mankind* and it deserves the same popularity.

The Hole has the same theme as many present day artistic works:
a warning of potential destruction by atomic explosion. Two building
workers, a white and a black man, are busy below ground preparing
the foundations of a big building. They yarn about this and that, and
get on to the familiar topic of the button: Who would press it? What
would happen? Could anything go wrong? Then we travel underground
as the voices go on talking and speculating, and see dug-outs, bomb-
proof shelters with listeners, watchers; then a rat gnawing a wire,
giving a false alarm. At the building site a crane drops its load and
then—the cataclysm. The black worker climbs up out of the hole and

53

Another Hubley masterpiece: THE HAT

sees, instead of the busy streets and buildings, a flat desolation. However, the scene gradually goes back to normal—the bomb has fallen, but only in the black's imagination, as a result of his train of thought followed by the crash of the crane accident.

The Hat is another cartoon with a moral. A little fat white soldier is patrolling one side of a frontier, a tall thin black soldier the other. The black soldier drops his hat on the wrong side. The white soldier will neither let him cross the line to pick it up, nor himself pick it up and give it back. The squirrels and rabbits can hop over the border as the spirit moves them, but the human beings are stuck like glue in their own rigmarole.

Both the cartoons are drawn and coloured in a pleasant, accomplished style with something like a crayon or pastel effect. André Martin describes Hubley as a master of "rough animation" by which he means that Hubley leaves his drawing with the sketch stage (the bones) showing through in the finished film and refuses to apply the process called *cleaning* by which "rough lines are smoothed out and their native forcefulness replaced by bland sterility." Most of the work

54

of Disney and other conventional cartoonists is overdone, over-finished in this way. There is a story that Frank Lloyd Wright, struck by the artistic qualities of a rough sketch he saw when being shown over the Disney studios, said "You should make all your films like this." The remark was not appreciated. Another feature of both *The Hole* and *The Hat* is the very effective use of rich accents on the soundtrack.

It is characteristic of Hubley's kindly outlook that the atomic explosion in *The Hole* is only an imaginary one, although in *The Hat* there is no solution to the problem of crossing the frontier. The benevolent, good-humoured character of Hubley's films may be seen as a limitation, and it is true that he never attains the tragic, or comic intensity of artists with less reserve. Nevertheless in addition to the fine qualities of his style, there is a dignity about his work which commands respect.

Some of Hubley's recent pictures have become stronger in subject matter and harsher in style. *Eggs* (1971), looks well forward to a grim future with machine-like characters called Death and Genetrix living in an ungraceful world where a couple require a permit to have a child and people, by benefit of transplant operations, are faced with the prospect of living for 200 years and more. However, the delightful *Windy Day* (1968) has the same accomplished painterly style and winning voices as Hubley's earlier films.

★   ★   ★

Ernest Pintoff is well qualified to play Impudence to Hubley's Dignity. He made his *début* with UPA which he joined in 1957. He created the character of *Flebus* for Terry Toons, a comic little gem featuring a tiny character drawn with ironic economy of line in a living wide-screen tradition. In Pintoff there is more of the comic cartoonist, less of the artist than in Hubley, and his later work has more in common with the UPA style. After leaving UPA he was mostly engaged in TV commercials, but the few cinema cartoons he has made are outstanding for their comic originality. *The Violinist* tells the story of Hapless Harry who scrapes his violin in the streets. He is advised that his playing will improve if he suffers and becomes miserable. So it does, but as he can't stand being miserable, he finishes by going back to happiness and bad music. *The Interview* depicts a jazz musician holding forth to a radio interviewer. Both parties grow more and more off-beam, less coherent, less in touch, until communication breaks down altogether. As with all Pintoff's films the satirical dialogue is an integral part of the performance. In *The Critic* the screen is filled with abstract shapes, but on the soundtrack the tired, croaking voice of an unseen spectator sends the whole thing up. *The Old Man and the Flower* is about violence, a bitter film quite unlike Hubley's work. In the end the old man is left ill-treated, unavenged, bereft of his flower—but he carries on. Since this cartoon Pintoff has made a short live-action, expressionist film, *The Shoes,* and more recently still a feature, *Harvey Middleman Fireman*. It looks as though he himself is lost to the cartoon world. However, the latest film from Pintoff's studio is a very individual cartoon called *Howard* by a new director, **Leonard Glasser.** Its scrawling black figures presented without backgrounds, and its long, involved captions in block-like *art nouveau* lettering develop a crazy internal triangle: the plight of Howard who speaks so beautifully and moves so gracefully, but is committed to the company of Howard suffering from deafness, and Howard determined to assert his absolute equality.

TELEVISION INFLUENCE

At the beginning of the Fifties UPA were on the crest of the wave. They had successfully challenged Disney, created new, universally popular characters, established a new style, expanded to New York and opened a London office. In 1956 Bosustow announced several projects for feature films: *The White Deer* based on Thurber, *Don Quixote,* Johnson's *Volpone, Helen of Troy.* But none of these materialised, and though they made two longer films, *Magoo's Christmas Carol* and *Gay Purr-ee,* and a feature, *Magoo's Arabian Nights,* UPA suffered a setback. In 1958 they had to close their New York studio, although in Burbank, California, they were still producing half-a-million dollars worth of commercials and other films for television. In 1961 Bosustow sold his interest and left in order to make travel and educational films,[1] but UPA continue. In 1964 David Rider wrote in *Films and Filming:* "UPA. Still there and they will make 26 half-hour stories for TV, featuring Mr. Magoo."

No doubt a good deal of UPA's original fire was lacking for they had lost several of their best artists and a *Ham and Hattie* series introduced in the late Fifties was not up to their best standard. But this change in their fortunes represented also a general alteration in conditions, common to most western countries, which has pushed cartoons out of cinema, leaving them to find new markets in television. There are several reasons for the change.

First, the pattern of cinema-going has altered radically. When the cinema was the only form of mass entertainment it attracted a weekly

---

[1] A cartoon from Stephen Bosustow Productions *Joshua in a Box* (John Lange) appeared at the 1971 Annecy Festival, a witty trifle pointing out that we create our own personal prisons.

audience who went regardless of the title of the film or critical report about it; they simply went to "the pictures." However, the cartoon (again not any special cartoon) was a customary part of "the pictures" and exhibitors were obliged to put a cartoon in their customers' shopping-bags along with the other goods. Now, this uncritical audience seeking easy distraction had turned to television, and the cinema can only draw an audience to see a particular film which they have read or heard about. Under these circumstances attention will naturally be concentrated on the feature.

An audience will come to see a good feature whether or not it is accompanied by a first-rate cartoon. Thus there is no incentive to the exhibitor to spend his money hiring cartoons which in any case are relatively expensive compared with other shorts. Because critical attention is concentrated on the feature, the standard of feature films shown may be better—but the supporting programme suffers. Programmes of short cartoons by themselves will not generally attract an audience, or only the casual shopping or travelling audience who have an hour to spare. Hence the occasional news and cartoon cinema in big centres or railway stations. Again this is an audience which goes regardless of what is playing, no doubt the reason why the programmes at these cinemas are usually indifferent in quality.

★   ★   ★

In television the conditions are different again. Feature films are popular and many old (and not so old) movies can be seen on TV. But there is an enormous audience seeking an infinite variety of programmes, there is plenty of money to pay for shorts, and they appear, not as part of a programme in the cinema sense, but in their own right. Thus there is a definite place for the cartoon or puppet picture, especially now that colour TV is steadily spreading. Perhaps also, the cartoon, as an art of miniature precision, can be more easily adapted to the small screen than the live-action feature whose strength is in its breadth of treatment and expanse of vision. So far animation has been kept to children's-bedtime viewing hours, but this is not to say that a few adults do not sneak a look at the brighter series, for instance at the BBC's *Magic Roundabout* with its clever dialogue.

Where there is commercial television, animation has had consistent success in the field of advertising. In some ways live photography is a little uneasy in commercial harness. Advertisers present an unreal world in which owners of particular brands of refrigerators, cars, carpets and so on, will be beautiful, secure, successful in business, in love, in life. There is something incongruous between this fake dream and the reality of the photographic medium. Often in an attempt to reduce its harsh realism the photograph is made misty, or sparkled with stars, or used to show some unreal juxtaposition—a watch in a bottle of whisky, a cow in a drawing room.

Some of the most successful advertising gets away from realism and makes the customer laugh by using a cartoon or puppet figure. For years Guinness have based their successful advertising on humour, including several cartoon films. In other ways animation is a good vehicle because it can be highly polished, perfectly timed, can achieve sharp humour, satire, striking visual effects, utter clarity or wild surrealism.

As the television market has developed, animation has turned more and more towards TV and away from the cinema. First there are the commercials—most rewarding financially, and also, in trade circles at least, conferring prestige if they win awards or are of outstanding quality. Then there are TV series, based generally on a particular character or characters, often a funny man. In addition individual entertainment shorts and even feature-length cartoons are beginning to be made for television, though an expensive feature like *The Yellow Submarine* or *The Aristocats* will obviously go for the bigger money of a cinema career if this is possible. The new development has enlarged the audience for animation and brought prosperity to many studios. As will be seen later it is this new market which will make investment in computer and other new techniques possible. Cinema fans may regret an embellishment that has been lost, but they should recognise that if animation had had to depend on the cinema alone, it would by now be a lost art.

THE TEX AVERY SCHOOL

In an interview in 1956, Bosustow said that UPA avoided "hurt gags." There is no violence in *Gerald McBoing Boing* or *Willie the Kid*. Magoo is constantly threatened with disaster, but always avoids it. However there is a postwar group of American cartoonists whose whole work is based on violence, break-neck, unremitting, extreme violence; their avatar is **Tex Avery,** their names are Robert McKimson, Chuck Jones, Friz Freleng (Warners); William Hanna and Joe Barbera (M-G-M); and Walter Lantz (Universal).

Tex Avery began making cartoons in 1930, working on *Aesop's Fables* with Charles Mintz, then working with Walter Lantz on the *Oswald the Rabbit* series. Before the war he collaborated with Chuck Jones at Warners, and between them they developed *Bugs Bunny,* said to have been invented by another animator at Warners, Bob Clampett, who has now branched into making puppet films for TV. One of Avery's characters is a duck who appears in *Lucky Ducky* (1948), a cartoon packed with gags. It starts with the heroine doing a striptease dance as she comes out of the egg, going on to out-manoeuvre at every turn two duck-shooters, lanky, flop-eared hounds, who finish the day with empty bags and long faces. Another character is Droopy, a pint-sized hound who appears in many pictures. In *Droopy Outfoxed* there is a wild fox-hunt, the screen full of hounds and foxes. Droopy does better than the bigger hounds, but it is the foxes who carry the day ending up by enjoying the hunt dinner, while the hounds are shut outside. There are many neat gags, one depicting Mr. Fox as the perfect English gentleman, who throughout the break-neck contortions of the action, carries a cup of tea in one hand, taking a polite sip between rounds. Another well-known character is *Chilly Willy,* a penguin.

In some cartoons Avery is an anarchic film-maker obsessed with changes in size, with cosmic destruction. In one of his films a goat eats the moon and then the cinema screen. In another a baby kangaroo jumps into its mother's pouch, the mother follows, disappearing into her own inside. A typical early film is *Kingsize Canary* (1947), in which a cat feeds a canary on magic *Jumbo Gro* to make it a better size for eating. The canary swells out as big as a man and attacks the cat, then these two plus a dog and a mouse take turns to drink the magic potion. Turn and turn about they grow and the film ends with the cat and the mouse as two King Kongs rearing above the skyscrapers of New York and finally dancing on a world hardly big enough to bear them. A reviewer wrote of Avery's film *The Cat That Hated People* (1949), "it is not remarkable for the subtlety of its line or colour, but for its ruthless, anarchistic fantasy which is quite uncompromising in its pace and extravagance." Avery has been called "a Walt Disney who has read Kafka."

★　　★　　★

Warner's leading cartoonists were for some time Chuck Jones, Friz Freleng and Robert McKimson, though both Chuck Jones and Freleng now have their own production companies, Chuck Jones with Les Goldman (Tower 12) and Freleng with David De Patie (De Patie-Freleng). **Chuck Jones** as we have said helped to develop *Bugs Bunny* and made a good few films with this character. His *Rabbit of Seville* (1949) is a beautifully worked-out exercise, matching Rossini's music with some uproarious slapstick as Bugs rushes into the opera-house to sing, hotly pursued by a Magoo-like hunter. Bugs then proceeds to perform with tremendous verve, at the same time wickedly tormenting his tormentor. A much later effort, *The Abominable Snowman* (1961), shows us Bugs Bunny and Daffy Duck trying to escape a huge Snowman who has a passion for cuddling bunnies. Bugs shows fiendish ingenuity in disguising Daffy as a rabbit and himself as a duck. They finally escape when the Snowman chases them to Florida and melts away. Chuck Jones has made many cartoons featuring E. Coyote (a rather mangy specimen) hopelessly chasing Mimi, the Road Runner (a kind of minor ostrich with a cry like "Beep Beep" and the speed of an electric hare). Some titles are *Beep Prepared, Gee Whiz-z-z,* and *Lickety Splat.* The action is at virtually electronic speed, the landscapes are aridity itself—bottomless canyons, rocky gorges, vertical cliffs—the gags involve explosives, avalanches of rocks, grim machines. The whole presents a singularly harsh, forbidding catalogue of violence, the two participants going through their never-ending chase routine as if doomed victims of an undying curse. Chuck Jones created another character, *Private Snafu,* during the war and also worked with UPA directing *Hell Bent for Election* in 1944. He won an Academy Award in 1966 with his *Dot and the Line,* and has recently made, with Abe Levitow, a feature movie combining animation with live-action, *The Phantom Tollbooth* (1969). The picture is taken from a novel by Norton Juster, well-known in the United States, and the main characters are a little boy, Milo, and his animal friends. Chuck Jones has grown in stature over the years and, with a large and varied body of work to his credit, is now a leading figure in the animation world.

★   ★   ★

Friz Freleng has made *Sam the Pirate, Tweety Pie and Sylvester* (1947), *Dog Pounded, Speedy Gonzales, Captain Hareblower* and *Nighty Night Bugs* (1958). Sylvester is a rather scruffy cat with a furtive manner always stalking the insufferably smug Tweety Pie (a featherless little bird), and always getting the worst of it. *Sandy Claws* (1955) shows Tweety Pie in his cage being given a beach outing by grandma, while Sylvester stalks him in all possible ways. There is a memorable scene, after Sylvester's motor boat has had its bottom ripped out on a rock, which shows Sylvester bravely saluting and standing at attention as he sinks steadily into the deep. *Speedy Gonzales* is another formidable mouse, a rather rakish man-about-town. There is a new series recently introduced by DePatie Freleng called *Roland and the Ratfink* and they are currently making a cartoon version of *The Wizard of Oz.* In the States, their *Pink Panther* character is popular on TV.

Robert McKimson's creatures include Daffy Duck and Elmer Fudd and among his films are *The Mousemerised Cat* (1946), *Hop Look* *and Listen* (1947), *No Parking Hare* (1953), *Dime to Retire* (1954), *Mousetaken Identity* (1957), *The Mouse That Jack Built, Wind Blown Hare* (Bugs Bunny), and many more. Recently McKimson at Warners has produced a *Cool Cat* series featuring a hippy tiger, and cartoons are planned with the Keystone Kops and a new character, Merlin the Magic Mouse. As we can see from the titles these three animators have frequently swapped characters, though each of them seems to have had their special favourites.

★ ★ ★

At M-G-M the principal characters are *Tom and Jerry,* created by Hanna and Barbera and Fred Quimby. They are another cat-and-mouse pair eternally at daggers drawn, each bashing the other though Tom usually gets the worst of it. In *Mouse for Sale* (1955), the ebb and flow of their bickering is built round a situation in which Jerry keeps disguising himself as a *white* mouse so as to get adopted, protected, fed and petted, by an all-powerful human being. There is a rich flow of invention as Tom unmasks one "white" disguise only to be faced with another. In *The Cat Concerto* (1946), Tom playing Liszt in a concert, disturbs Jerry who is asleep inside the grand piano. Again with brilliant invention the piece is kept going right through their fighting, though they batter the piano with more-than-somewhat unorthodox techniques. Since 1957 **William Hanna and Joseph Barbera** have had their own production company and have created new characters for television: *Ruff and Reddy, Quick Draw McGraw, Huckleberry Hound,* and most popular of all the *Flintstones,* a stone-age family.

Because of their television work they are perhaps the best known animators in the States. Their output is terrifying. They have made a hundred to two hundred *Tom and Jerry* cartoons, and currently are said to turn out 25,000 feet of film a week for television. Their television cartoons are highly mechanised. The different positions of the body have been rationalised and classified by numbers. The positions of the head, the mouth, the limbs, the body, vibration as a result of shock, entry, exit—everything is numbered. To make a new sequence it is sufficient to plan the sound carefully, for there is a lot of dialogue, and then simply draft a script which gives the numbers of the key, feed it into a computer, and the machine will do the rest. Animators no longer have to draw successive movements but merely make lists of numbers. This highly rationalised technique has been used, not only for Hanna and Barbera productions but several other cartoon series for TV: *Bono the Clown, Rod Rocket, Space Hero, Crusader Rabbit, King Leonard, Deputy Dawg.* The resultant cartoons are decidedly inferior, but this may be due to the artists becoming stale and running out of ideas as much as to the methods used. Labour-saving devices are not all bad, and the animated film-maker would be wrong to reject them. They are discussed further in the last chapter. However, though rationalisation and machines may enable mass production of celluloid, they cannot supply mass production of ideas.

At Universal there is Walter Lantz's *Woody Woodpecker, Andy Panda, Oswald,* and at 20th Century-Fox Paul Terry's *Mighty Mouse,* an animal imitation of Superman. *Popeye the Sailor* goes marching on, appearing on television, directed by I. Sparber, but a pale reflection of the original. Popeye series have also been made by Halas and Batchelor in London and Gene Deitch in Prague.

★　　★　　★

The best of these cartoons are often the fairly early ones: *Kitty Foiled, Mouse Trouble, The Cat and the Mermouse* in the Tom-and-Jerry series; or *Bugs Bunny and the Three Bears, Bugs Bunny Rides Again, Mississippi Hare, Frigid Hare,* in the Bugs Bunny series; or Tex Avery's *Shooting of Dan MacGoo, Half-Pint Pigmy, Slap-happy Lion* as well as the films mentioned in detail; or *I Taw a Putty Tat* in the Sylvester-Tweety Pie saga. And the best of them do have a cracking pace and are full of invention. They had a new formula, a new vigour, and they made Disney seem dull and slow. At their occasional best their gags are cool and sophisticated, and have a nonchalant cavalier *style.* Chuck Jones, in one of his films *Now Hear This,* instead of the usual sound effect shows a notice: GIGANTIC EXPLOSION. This is fine. But in the long run the violence palls, the formula becomes stereotyped, we tire of the endless repetition of virtually the same situation, the absence of any plot, any subtlety, any relief from the bang-bang-bang of two characters chasing and bashing each other. French writers such as Robert Benayoun have praised these cartoonists, especially Avery, up to the skies: "Their structure, their equilibrium and geometry, make them at the same time impenetrable and sublime." They have compared them with Swift and de Sade. This is romantic moonshine, on a par with certain French critics' view of Hitchcock as a combination of profound philosopher and psychological genius with superhuman insight.

As one sees the average rag-bag collection of these cartoons in, say, a news cinema the result is often stunning in its repetitive violence and lack of originality or wit. At the same time one is astonished at the vigour and fertility of the vintage samples. Some of this unevenness of quality is no doubt due to the quantity of pictures turned out. As Chuck Jones said, "Since leaving UPA John Hubley has only made ten films, while at Warners I have made about 150." Disney made as many cartoons but spread over a longer period and with several hands helping to diversify the gags. Possibly an important factor is that, since all these cartoons depend on a chase or fight situation, the main action tends to be similar. Also the violent situations limit the development of the characters who hardly differ from one another. Thus to succeed they need a really bright idea for the central situation and then an absolute flood of gags to keep it going. Unfortunately when they start scraping the barrel, there is much repetition and the same gags crop up again and again. Sometimes they manage (Chuck Jones for example) to parody themselves in a witty, sophisticated incident, but this happens only occasionally. In one unhappy programme I saw a very average Tom and Jerry followed by a "Columbia Favourite"—*Leave Us to Chase It*—depicting a cat-and-mouse chase with situations, gags and even the characters themselves, an indistinguishable copy of the Tom and Jerry which had preceded it.

The drawing and colouring of the Tex Avery school is very similar to Disney, and though its exponents are all accomplished artists, they work within the formula of bright story-book pictures, and do not allow wide variety or free play for individual artistic styles. Perhaps these would be out of place in this ever-popular world of violence. A world so popular that perhaps it will absorb the whole film scene, since the latest Bond film *Diamonds Are Forever* in its faceless characterisation and inventive destruction can be seen as a live counterpart of a Bugs-Bunny-Sylvester-Beep-Beep cartoon.

★　　★　　★

Before leaving the commercial scene, mention should be made of **Saul Bass,** who has transformed the credit titles of feature films, in many cases by using animation. In the past credit titles consisted simply of lists of names put on a moving drum or on cards, and photographed. There would generally be some art-work to set off the names of the film-makers and the cast, but this decoration was usually unobtrusive, undistinguished, and bore little relation to the subject of the film. Saul Bass's credits consist of moving drawing, striking and attractive in itself, and cleverly related to the film, often adding considerably to its impact. To quote a writer in *Time*, "Bass's stalking cat was far and away the best thing in *Walk on the Wild Side* . . . for *The Seven Year Itch* . . . the colours and layout were as visually delightful as a Mondriaan in motion and the *t* in *Itch* scratched itself. He drew the fixed and crippled hand on *The Man with the Golden Arm* and the jig-sawed corpse of *Anatomy of a Murder*. For *Vertigo* he let his spook imagination run even further . . ."

Many animators have followed in his path with success, for instance Alexeïeff's credits for Orson Welles's *The Trial* (1962). Hubley and other Americans have been responsible for fine work, and the credits of Dick Williams and other British animators are mentioned elsewhere.

AVANT-GARDE, EXPERIMENTAL AND RECENT WORK

Cartoon production in the States has overwhelmingly been of commercial cartoons, and breakaway groups like UPA also aim primarily at popular entertainment, even if not in exactly the same orthodox style. There are however a growing number of eccentrics whose work is as idiosyncratic and sometimes as baffling as the most abstruse styles of modern painting. These are personal films made by individuals often working alone, sometimes making only one film as an experiment. Even if the results are not always entirely successful the work is important because it breaks new ground, because it is a growing point which may start future trends. By their nature it is difficult to write systematically about these films. Their distribution is haphazard and their publicity and information services non-existent. One can only mention the films one happens to have seen or read about, and the information gleaned about their makers.

Avant-garde film-making originated in Europe, and in this field the cartoon has followed, on the one hand, the live-action film and abstract experiments with the camera. On the other hand it has been influenced by movements in art, abstract painting, surrealism, futurism. One pioneer was the German, **Oscar Fischinger,** a follower of Ruttmann, who made abstract cartoons as visual accompaniment to music on the soundtrack. Hans Richter writes: "The forms in themselves were quite meaningless but his films were unique because of the solid unity of sound and picture. I remember with delight his Brahms' *Hungarian Dance.*" This is a short film made in 1931 in which sharply-outlined patches of light dance across the screen and change shape in time to the music. The technique is remarkable, and the composition is lively and interesting enough to hold the spectator for the six minutes the film lasts. Another film, *Composition in Blue* (1937), using coloured strips and cylinders, is heavier, more massive in its effects, but still impressive. In about 1938 Fischinger emigrated to America where he has made *Optical Poem, Allegretto, An American March.* He collaborated with Disney on the Bach sequence of *Fantasia* and was active for a long time in Hollywood.

Mary Ellen Bute's work is important, ranging from a silent film

Synchronisation (1934), with Schillinger and Jacob, to several films animating objects made with Ted Nemeth. Fischinger worked with two-dimensional animated drawings: Miss Bute concentrated rather on three-dimensional substances: ping-pong balls, paper-cutouts, sculptured models, cellophane, rhinestones, buttons. Some titles are *Anitra's Dance* (1936), *Evening Star* (1937), *Parabola* (1938), *Toccata and Fugue* (1940), *Tarantella, Spook Sport* (1941).

The painters, **John and James Whitney,** have pioneered in sound as well as in cartoon form, both sound and image being entirely abstract. The synthetic sound of their films is created by "an optical wedge" oscillating "over a light slit, by the movement of pendulums." The images are composed first in black-and-white sketches, then (by optical printer, pantograph and colour filters) are developed to cinematic proportions, given movement and colour, and are further varied by multiple-exposures, magnification, reduction and inversion. By these means they have made five short *Exercises* during the Fifties. More recent work includes "action painting" on film in *Celery Stalks at Midnight* (1951–58). James Whitney has made *Yantra,* completed in 1960 and covering a wide range of material, but mainly presenting configurations of simple elements, and also *Lapis* (1966). John Whitney worked at UPA and collaborated with Saul Bass on the credits for *Vertigo.* In the Sixties he has developed a specialised animation computer, producing *Catalogue,* a "brilliant display of floral patterns" and *Permutations* (1967), while his sons, Michael, John and Mark, have all made their own computer films.

Douglas Crockett (*Fantasmagoria, The Chase, Glenn Falls, Sequence, Long Bodies*) improvised by spreading oil colours on glass, adding, subtracting and manipulating them by means of razor-blades, brushes and fingers. He used non-drying oils mixed with the colours, adding other glass levels, and photographing through the glass. Writing in 1948 Lewis Jacobs also mentions Joseph Vogel's *House of Cards,* and Chester Kessler's *Plague Summer.* **Hy Hirsh** has made a good many abstract films. *Divertissement Rococo* is described as "composed entirely of oscilloscope and other moving artificial patterns." *Gyromorphosis,* although a very striking abstract record of moving shapes and colours, is not strictly animation, but a live-action recreation of the construction-sculpture made by the Dutch artist, Constant Nieuwenhuys of Amsterdam.

Active in more recent years are Carmen D'Avino, Robert Breer, Morton and Mildred Goldscholl and Stan Vanderbeek. **Carmen D'Avino** makes films from objects. The camera lingers on some stones in a river-bed, rapidly they grow colours, stripes of blue, red, yellow, green; or we see a piano and a gramophone (*Pianissimo*) which bit by bit turn all the shades of the rainbow; the piano keys coloured, striped, starred, chequered, the gramophone a spectral disc. In a recent film, *A Finnish Fable,* a number of female clothes-dummies undergo the same garish painting. The technique is limited but it is unpretentious and gay, a form of vicarious doodling. **The Goldscholls** also make films from objects. *Envelope Jive* amusingly brings alive envelopes of every size, shape and colour. *Intergalactic Zoo* creates strange creatures out of strings of beads accompanied by captions in an invented language and a surrealistic commentary about these Martians . . . It is more successful in evoking a mad other-life than many serious science-fiction stories. Their most recent short is *Up Is Down,* about a disorientated boy.

Robert Breer is an abstract painter and has made some odd cartoons. From his first films *Frame by Frame* (1952) and *Form Phases* (1955–56), he announced his indifference to realistic movement. *Form Phases No. 4* is a neatly composed abstract film, in which the movement of the elements is original and interesting, and the functional unity between the individual units of the composition is well maintained. In the copy I saw, it was followed by a thirty-second joke—*The Miracle,* which shows the Pope blessing the faithful. He juggles first with a golden halo, then with his own head, while a spectator gets a golden dazzle in her field-glasses. This is skilful and good fun, but Breer has become more and more difficult. Even in the more representational of his later films, *A Man and His Dog Out for Air* (1958) and *Horse over Tea Kettle* (1963), little objects and characters appear on the screen and disappear with great rapidity and without any easily discernible relationship. In *Jamestown Baloos* (1957), and *Blazes* (1961), he has a different picture with a different subject on every single frame of the film, to provide twenty-four shocks a second for the staggering spectator. André Martin writes: "These fragments of pure animation are aimed at cutting off both the memory of what one has seen and any chance of foreseeing what is to come, so as to concentrate on the pure essence of animation." At statements like this one can only hold one's breath in admiration. In an interview Breer himself says, "This film (*A Man and His Dog Out for Air*) like most of my films begins in the middle and goes towards the two ends . . . the final result cannot be exactly predicted . . . I am sorry if my films bore people, I would rather they made them angry." Breer's *BLP3* (1970) uses a single line twisting on the screen to describe imperialist expansion and its aftermath.

Stan Vanderbeek is another experimenter, on the edge perhaps of animation. In an early work, *Wheeeels,* collage cut-outs are animated in a neo-dada whimsey. *Science Friction* (1960) and *Breathdeath* are similar in technique, a writer describing the latter as "a collage-animation that cuts up photos and newsreel film and re-assembles them, producing a mixture of unexplainable fact and inexplicable act." *Panels for the Walls of the World* uses videotape control to produce an electronic *collage.* Another individualistic worker, **John Grunberger,** besides other techniques, has used glued-on acetate and paint applied direct to film (in *Crystal Vision* and *Inflorescence,* 1971) thus obtaining hard-edged crystal reactions and breaking up light with special effects on the screen. **Eliot Noyes** at Harvard University has made a film of clay figures, *Clay,* which presents a frightening picture of living matter endlessly changing, growing, struggling, devouring, being devoured. A second picture made for the Canadian National Film Board, *In a Box* (1969), shows a human-being building his own personal, isolating habitation.

Jordan Belson is a film-maker who has recently received critical praise, though he has been making abstract movies since the Forties. Titles are *Transmutation* (1947), *Improvisation* (1948), *Mambo, Caravan, Mandala* and *Bop Scotch* (1952–53), and in the Sixties, *Allures, Reentry, Phenomena, Samadhi, Momentum.* In his earlier pictures he used "scroll animation, improvised abstract composition, and stop-action animation of natural forms and surfaces"; in his later work he has used computer animation. An enthusiastic account is given by Gene Youngblood in his book "Expanded Cinema." *Phenomena* "is a film of outer-space rather than earth space." Of *Samadhi* Belson himself said "After it was finished I felt I should have died. I was rather amazed I didn't." Youngblood calls it "a cyclone of dynamic form and colour." In *Momentum* there is "a soul-shaking roar," "towering shards of luminescent colour reach deeper levels of the mind" and "the translucent realms of kinaesthesia leave one speechless." To sum up, "it is a calm, objective experience of concrete imagery that manages to suggest abstract concepts without becoming particularly symbolic." It will be interesting to see what Belson does next. One could go on adding names as further experimenters come to notice: Norman Rubington, Dwinell Grant (*Themis Contra-Themis,* 1941), Mylon Merian (*Abstract Films,* 1942), James E. Davis (*Light Reflections,* 1948, *Analogies,* 1953), Hugo Latelin (*Colour Designs,* 1948), Francis Lee (*Le Bijou, Idyll,* 1947), Roger Bruce Rogers (*Toccata Manhattan,* 1949).

The creation of abstract patterns on film has been called "cineplastics," but the word should be used with reserve. *Plastic* in art means three-dimensional as opposed to two-dimensional work so that object and puppet animation and live-action would qualify for the description. *Collage,* cut-out shapes and drawn animation would not. Writing in the Fifties a critic commented: "Though cineplastics is one of the most original forms of cinema . . . it is the hardest in which to achieve a good result. American experimenters . . . tirelessly explore designs, lights, colours, adding sound in an attempt to give life to the otherwise dead flow of images . . . They . . . mostly display technical crudeness, repetitiousness and unoriginality." However, the more recent work of Belson, the Whitneys, Stan Brakhage and John Stehura, besides those using videotape or manipulated cathode-ray images (Terry Riley, Nam June Paik, Aldo Tambellini), shows a wider range of material, a freer flow, a richer vision, due largely to the more varied technical resources available. Gene Youngblood, the prophet of what he calls "expanded" or "synaesthetic" cinema (meaning *avant-garde* or abstract[1] movies whether animated or not) writes: "The new cinema has emerged as the only aesthetic language to match the environment in which we live" and "it promises to dominate all image-making."

★   ★   ★

Teru Murakami and **Fred Wolf,** more orthodox, understandable and witty, have worked in England as well as America, and are close in style and content to the British school. Murakami's *The Insects* shows a struggle between a man and a swarm of midgets which ends in the midgets carrying off the man's body. Very funny but sinister too. *The Top* presents a Dante-esque view of the world with a sharply-defined, geographical heaven at the top of the screen. There is room at the top, but it is a struggle to get there and even those who succeed are not sure of a permanent place. In *Breath* the characters, men and women, breathe in and out clouds of sweet or poisonous ideas, feelings and even other people. Among other films, Fred Wolf has made *The Bird* in which a bird who brings a man and a woman together is eaten by the man after he has finished with the woman. *The Box* (1968) gives us an allegory with a surprise ending concerning a series of mysterious boxes which are brought into a bar. The latest Wolf-Murakami film, *The Point,* is a longish fable about a boy, Oblio, exiled from a country of pointed people to "the pointless forest" where he and his dog Errol meet Alice-in-Wonderland creatures and adventures. The film is by Harry Nilsson and the story narrated by Dustin Hoffman.

Another recent name is **Paul Julian** who with **Les Goldman** made

---

[1] Youngblood claims these films are "not abstract but concrete." He justifies his terminology, but there seems no reason to depart from the common usage (which is generally understood) of talking about *abstract films* by analogy with *abstract paintings* and as opposed not to concrete, but to representational, films and paintings.

The Hangman for Tower 12, based on a narrative poem by Maurice Ogden. If the verse recalls the days of melodramatic recitation, the images which accompany it are impressive. A talented newcomer among directors is **Bill Melendez** who has made for television *Babar the Elephant* and also a series from the comic strip *Peanuts* featuring a moon-faced little boy, Charlie Brown, with an endearing dog, Snoopy. Charlie has many girl friends—Cathy, Violet, Lucy and the gimlet-eyed Pigpen. The strip was created by the cartoonist Schultz and the jokes are off-beat, good-humoured and often profound. Melendez went on to make a feature, *A Boy Named Charlie Brown*,[2] which has all the charm and wit of the short films. Melendez's short *Rainbow Bear* is a poetic creation, shot with colour in the style of folk-art and with simple, effective rhymes.

A number of new American animators were praised for films at the 1971 Annecy Festival. There was Jim Duffy's *Digging* and *The Weight Lifter;* James Gore's *Dream of the Sphinx,* creating a tense atmosphere with silent visuals and in style reminiscent of Picasso's drawings; and *Simon Says* by Anestos Trichonis, a grim allegory of war based on a parlour game.

★   ★   ★

Many of these animators are on the borderline between *avant-garde* and orthodox work, a borderline which is now much less sharply defined. There is much vigorous film-making among underground, student, artist, and semi-professional groups which has had a wide influence reaching into the most conservative studios. The new comics too, for example "Zap" comics and "Mad Magazine" have lent their styles to some animated films. A case in point is Robert Mitchell and Dale Case's *The Further Adventures of Uncle Sam* (1970), in which science fiction creatures kidnap the Statue of Liberty who is rescued by a diminutive Uncle Sam and an Eagle. There is Mitchell and Swarthe's *K-9000: A Space Oddity* which features the famous His-Master's-Voice terrier in a space fantasy. Or again there is Bob Kurtz's *My Son the King* in which Solomon and Sheba are shown as scratchy figures, Solomon kosher from head to toe and complete with Jewish mum. Typical of the new scene (man) is a feature cartoon, *Fritz the Cat,* by Robert Crumb and Ralph Bakshi. Moving at a cracking pace

---

[2] The most recent feature cartoon from the studio, *Snoopy Come Home,* tells the brave story of Charlie Brown's dog, and how he goes back for a time to a former owner, coping stoically throughout with the hostility of an anti-dog world. By now Schultz has created a world of make-believe which in its warm quiet humour, insight and compassion, will bear comparison with any other children's classic. These recent feature films are entirely successful in transferring the short strip cartoon to a larger canvas, and surely they will go on from strength to strength, gaining popularity with children and grown-ups wherever and whenever they are shown.

and brilliantly drawn, it follows the randy Fritz and his pals through a series of sex orgies, drug sessions, bar-room brawls, fights with the pigs, then going West to Gothic hide-outs, tortures and bomb-plots. In the climax Fritz, blown up, dying in hospital, philosophising about life surrounded by weeping girl-friends, suddenly revives, rejuvenated at the thought of sex, throws off his bandages and turns his bed into an amorous battle-field. Scandalous, irreverent, satiric but pulsing with life, *Fritz the Cat,* though unlikely to go on the Disney circuits, is a major work. However, even the Disney studio in *It's Tough To Be a Bird* (1969), blossoms into a pastiche style using a collage of old illustrations, advertisements and the like. The American scene is changing, and we can no longer say that the accepted cartoon form is the sadism and stereotype of commerce, with any experiment confined to a lunatic fringe.

From the hilarious 1972 feature cartoon, FRITZ THE CAT

5. Animation in Canada and Britain

Unlike the United States, Canada has had virtually no commercially viable film production, and film-making has centred round the National Film Board which was founded in 1939 by John Grierson. When Grierson went back to the U.K. he left behind a treasure he had found in his native Scotland: **Norman McLaren.** It was perhaps the best of the good things he did for Canada. The National Film Board has put Canada in a class by itself so far as short films are concerned, ahead of the United States, England and virtually every continental country. And the greatest individual talent working for the NFB is undoubtedly McLaren.

McLaren was born and educated in Scotland. He made his first film in 1933 at the age of nineteen, when he was still a student at art-school. It was called *Seven till Five,* a record of a day's events at the school. In 1935 he made his first animated film, *Camera Makes Whoopee,* which included cartoon work, models and animation of objects. In 1937 he joined Grierson's GPO Unit and made four films including a documentary on the telephone directory called *Book Bargain,* and *Love on the Wing,* a picture with images drawn direct on film, advertising the new air-mail service. From 1939 to 1942 there were another dozen films: nearly all drawing direct on celluloid, some in abstract colour. The technique had been originated by Len Lye, but McLaren developed it and made it known.

He was at the National Film Board in 1941, in at the beginning, and by 1943 had formed an animation unit which included Dunning, Ladouceur, Jodoin, McKay and Grant Munro. In 1943 came *Dollar Dance,* drawn on celluloid with moving backgrounds; in 1944 *Alouette* from cut-out paper, in 1945 to 1947, *C'est l'aviron, Là-Haut sur ces montagnes, Phantasy on a Nineteenth Century Painting,* and *La Poulette grise,* all using gouache or pastels and given a form of movement by continuous tracking and dissolving. This group of films tends to have a slow mysterious rhythm, the colours are subdued, the music soft and gentle, all combining to give a mood of muted tranquillity. In *C'est l'aviron* the continual forward tracking over the rocking bow of a boat is almost hypnotic.

Up until now McLaren's drawing on celluloid had been marked out like photographed film in individual frames. In *Begone Dull Care* (1949), he used the strip of film as a long continuous ribbon, his lines and patterns flowing on, ignoring the stop-go, stop-go frame-division

The art of Norman McLaren: above left, CANON,
above right, LE MERLE, opposite, McLaren drawing
directly on 35mm film with ordinary pen and India ink

which is part of the technique of photography. *Serenal* (1959), *Vertical Lines* (1960), and *Horizontal Lines* (1962), are similar in technique. Since in projection the film will be artificially divided into frames by the movement of the projector the difference will not be evident to an audience, but it may be argued that the method makes possible for the artist a different approach with more flexibility and freedom, which will communicate itself in his finished work.

In 1952 McLaren made one of his most important and most popular films, *Neighbours,* again using a new technique: the animation of living actors. The film is a fable of aggression and war. Two men are sitting peacefully on a lawn in deck-chairs when a flower appears on the boundary of their properties. In the quarrel that ensues the flower is destroyed, and the men are killed. Two of McLaren's colleagues, themselves animators, took the parts: Jean Paul Ladouceur and Grant Munro. Such a combination very likely facilitated the making of a film which, posing the actors twenty-four times a second, initiated a technique which was not only new but more difficult in some ways than animation of drawings, puppets or objects. *Neighbours* is stylised in a gay, fairy-tale manner, in telling contrast to the grim allegory. The actors, shot in odd attitudes, moving mechanically, are more human than marionettes, more doll-like than humans. The combination of realism and formalism is effective for a moral fable, and McLaren's control over his material is perfect.

Having once used the technique of pixillation McLaren came back to it in *Two Bagatelles* made in the same year, in *Chairy Tale* (1957), in *Opening Speech* (1960), in the credits of *Christmas Cracker* (1963), and in *Canon* (1964). None of them except *Canon,* in my

72

view McLaren's finest film, compares with *Neighbours* which despite its obvious theme has a strong impact. *Two Bagatelles* is simply an exercise, which shows Grant Munro jittering about in a march and a waltz. *Chairy Tale* and *Opening Speech,* lively but minor jokes, both combine animation of live actors with animation of objects, and both appropriately enough illustrate the malignant resistance of the inanimate world to human manipulation. *Chairy Tale* shows a man (Claude Jutra) struggling to sit on an unwilling chair; *Opening Speech* shows McLaren himself, trying to master a recalcitrant microphone. In *Christmas Cracker* only the credits and inserts are by McLaren, the rest by Gerald Potterton.

Canon is technically one of McLaren's richest and most complex films, and includes cartoon animation, animation of cut-out shapes, of objects, of human actors and even of a cat. With the perfect craftsmanship typical of all his work, it illustrates a theme which has evidently fascinated him and which he has presented more fully on paper; the translation of musical forms into visual terms. The precision of musical form suits McLaren's turn of mind, and he has drawn diagrams illustrating the *Theme and Variations* and the *Fugue* as well as the *Canon*. A canon is a tune like *Three Blind Mice,* contrapuntal music similar to the fugue, in which the same melodic line overlaps; it may be at different intervals, or inverted, expanded, or contracted. McLaren in the film illustrates this, first by means of toy alphabet-blocks, then (delightfully) by having a man, a woman and a cat march across the screen repeating the same movements (melodies) at different stages. Somehow although the film is quite abstract it is full of feeling and has something rich and satisfying about it, a depth of originality and a "felt" strength of purpose. Another shorter exercise in the visual translation of music is *Synchromy* (1971), but being entirely abstract it is less rich and entertaining than *Canon*.

A further technique to be discussed, used most successfully in *Le Merle* (1958) and *Rythmetic* (1956), is that of cut-out shapes. This style of animation lies between cartoon and animation of objects. In general the cut-out "components" remain the same between frames and are re-arranged into different pictures, positions or patterns: but if he wishes the artist is still at liberty to change their shape occasionally as in the case of a drawing. The first use of the technique was by Emile Cohl who sometimes used simple jointed cardboard figures, but McLaren was possibly the first to revive it in *Alouette,* a three-minute illustration of the French Canadian folksong made in 1944. *Rythmetic* is an exercise in patterns of figures, moving, proliferating, changing into odd shapes. *Le Merle* (*The Blackbird*) is another folk-song like

Alouette, but an advance on it, and McLaren's wittiest film. It is about a bird which loses different parts of its body only to grow them again two-, three-, four- . . . ten-fold, a creature constructed entirely of sticks with two circles for eyes. In the course of loss and regeneration, it goes through all kinds of metamorphoses: it plays ball with its eye, juggles with its ribs, becomes an Indian totem, a game of noughts-and-crosses, a kind of round game and so on. The film is just right—has the lightest touch, goes at an easy spanking pace, is packed with ideas, is short and sweet, clear and charming.

In *Pas de deux* (1968), McLaren revived the chronophotography used by Marey in 1888 to analyse human movement, and presented it in a modern form, illustrating with tenderness and beauty the steps of two ballet dancers. The motion is staggered and superimposed in an optical printer to obtain a stroboscopic effect. (A two-frame stagger gives a rapid chain of images, a twenty-frame stagger a slow sequence.) At the same time the pace has been slowed to the gracious dignity of a musical *andante,* and rightly rejecting colour, the picture has been given the well-defined outline of black-and-white photography. Then as the limbs move they leave an outline of each separate position, as it were each frame, on the screen, so that time is transformed into space, and we see not two dancers but forty-eight, not four arms but ninety-six, each of them echoing, reflecting, extending the meaning of all the rest. The film has diversity yet unity; it is simple yet complex; it is exciting yet satisfying; and once again McLaren has given us an entirely original yet perfectly-finished artistic creation.

McLaren's work has been discussed under the different techniques he used, because the importance of technique in his work is both a strength and a limitation. If he deserves to be called great, it is as a craftsman and an innovator. The immaculate perfection he has achieved in many different styles, the precise effects, the fine detail—the result one feels of days of unassuming, patient, loving labour—these are McLaren's glory, his claim to fame. With them there is a shy humour, a modest understatement, a scrupulous honesty. But at the same time one feels there is a lack of fire, and the pain and passion of an artist powerfully moved to deep feeling and burning to communicate his emotion, are largely missing. McLaren's modesty and reserve can be seen if not as weaknesses, at least as limitations. As a dramatic art the cinema can express the deepest human experiences and emotions, and McLaren's work stops short of engaging the medium to its fullest extent. Nevertheless what he lacks in breadth he has gained in depth, and he has shown that the cinema can express the same beauty as the art of the sculptor, the jeweller, the carver, the designer. Of their kind his best films are great works of art and should be recognised as such.

OTHER CANADIAN ANIMATORS

Quite apart from his own artistic achievement, McLaren deserves credit for his encouragement of other animators. Instead of dominating and exploiting as a less generous personality might have done he has been content to allow the growth of individual talents, quite different from his own. Grant Munro, René Jodoin, Jim McKay, Colin Low, George Dunning, Wolf Koenig, Evelyn Lambart, Gerald Potterton and others have achieved fine individual creations while working at the National Film Board, to a greater or lesser extent in collaboration with McLaren and each other. In some cases functions have been interchangeable and in some films many names appear in the credit titles. Most animated films are a joint effort; what distinguishes NFB films, like those of UPA, is that they are a democratic joint effort, in contrast to the hierarchy of Disney and other studios.

Grant Munro first worked as a freak sculptor creating a work called *Japanese Fortress* made out of praline and another called *Salt of the Earth* made from sodium chloride itself. His first films were *The Man on the Flying Trapeze* (1945), a clown cartoon, and *My Darling Clementine,* an illustration of the song. With Jim McKay he made *André's Grand Tour* using characters fashioned out of coloured paper. In *Oh No John* he used thousands of black crosses in squares to represent vehicles. *Sur Le Pont d'Avignon* was a puppet film as was *Funny Mic Mac* (1953). *Huff and Puff* (1956), co-director Gerald Potterton, was made for the Canadian air-force on the subject of physical fitness.

René Jodoin is best known for his illustration of folk songs and he worked on several films in a *Let's All Sing Together* series including *Square Dance* (1944). He worked with McLaren on *Alouette* and *Chalk River Ballet.* His latest films are: *Dance Squared* (1961), made with Trevor Fletcher, the mathematician mentioned below, a film made of geometrical shapes which in a novel way provides illustration for children of mathematical combinations; and, most recently, *Notes sur un triangle* (1966).

Evelyn Lambart has mostly collaborated with McLaren, but has herself made a few films including *O Canada* (1952) and a little teaching film *The Lever* (1966). She is an expert in setting up technical experiments in film-making, having earlier studied mathematics and physics. One of her first projects at the Film Board was the drawing of diagrams and maps for the *World in Action* series, and a complete short film called *Maps in Action*. Her latest work is *Paradise Lost* (1971), a film about pollution of the environment.

Wolf Koenig was born in Germany, studied art, and joined the Film Board in 1948. Besides being mainly responsible for the cartoon *It's a Crime,* he has worked as cameraman (*Neighbours*), script-writer (*Romance of Transportation*), and collaborated on several documentary films and films made from still photos: *Corral* (1953), *City of Gold* (1955), *Fish Spoilage Control* (1956), *Lonely Boy* (1962). Koenig is currently working on an animated film, *Winter in Canada,* and a project on Stravinsky. He also recently took over from McLaren the function of producer in charge of the animation section. His responsibility is shared with **Robert Verral** as Art Director, whose films include *A Is for Architecture, The Great Toy Robbery,* and *Energy and Matter* (1966).

Derek Lamb has made a number of films for the National Film Board. He worked on *Hors d'oeuvres, Pot pourri* and *The Great Toy Robbery,* but is best known for *I Know an Old Lady Who Swallowed a Fly,* an illustration of the popular song, similar in style to UPA but with something in common too with the English surrealist school. He left Canada, worked for a time with Halas and Batchelor, and now lectures on animation at Harvard University.

Colin Low studied at the Calgary Art School, joined the NFB in 1945 and with Dunning made *Cadet Rousselle,* then a didactic film *Time and Land.* After studying in Stockholm he returned to the NFB and in 1950 made *Work Team, The Time of the Beaver,* and (with Verral and Koenig) his most popular film, the amusing *Romance of Transportation* (1952), rather in the UPA style. He was co-director of the film *Universe* (1960), a striking re-creation of the heavens which included a certain amount of animation.

Jim McKay joined the NFB in 1942 as a caricaturist and his first films were in a series *Chants Populaires,* for example *Filez Filez O Mon Navire.* Then followed two propaganda films, *Bid It Up Sucker* and *Joe Dope Helps Cause Inflation. Stitch & Save* was in an extremely simple style of drawing and *Ten Little Farmers* (1946), used coloured, cardboard cut-out figures. In 1940 he left NFB to form *Graphic Associates* with Dunning and in 1956 joined *Batten Films.*

Gerald Potterton started in England with the Grasshopper Group, joined NFB in 1954 and assisted in several films besides directing *Fish Spoilage Control, My Financial Career* (1960), and *Christmas Crackers* (1964). *My Financial Career* is taken from a Stephen Leacock story, but the humour, leaning heavily on Leacock's writing, is not entirely suitable for a cartoon, despite lively drawing. He has gone on to make

Cool McCool, The Quiet Racket, Superbus and *Charge of the Snow Brigade*. A trilogy on Pinter characters with the playwright's fragmented dialogue and failure to communicate, includes *Last to Go* (1971), which uses the voices of Pinter himself and Donald Pleasence.

Another experimenter with techniques is Ryan Larkin. His *Syrinx* (1965) is the story of a nymph turned into a reed, and the black-and-white drawing goes through a series of transformations, moving, changing, creeping into new shapes and forms. *Walking* (1970) is a study of human motion obtaining interesting effects of rhythmic movement in restrained monochrome.

In recent years new names from the National Film Board have come to the fore. Some of the films use animation to present a scientific or social theme. Sidney Goldsmith's *Fields of Space* and Pierre Hébert's *Elementary Notions of Genetics* have been described as showing great skill but proving dull in presentation. Mike Mills's *Evolution* is an odd essay on the subject and shows strange creatures coupling, giving birth, devouring one another, one of them in the end swallowing the film titles.

Scene from SYRINX, by Ryan Larkin

Other films are based (as are many Canadian cartoons) on popular songs: Laurent Coderre's *The Macadam Flower,* Pierre Moretti's *The Frozen Brain* (1970), and Bernard Longpré's *Tête en fleurs. Where There's Smoke* (1971) is an uproarious anti-smoking cartoon made for the Ministry of Health. It is in short explosive incidents contributed by twelve animators including seven newcomers.

★   ★   ★

The National Film Board dominates. But Canada sports a few independents: Cioni Carpi, Trevor Fletcher, and Al Sens.

Cioni Carpi in *Lines and the Maya Bird* (1961), *The Cat Here and There* (1962) and *The Bird Is Good* (1963), builds variations on an austere drawing in ink-coloured pencil in the tradition of free animation. Also by Carpi is *Chronograms,* an interesting abstract film shown at Annecy in 1962. **Trevor Fletcher** is an English mathematician but he has made a film in which mathematical formulae in graphic form are used aesthetically: *Four Line Conics.* It is beautifully finished, satisfying to watch, and presumably of some value from a mathematical point of view.

Al Sens—*The See Hear Talk Dream and Act Film* and *The Sorcerer* —has some resemblances to Robert Breer, but he uses more easily identifiable images. His violently caricatured figures are forceful and funny. Al Sens makes his very personal films working alone and he uses methods to match. His own account is worth quoting at length. It makes an interesting comparison with what is said in other chapters about mechanical methods and the assembly lines of the big commercial studios: "I have endeavoured to create techniques which help to eliminate the multitude of cels usually required. A technique I have called the "spit technique" consists in drawing and erasing right under the camera. Although this results in a crude, almost vulgar sort of graphics it does give vitality to the image and the movement. I have used the black-and-white "spit" method plus colour on top in the *See Hear* film. *The Sorcerer* was done in Hubley-like double-exposure (*Moonbird*) while *The Puppet Dream* was done on newsprint with water-colour and then back-lit. These are economical ways of working though they have certain limitations. Have also tried to incorporate "Live" bits and "experimental" type things into the animated film to give it another dimension and counterpoint the image with sounds from unrelated objects or scenes. Believe this can be used to recreate the flare-ups from the unconscious, the dreams, fantasy, nightmares and breakdowns that are all part of man's inner life." Al Sens's latest film was *New World,* shown at the 1971 Annecy Festival.

The spit method, employed by Al Sens for
THE SEE HEAR TALK DREAM AND ACT FILM

Canada's contribution to animation has been a substantial one, particularly in relation to her movie-making as a whole. No doubt because of the influence of the NFB, the work is as often serious as comic, using personal styles, new techniques, eschewing the violence and triviality of the popular cartoon, frequently with an instructional or didactic bent. Some critics may find it lacking on the lighter side, but it is a welcome counterbalance to the flood of animation in other countries where cartoons and puppets are not allowed out of the nursery.

BRITAIN

Between Canada and Britain there has been a lot of interchange. McLaren and Potterton started in Britain; Dick Williams and George Dunning have come to this country from Canada; Trevor Fletcher and Potterton have come back to work here. In general international links and cross-currents have been strong in the animation field. Disney's influence has been world-wide and lifeless imitations of his style have appeared in many countries, notably Russia, China and Japan. The influence of UPA and McLaren has been strong on the continent, as has Trnka's influence on puppet films everywhere. Gene Deitch of UPA has for many years been working in Prague. Bretislav Pojar, one of the best Czech animators, Peter Foldes from France, and Zlatko Grgić have worked in Canada with the National Film Board. The British school has had a world-wide impact with its wild surrealist humour; and Britain's use of cartoons for instruction and propaganda which developed during the war, has spread to many countries.

★   ★   ★

English cartoons were among the earliest made, and Walter Booth (as mentioned in Chapter Two) may even have preceded Emile Cohl. None of the English artists had Cohl's fertility and by the Twenties, as in France, American cartoons seem to have captured the British market. In 1914 the artist Harry Furniss made several films (*War Cartoons, Peace and War Pencillings*, etc.) as did Sidney Aldridge (*War Skits*), Dudley Tempest (*Merry War Jottings*) and Dudley Buxton (*War Cartoon Series*—plus *How to Run a Cinema* and other cartoons in 1917). In 1914 and 1915 Lancelot Speed produced eight *Bully Boy* cartoons. Speed made *Tommy Atkins* and *Britain's Effort* in 1918, and in 1921 a *Pip Squeak and Wilfred* series in twenty-six episodes for Astra Films taken from the famous newspaper strip which still keeps going today, fifty years later. Tom Webster, well known as an illustrator, made *Charlie at the Front* and *Charlie Joins the Navy* in 1918, a series based on his character *Tishy*, in 1922 and 1923, and in 1926 *Alfred and Steve*. G. E. Studdy made his first film cartoons *Studdvis War Studies* in 1914, and in 1924 to 1926 brought his celebrated puppy, *Bonzo* to the screen in twenty-six or more cartoons including *Bonzolino* and *Bonzo Broadcasted*. Though the stills look attractive, somehow Bonzo never became as popular in the cinema as in the magazine world. The longest-lived of the early English animators was **Anson Dyer.** In 1917 he made five cartoons including *The Kaiser's Record* and *Agitated Adverts*, in 1918 a further five including *Foch the Man*. In 1919 he made an *Uncle Remus* series and burlesque adaptations of Shakespeare—*The Merchant of Venice, 'Amlet, Othello, The Taming of the Shrew* as well as animation sequences for Maurice Elvey's feature *Nelson*. In the Thirties Dyer introduced American studio methods into England and, besides commercials, made a number of entertainment cartoons including *Carmen* and *Three Ha'pence a Foot*.

Georg Pal, a Hungarian who worked at first in Holland also made a good few films in England then later worked in the U.S.A. He specialised in puppet films, many of them for advertising. *Aladdin, Sinbad, On Parade, Jasper Goes Hunting, Jasper's Close Shave,* are some of his films. It was Georg Pal who gave Halas his start in the field of animation. Pal used wooden marionettes, wire-jointed, but they were brought alive by the true methods of animation.

Among the most original and liveliest of the earlier animators was **Len Lye.** Lye is a New Zealander born at Christchurch in 1901. He studied art not only in New Zealand but in the South Seas where he was influenced by the styles of the Polynesians. He appears to have made his first film cartoon in 1928, and in the Thirties he was employed by the GPO unit. He worked on a number of live-action films, *North or North West, Kill or Be Killed, Swinging the Lambeth Walk,* before inventing the technique which made his name: drawing and painting direct on the film.[1] *Colour Box,* made in 1935, was the first film to use this new technique and it is achieved with astonishing accuracy, finely formed and finished. Dots, lines, patterns, arabesques, dance and mingle on the screen; the technique seems to have sprung to life in its full perfection. *Trade Tattoo,* made two years later, could even be regarded as a setback. The patterns are more perfect, but more mechanical. They are set in double-exposure against live-action sequences which have been shot in a one-colour process and given the quality of a block engraving. They show workers in transport, commerce, industry, while hopping letters give us the GPO message: "Trade-is-sustained-by-the-mails." Lye was a pioneer and although his technique was taken up and developed by McLaren, his films were never popular, and he was not able to make a career in the cinema. He returned to the fine arts and a year or two ago he was working in New York on moving sculptures which produce their own music.

★   ★   ★

In Britain as in other countries there is some divergence of style between the older established studios and the new, younger animators: Halas and Batchelor on the one hand, and George Dunning, Bob Godfrey, Dick Williams on the other. But as in other fields, the divergence is less violent and less marked than in America. The conservatives are not so conservative, the commercial film-makers are not so commercial, the *avant-garde* is not so *avant-garde.*

---

[1] Man Ray is said to have drawn on film in 1923 in *La Retour à la raison,* but nothing seems to have survived.

Opposite: Halas and Batchelor's ANIMAL FARM (above) and an early English cartoon BONZO

The largest and most successful of the long-established studios is **Halas and Batchelor.** John Halas was born in 1912 in Budapest, and studied animation with Georg Pal. He worked in Hungary then came to England in 1936 to work on an early English colour cartoon, *Music Man.* Joy Batchelor was in the same film unit, and after a period of working as commercial artists, they founded the cartoon company of Halas and Batchelor in 1940. Today they are bigger and more prosperous than ever, and their work is known all over the world. During the war and postwar years, Halas and Batchelor made many information and propaganda cartoons, inventing a character called Robinson Charlie, the man in the street, the average citizen. Scientific, industrial and promotional films and over 750 commercials have continued to form the bread-and-butter of the studio right up to the present, though many of them have high entertainment value as well: for example *All Lit Up* (1956), made for the Gas Council, or *For Better For Worse,* a satiric view of television made for Philips. In this field British work, encouraged by the Government during the war, led the way, and is still among the best in the world. For explaining certain scientific, industrial processes the cartoon medium is unrivalled, but for many audiences it is important that the films should have an infusion of humour and a lightness of touch, and Halas and Batchelor have been very successful in achieving this. *Dustbin Parade, To Your Health* (directed by Philip Stapp) and *The Colombo Plan,* are models of their kind. *Flow Diagram,* director Harold Whitaker, gives an explanation of problem analysis and programming while at the same time hilariously depicts how to wash (or not to wash) a dog. *What Is a Computer* (1970) is a recent production.

Halas and Batchelor produced the first British feature-length cartoon, *Animal Farm,* three years in the making and released in 1954. It was a straightforward adaptation of George Orwell's political fable, according to some critics too straightforward, although William Whitebait wrote: "In times which have made a strip-cartoon of the *Iliad* we may at least be thankful for the boldness and restraint of *Animal Farm* and the prospect of new sources to be tapped." Seen today one feels that this is as good a screen translation as possible despite the substitution of a happy ending, but the savage, Swiftian irony of the original is untranslatable, and remains locked in Orwell's shining prose, polished as hard as a bone. From a financial point of view the film was probably too good; something more trite, directed at an audience of children, would have made more money. A projected *Pilgrim's Progress* combining live actors for human characters with animated cartoon for the devils, angels and monsters, was abandoned, but entertainment shorts continued, mainly after 1956, for television.

The studio's principal cinema shorts are *Magic Canvas* (1951), an abstract colour cartoon, *The Owl and the Pussy Cat* (1953), *The History of the Cinema* (1956), and *Automania 2000* (1963). For television their first film was *The World of Little Ig,* the story of a prehistoric family. Then came a series of modern fables oddly called Habatales, which included *The Cultured Ape, The Widow and the Pig;* and then a series about a cheerful, little blunderer called *Foofoo,* a stout heroine, Mimi, and a villain, Gogo. Another series in paper sculpture featured *Snip the Magic Scissors* and three dogs: Snap, Snarl, and Sniff. These were all made for ABC television. In 1961 they even made six Popeye films. More recently they have made a very successful series for the BBC (several of them directed by Harold Whitaker) based on Gerald Hoffnung's drawings: *The Hoffnung Symphony Orchestra, The Palm Court Orchestra, Professor Ya-Ya's Memoirs* and so on. In 1966 they completed a full-length cartoon version of Gilbert and Sullivan's *Ruddigore,* an excellent interpretation of the original which failed to find the criticism or the audience it deserved.

The following are some of their most recent films. *The Question* (1967) was a neat allegory (story by Stan Hayward) about a question mark and all the uses to which it can be put. *Flurina,* a film for children from Alois Carigiet's book, was in an agreeable coloured-illustration style. In 1969 came a fairy-tale series in collaboration with Encyclopaedia Britannica Films—*The Frog Prince, Rumpelstiltskin, Hansel and Gretel* etc. One of their most recent movies, *Children and Cars* (1970), is based on youngsters' fantastic notions about motor-cars and on the children's own drawings, with gay colouring, lively animation, and young voices explaining their extraordinary contraptions with the gravity of university professors.

Halas and Batchelor have been established now for nearly forty years and have produced an enormous number of cartoons in a wide variety of styles. If occasionally their inspiration has flagged and they have fallen into banality, this is hardly to be wondered at, and their best work is of high quality, superior to the equally prolific Jean Image in France or for that matter to the product of commercial studios in the States. If they have not attained the inspired lunacy of some of the newer studios such as Biographic, they have a more impressive body of work behind them and have won a permanent and leading place in the history of British animation. They can also claim to have trained and encouraged many animators who have gone on to work elsewhere, and John Halas has been active in promoting ASIFA, an international association of professional animators. The studio has recently merged with Tyne Tees Television, but will retain its identity and continue to produce films and commercials for cinema as well as TV.

★　　★　　★

There are other studios, notably **Larkins,** which have specialised in the sponsored and instructional cartoon. Beryl Stevens has been responsible for some of Larkins' best work, a series of sponsored cartoons for Barclay's Bank beginning with *Put Una Money for There* in 1956. This was a little story with Negro voices and Negro characters about the virtues of safe deposit, charming and perfectly suited to its purpose and its audience. *Man of No Account* (with Dick Taylor), *The Banking Game* and *The Bargain* followed. *The Curious History of Money* (1969) is another bank film, entertaining and informative; *Refining* (1970), made for BP, combines live-action and animation; *The Square Deal* (1971, director Douglas Jensen) traces the development of modern insurance practice; while *The Electron's Tale,* directed by Bob Godfrey, gives a light-hearted account of the whys and wherefores of electric energy.

Other studios in the commercial and sponsored field include Dart Films (Trevor Bond) which made the credit titles for *Doctor No* and *From Russia with Love;* World Wide animation (Peter Bradford) and Guild Animation (Charles Legg), the two latter specialising in teaching or research movies. World Wide's work includes *Physics and Chemistry of Water* and *Crystal Diodes Part I,* while among others Guild have made *Cyclone Burner, Reactor Systems, Protein and Health.*[1] A relatively new studio is Wyatt Cattaneo, who have been active mainly in the TV commercial field since 1965. Their entertainment shorts include *The Fairy Story* and *I Love You,* both 1968. New projects include *Cafe Bar, The 'Eart of Living* and a cartoon for Decca based on Saint Saens's *Carnival of the Animals.* Richard Taylor, formerly with Larkins, established his own studio in 1968. His cartoon shorts include *Revolution* (a personal film about government power, four years in the making), *The Rise of Parnassus Needy* (banking), *The Princess and the Wonderful Weaver* (wool), *Tell Mummy* and *Don't Talk to Strangers* (two safety films for the COI), *Motorway Fog* and a TV series for the BBC *Crystal Tipps and Alistair,* 1971. Tony Cuthbert Cartoons is another new studio working on commercials.

---

[1] Cartoons are also extensively used for instructional films in the States, a typical director being Lee Blair of Film and TV Graphics, New York, whose films include: *ABC of Auto Engines* (1945), *Man Learns to Farm* (1950), *ABC of Diesel Engines* (1952), *Eye in the Sky* (1961) and *Nothing to Sneeze At* (1962).

Nick Spargo (*Dinosaur, Flags, Joe and Petunia, Genius Man, Shell Duel* and *Arnold Doodle*) and Derek Phillips (*The Battle, The Fan, A Passing Phase, The Greater Community Animal* and *Same but Different*) are also talented artists working in commercial and sponsored cartoons.

★ ★ ★

Amateur film-making flourishes in many countries, but animation is less attractive to amateurs than live-action, because of the immense labour involved and the need to have a camera which will operate frame-by-frame. Nevertheless in Great Britain a good few animated cartoons have been made by amateurs and one group, **The Grasshopper Group,** has gained a reputation which professionals might envy. The founder of the group and director of their animated films is John Daborn (born in 1929) who studied at the Kingston School of Art. An early film, *The History of Walton* (1952), was a documentary history of the town on the Thames. In two films made with Gerald Potterton, *Two's Company* (1953), and *Bride and Groom* (1956), he developed McLaren's pixillated technique. Most successful, however, was *The Battle of Wangapore,* a comic evocation of Kipling's India and the North-West Frontier, which won the Grand Prix at the 1955 Cannes Amateur Festival. Since then Daborn has made *Leave No Litter* (1966), and a cartoon based on the Greek Myth, *Cupid and Psyche.* **Stuart Wynn Jones** started with the Grasshoppers then worked for Halas and Batchelor. His first work, *Short Spell,* is an animated alphabet drawn direct on film, soundtrack as well as visuals. Then he made two abstract films, *Raving Waving* and *Billowing Bellowing. The Rejected Rose* is a more orthodox story of an artist who paints in order to impress someone, becomes so interested that he no longer cares about impressing anyone, and succeeds in impressing everyone. *The Spark* combines live action with a cartoon spark, animated by scratching on the film like Robert Breer's *Miracle.* Finally his latest film, *Optic Ticklers,* is a lively series of visual and verbal puns using a *collage* technique both for the soundtrack and the visuals.

★ ★ ★

Within about the last fifteen years, three animators have given Britain a reputation abroad as leading exponents of the cinema of the absurd: Bob Godfrey, George Dunning and Dick Williams. To them should be added Stan Hayward, ideas man rather than scriptwriter, and at **Biographic,** Nancy Hanna, Keith Learner and Vera Linnecar. Despite close relationships, the leading three, Godfrey, Dunning and Williams have individual differences. Godfrey is the shaggiest and cuts deepest where sex is concerned. Dunning is more of a stylist and has developed a liquid painting style derived from Bartosch. Williams takes his ideas more seriously and has tackled more ambitious projects. Their work is sometimes called "goon" humour but the description is inexact. The Goons descended via Tommy Handley from a radio—and before that from a music hall—tradition, essentially spoken and rooted in the English language. The Goons had a vast audience in England and none abroad, their humour was untranslatable, their acts not for export. Contrariwise the cartoons of Godfrey, Dunning and Williams have reached audiences abroad more easily—and received more acclaim from critics overseas—than they have in England. In England the Goons were a household word; the cartoon school is practically unknown. Like many animators their bread-and-butter is anonymous TV advertising or sponsored work while their entertainment shorts, financially unrewarding, were made for the cinema, but because of circuit controls and programme patterns, reached only a minority cinema audience. There have been other influences in the English cartoon collectively more important than the Goons. One could go back to the surrealist worlds of Lear and Lewis Carroll, the light verse of Harry Graham, Belloc and T. S. Eliot. In the newspapers there has been the deadpan lunacy of Beachcomber, *This England* in the "New Statesman," the satire of Giles and his anarchic midgets, of "Oz" and "Private Eye." Again there is the work of *objets-trouvés* sculptors, Bruce Lacey's crazy collections, the vogue of Victoriana and the like as fun objects, op art, pop art, and even modern fancy-dress fashion modes.

★   ★   ★

George Dunning was born in Toronto in 1920 and studied at the Ontario College of Art. He joined the National Film Board in 1943, his first film being *Grim Pastures* (1943), *J'ai tant dansé* (from *Chants populaires*) (1944), then *Three Blind Mice* and *Cadet rousselle* (1947), made with Colin Low. These films show an individual style, perhaps more strongly than any other of the National Film Board animators except McLaren. *Cadet rousselle* is a visual illustration of a French folk-song dating from 1792. It has been classified as a puppet film, although it looks like a cartoon, as the characters are made from flat, metal shapes painted and jointed. It has rich coloured backgrounds and both the human beings and the animals (cats, dogs and mice) are highly individual. Dunning and McKay left the National Film Board in 1949 and set up their own company *Graphic Associates*. Dunning came to England in 1956 and established *TV Cartoons*. He has made a lot of sponsored films and TV commercials including *Discovery— Penicillin, The Adventures of Thud and Blunder*, a safety film for the

Design from Richard Williams's I VOR PITTFALKS (above), and still from Wyatt Cattaneo's THE FAIRY STORY (below)

Four frames from THE YELLOW SUBMARINE

Coal Board, *Mr. Know-How* for the Gas Council, and *Visible Manifestations,* a film about the famous Shell sign. In 1967 he worked on what must be the only triple-screen cartoon ever made: *Canada Is My Piano* for the Montreal Exhibition. He has also made a number of TV series, for instance *The Beatles* and *Cool McCool*. His cinema films include *The Apple, The Everchanging Motor Car* and *The Flying Man*. Most interesting of these is *The Flying Man,* a three minute film using blobs of watercolour which float nebulously on the screen without the clear line used in all conventional and much modern work. He is said to have developed the technique by painting on glass, following Bartosch who hints at it in *L'Idée,* but Dunning has taken it further and used it with colour so that it becomes more meaningful, since colour is in a sense opposed to line. Dunning has used the same method for a longer film, *The Ladder,* and *Damon the Mower,* 1971 (on an

Andrew Marvell poem) and a similar technique has also been used effectively by the Polish animator, Witold Giersz.

Dunning's themes are strongly surrealist, stemming from Carroll and Kafka. The irrationality of *The Wardrobe* was followed by the mystery of *The Flying Man*. One man flaps strangely about in space, airborne, another comes on with a dog and tries to emulate him but fails. That is all, yet the film has a curiously strong atmosphere. *The Apple* features a determined chap after the only apple on the tree. Frustrated time after time he persists undaunted. Famished? Suffering from apple-starvation? When he finally gets the apple he scutters up to a secret attic where a small boy and dozens of split apples testify to a William Tell complex. Hints at secret vices? It is a mad, suggestive film.

Dunning has crowned his career with the feature-length cartoon, *The Yellow Submarine* (1968). Based on the Beatles' popular song, the story begins in the happy kingdom of Peppercorn, suddenly subject to a full-scale attack by the Blue Meanies whose missiles turn their enemies to stone. Only Old Fred, conductor of the band, manages to escape in the Yellow Submarine and makes his way to Liverpool where he persuades Ringo and his pals—John, Paul and George—to come to the rescue. They all go aboard the submarine and after many adventures involving the Nowhere Man, the Boob and others, they reach the Kingdom of Peppercorn, conquer the Blue Meanies with LOVE, and restore the inhabitants to their happy state. The picture unrolls on the screen in a profusion of rich imagery, one marvel crowding after another, a modern Arabian Nights Entertainment but in many different styles—ranging from Beardsley (the elongated Apple Bonkers) to *art nouveau* via Dali (limp watches), Rauschenberg, op art and pop art. Dunning's was the controlling hand, but none of his previous styles is apparent in the movie. Though the list of credits is an enormous one, a major influence on the design was that of a German animator, Heinz Edelman. The caricatures of the Beatles and the idea of using them in a cartoon no doubt arose from a previous TV series on them which Dunning made a year before. The film with its pop-star characters, lively invention and modern styles was immediately popular, an artistic and financial success. It looks like being a landmark in animation history, and seems to have had influence in encouraging feature-cartoon production elsewhere.

Dunning's latest film *Moon Rock 10* is a curious space fantasy in style similar to some sequences of *The Yellow Submarine* with a pale astronaut attacked by gaily-coloured monsters who one by one explode leaving nothing behind. It is a mysterious creation with a style all its own. Two recent shorts directed by Alan Ball for TV Cartoons are *A Sense of Responsibility* and *The Self-Rescue Breathing Apparatus,* the former a chain of disasters starting with carelessness in a coal-mine and ending with the British Isles sinking beneath the waves. Another TV Cartoons animator, Jack Stokes, has set up his own studio and made animated credits for Hammer's space thriller, *Moon Zero Two* (1970).

★   ★   ★

Bob Godfrey, born in Australia, started at Larkins studio, and while there made *Watch the Birdie* (1953), remarkable for its drawings of endless varieties of cartoon birds distinguished by their scornful, ogling eyes. His first real body-blow at audience composure was *Polygamous Polonius* (1959), a wild sex romp in which Polonius tries every trick in the book to break the bonds of matrimony only to finish at the end with a whole screenful of battle-axes instead of one. Then came the *Do-it-Yourself Cartoon Kit,* one of the funniest cartoons ever made. The audience is offered the works: "Somebody . . . chasing somebody else . . . in any direction . . . at any speed . . . Go on . . . until you run out of colours . . . then follow up with paper . . . bits of string . . . old boxes . . . anything." It is offered an assortment of noises: an *oing,* a *brrr,* a *whee* and a *clunk.* There is a jointed figure with eyes that roll, teeth that chatter, toes that wiggle, and an arm that waves the Union Jack. By the end the cartoon and the audience have been reduced to pulp. *The Plain Man's Guide to Advertising* didn't seem to hit the spot quite so exactly, nor did *The Rise and Fall of Emily Sprod,* but with *Alf Bill and Fred* (1964), the story of a little man who won the pools and left his pals, a duck and a dog, Godfrey was back in the ring and taking on all comers. The same with the *Morse Code Melody,* a mechanised Victorian head frantically singing, and *One Man Band* (1965). Up to standard too is *The Battle of New Orleans,* an earlier film in accelerated motion, which shows a musical quartet playing for dear life as they gradually sink deeper and deeper in the mud.

In the later Sixties, Godfrey left Biographic to go it alone, and Vera Linnecar and Keith Learner have carried on the studio. To date they have made *Gold Whiskers,* a parody of James Bond, *Springtime for Samantha* and (back to Godfrey's form) *Do Be Careful Boys. Do Be Careful Boys* is about a porter called Charlie Burk who busts every case he handles because he just doesn't care. Then he consults a psychiatrist with an accent like Limberg cheese, who gives Charlie nightmares describing what life would be like if everybody threw things about, and makes a practical suggestion: "Why take it out on the

Photo-animation montage from a "Wimpy" commercial by Bob Godfrey

vegetables, give it to your wife instead." After this inspiring consultation, Charlie is a reformed character. At the beginning of the film the characters are introduced by musical-comedy songs, a novel and effective touch. Recently Biographic have made *Living Tomorrow* for the COI and an entertainment short, *The Trend Setter* (story Stan Hayward), about a leader of fashion who sends his tedious, fanatical imitators to their doom by staging a fake suicide. Godfrey has made the very funny *Whatever Happened to Uncle Fred* and *Henry 9 till 5,* and hit the jackpot once more with *Kama Sutra Rides Again,* a riotous and timely parody of the sex manual, presenting the stodgiest of British couples who with true-blue phlegm go leaping from one ridiculously acrobatic love-pose to the other.

★　★　★

Dick Williams, born in 1933, is another Canadian. He was never at the National Film Board, but worked with Dunning when the latter was at Graphic Associates. He came to England in 1955 and spent over three years making his first film, *The Little Island,* keeping his head above water by drawing for TV commercials. This story of three figures representing Truth, Beauty and Goodness, had a prodigious success. The film had a startling, jack-in-the-box style, and Tristram Carey's music added a great deal, but in the end it was the content which excited most comment. It is a film which raises questions rather than answers them. Truth, Beauty and Goodness are shown as harmless little men ("like pear-drops") on a desert-island. Harmless? Each of them is a monomaniac who tries to impress the others with his own special vision. Truth's vision is most abstract, patterned hints from many philosophies. Beauty favours flowers and flute-music and the mincing fantasies of esoterics. Goodness sees life as a crusade for the soul, the church militant, red with the blood of sacrifices. Then a fight breaks out between Goodness and Beauty who grow into terrifying monsters on a vast, expanding screen. Truth keeps the score on a ticking score-board, which turns into a shattering atomic bomb . . .

In *A Lecture on Man* Williams illustrated Christopher Logue's poem with a mixture of engraved anatomy-charts and various styles of drawing and painting. His *Love Me Love Me Love Me,* the story of a stuffed alligator called Charlie, its owner Thermus Fortitude, and the lovable Squidgy Bod, pushed his reputation a peg further up the board. He has a lot of projects in production. Most serious is *Circus Clowns,* in which the camera slowly explores the fine drawings he made during a long visit to Spain. Then comes a middle section of animation still to be made, and the camera comes back and ends with the drawings. In *The Sailor and the Devil* a square sailor with a smile like a scrubbing-brush sings about his adventure with the devil. There are staggering changes of colour and scale and it carries the punching style of *The Little Island* to a more violent pitch. *I Vor Pittfalks* is only finished as far as the introduction, a terrifying prologue with explosions on the soundtrack and the letters varying to suit the mood of the music. Williams has made credits for *A Funny Thing Happened On The Way To The Forum* (flies and Pompeian wall-painting in a nudging style), *What's New Pussycat?* (cupids and a glitter of curling letters), *The Liquidator* (a whirling black gunman), and *The Charge of the Light Brigade* (Victorian England satirised). He has also made a striking animated-film background for a New York stage show, *The Apple Tree,* with great jostling letters, and startling photos of the heroine as she bravely breasts her way to fame and fortune. Like other animators Dick Williams depends for subsistence on a flow of TV commercials, in his case of much originality and wit—*Guinness at the Albert Hall* (with the conductor balancing the whole choir on his shoulders), *Yellow Pages Pinball, Equitable Savings Builds.* His Oscar-winning cartoon, *A Christmas Carol,* sponsored by a merchant bank for American TV has superb ghosts and captures the authentic Dickens Christmas atmosphere in both its gay and sombre moods. A drawback is the extensive dialogue with lip-synch for however good the drawing it is impossible to animate in a naturalistic style without awkwardness. Talking or singing faces are better with the lips stylised, a good example being the American, Paul Glickman's *Calypso Singer*. The studio continues working on *Nasrudin,* an Arabian-Nights clown, who will eventually be the hero of a cartoon feature. The drawings for the film capture all the glittering detail and jewel-like colour of Persian and Indian art and it looks as though the finished cartoon will surpass anything else the studio has done.

★　　★　　★

At the outset the studios established in the Fifties and Sixties were a close-knit group, and one man, **Stan Hayward,** was responsible for the ideas behind many of the best cartoons. An Australian with a technical background, he wrote first for the Goon show. The finished pictures developed by different directors may be in different styles, but are still closely related as a list of story-boards indicates. Besides over a hundred commercials the following are some of the entertainment shorts which have come from Hayward's fertile mind—*The Wardrobe, The Apple, The Flying Man, The Ever-changing Motor Car* (Dunning), *Love Me Love Me Love Me* (Dick Williams), *Polygamous Polonius, Alf Bill and Fred, Whatever Happened to Uncle Fred, Rope Trick* (Godfrey), *The Fairy Tale, I Love You, Package Deal* (Cattaneo), *The Question* (Halas and Batchelor).

★　　★　　★

At the present time the excitement of a new movement has died away, the success of *The Yellow Submarine* has made shorts seem less of an achievement, and perhaps English animation is in need of fresh inspiration. At the same time (no doubt due to expanding TV and industrial markets) studios seem more prosperous and there are more of them. Perhaps, eventually, new thought will come from schools and colleges where film-making and film appreciation are increasingly finding a place in the curriculum—though not often alas, animation.[1] There is a good case for including animation courses in art colleges and/or universities. English animators, though they have led the way in instructional cartoons and have established a school of eccentric humour, have worked in fairly conventional styles and along conventional lines. There are still enormous possibilities for new, adventurous approaches to movement on the screen both graphic and plastic. On the one hand

---

[1] An exception is a cartoon from Bristol University, Nancy Edell's *Black Pudding,* a modern erotic fantasy in the vein of Bosch or Bruegel.

association with those training or trained as artists should bring stylistically broadening influences, while on the other hand the range of academic knowledge to be found in a university should help to make the most fruitful use of new techniques such as computer animation.

THE SQUARE DEAL, by Larkins (top left),
BE CAREFUL BOYS, by Biographic (top right), and
REVOLUTION, by Richard Taylor (below)

6. French Animation from Cohl to Kamler

Up to the Twenties the French scene was dominated by the work of Emile Cohl already discussed in Chapter Two. Cohl's 300th and last film was made in June 1923, an advertising cartoon for Publi-ciné, a company which had been founded by Lortak (Robert Collard) in 1919. As a result of recent researches in France it is claimed that Lortak was "quantitatively the most important in the whole history of French animation" and though a full filmography has not been established, his studio employed fifteen people, including André Rigal and Raoul Guérin, and went on making cartoons including many commercials, until 1945. Some titles are—*Joko le singe, Toto aviateur, Le Noël de Toto, Mecanicas et la machine à guérir, Le Canard au ciné* (a cartoon supplement to the weekly newsreel). However O'Galop (Marius Rossillon) connected with *Le Rire* was first to follow Cohl with two social-reform cartoons, *Le Taudis doit être vaincu* and *Le Circuit d'alcool* in 1912. Then in the Twenties he made several cartoons on subjects from La Fontaine: *Le Lièvre et la tortue, Le Loup et la cigogne.* O'Galop was apparently quite a character, facetious and unorthodox, his colleagues called him "Grand-pere Zig" while he called himself an "artistronome dessinémateur"!

The artist Benjamin Rabier, well-known for his animal portraits was responsible in 1916 for the drawing of some of Cohl's cartoons: *Flambeau chien perdu, Les Fiançailles de Flambeau* etc., and in the Twenties made his own films featuring Caramel and Columbine as well as *Les Animaux de Benjamin Rabier* and *La Queue en trompette.* A name thrown up by recent research is Albert Mourian, "the great unknown of French animation" who in 1921 made *Potiron sergent de ville, Potiron garçon de café* etc., using jointed figures and as hinges for the joints abandoning pins for chewing-gum, "the ideal material"! In 1922/23 he made a feature, *Gulliver in Lilliput,* combining a live actor with puppets, but of the original 180,000 frame-by-frame images (enough to run for three hours), only a few stills now remain.

★   ★   ★

Berthold Bartosch was also an architect, but in the film world he is known for *L'Idée,* a short cartoon made from Frans Masereel's woodcuts with music by Honegger, and produced in 1932. Bartosch had worked with Lotte Reiniger and made cartoons in Germany—*Communism, Animated Cards* (1919), *Battle of Skagarak* (1922), *Occupation of the Rhineland* (1925). *L'Idée* was revolutionary in the simplicity of its technique since it abandoned the smooth cel technique developed in

America, and used bold black-and-white figures cut out and roughly animated. L'Idée, representing the idea put forward by an author, a poet, or an artist in any field, is shown as a naked woman born from the brain of her creator. The artist puts her in an envelope and sends her forth, but those who receive the message, business-men, legislators and the like, are shocked. They dress her, chase her through the town, condemn her. Naked again, she meets the artist and they try to rouse the workers, but the artist is seized, tried and shot. L'Idée is reproduced in a newspaper, but war comes, and we see her as a spirit floating among the dead and dying. The social theme, the striking music and the new technique assured the film a *succès d'estime,* but it was not popular and had no successors.

★　★　★

Hector Hoppin and **Anthony Gross** displayed a style admirably suited to the cartoon medium. Gross was a well-known English painter and illustrator, Hector Hoppin an American artist. In a fluid style using cel technique, they nevertheless produced drawings that were fresh and different. *Joie de Vivre,* a present-day pastoral made in 1934, is a charming trifle. Through varied settings a workman pursues two girls to give back one of them her shoe. Coquettish, alarmed, the more he chases the more they run away until at last in a railway signal-box—capture, explanation, reconciliation—he rides into the clouds, with the two of them pillion, on his bicycle. The film is curiously erotic in its effect, the rhythmic movement of the girls, their billowing skirts, the way they are drawn: all these combine in a sensuous whole. In 1953, *Indian Rhapsody* gave another example of their style. It was an account of Phileas Fogg's journey across India and his rescue of an Indian widow from her funeral pyre. Looking at this delightful fragment, it seems a pity they were unable to achieve a full version of *Around the World in 80 Days* for Jules Verne's period flavour suits the cartoon.

★　★　★

A leading exponent of puppet films was **Ladislas Starevitch,** an insect-photographer born in Moscow who worked first in Russia and later in Paris, and made many films using marionettes from 1912 onwards. His Russian films were live-action and included *Insect Aviators* and *The Dragon Fly and the Ants.* In France from 1918 he made the puppet films—*Les Griffes d'Araignée, L'Epouvantail* (1921), *L'Horloge magique* (1927), *La Petite Parade* (1928). His most important film, *Le Roman de Renart,* is a sixty-minute feature and took ten years to make. Its animal characters are life-like but (Lo Duca suggests) one tires of its perfect competence, its novelty wears off and the resources of animation could be used for sharper, wittier, more telling effects.

However, others have praised his imagination, his gift of observation and his meticulous detail. He died in 1965 working on a puppet film *Comme Chien et Chat.* Following Starevitch were Pol Bianchi's *Fantoches Vivants* and Paul Diehl's *La Course du lièvre et du herisson.* In 1938 Jean Painlevé and the sculptor, René Bertrand, made *Barbe Bleue,* a film from plasticine models animated and shot in colour. This film was more effective, a macabre account of the fairy-tale told with a certain irony. Apparently the technique was one of considerable difficulty, increased by the fact that in some scenes there were as many as 300 separate figures. More recent is the feature-length puppet-film by Lou Bunin, *Alice in Wonderland,* made in 1948. Critics found it unequal but with moments of real beauty, in spirit faithful to the original, intelligently adapted, and far better than "Disney's hideous film."

Returning to the cartoon, another single effort was Albert Dubout's *Anatole fait du camping.* Dubout is celebrated for his fine line-drawings in French newspapers, sharp, satiric, cruelly revealing of class and human weaknesses. He planned a feature-length cartoon *Les Aventures des héros de la Tour de Nesle,* but only a fragment was released in 1947. Léontina Indelli is another artist worth mentioning, although her efforts in the cartoon field came to grief. *The Discovery of America* (1935) failed because of technical faults; *Le Coche et la mouche* was destroyed by fire.

★　★　★

A greater figure in the world of animation who has worked from 1933 to the present day, although with a small output, is **Alexandre Alexeïeff,** the inventor and sole exponent of the "pin-board." His wife Claire Parker has collaborated with him on all his films. Alexeïeff was born in Kazan in 1901, studied painting in Paris and designed ballet costumes and decor for Kommisarjevsky, Pitoëff, Jouvet and Baty. From 1926 he worked at wood engraving and lithographs, and developed very personal styles of etching and book illustration. In 1933, struck by Léger's *Ballet mécanique,* he turned to cinema, and using the pin-board technique made *Une Nuit sur le mont chauve,* a fantasy accompanied by Mussorgsky's music.

Alexeïeff's pin-board consists of a large board covered with pins the size of small nails, each of which can be raised or lowered. Using special rollers or in some cases adjusting the pins individually by hand, a pattern is created. When lit from the side the different heights of the pins and the different lengths of the resulting shadows combine to form a black-and-white picture rather like a steel engraving. It is a severe technique, but the very austerity of the resulting picture is effective for certain subjects. Humour is out: the tragic, the macabre, the serious, are the moods to suit this style. In 1935 Alexeïeff directed *La Belle au bois dormant,* a puppet presentation of themes from *The Sleeping Beauty* with designs by de la Rochefoucauld and music by Poulenc. The film is most curious. Some of its trick effects recall Cocteau. Vivid reds and black and midnight blue predominate; in the palace the prince passes through one magic door after another and through rooms peopled by transfixed figures. At the end there are midnight revels with wild dancing. Also in the Thirties Alexeïeff made a number of other outstanding commercials. In 1943 he made *En Passant* for the National Film Board, a film in their series *Chants Populaires,* illustrating Canadian folksongs. It was made on the pin-board and contains fine images of a squirrel in a cornfield, a church and a cock in a farmyard.

In 1951 Alexeïeff experimented with the patterns of a pendulum,[1] and applied the result in a number of films, e.g. *Sève de la terre* (1955). He has also made three films with Georges Violet: *Fumées, Masques* and *Nocturne.* In 1963 he produced with the pin-table his most ambitious film, *Le Nez,* taken from Gogol's strange tale of a man who loses his nose, and of a disembodied nose which haunts him.[2] *Pictures from an Exhibition* (1971) has Mussorgsky's music on the sound-track, and dreamy, turning pin-table images taken from the composer's childhood. Refined, almost remote, this technique of Alexeïeff's has not been copied, and seems likely to remain his own. Nevertheless the films he has produced are unique in their strange, other-world atmosphere. He has been called "the Einstein of animation," and his reputation among other film-makers is considerable.

★   ★   ★

Another leading figure in France with a larger output is **Paul Grimault,** born in 1905 at Neuilly-sur-Seine. For a long time he worked with André Sarrut in a company called *Les Gemeaux.* Financed by commercials they were able to make several very successful films during the late Thirties and Forties culminating in the feature film *La*

---

[1] Alexeïeff has made the following comment on his work (and Claire Parker's) on pendular movement: We construct *robots* controlled by compound pendulums or motor-powered mechanisms, which themselves control the movement in space of a "tracer," a small luminous object. These tracer movements are recorded on a single frame by a long exposure, and form a "totalized" solid. Then after changing the parameters which govern the robot, a fresh series of tracer movements is recorded on another frame—and so on. The degree of condensation is such that a final film of one minute may represent twelve hours of the tracer's movement. What is animated is not a natural solid, but a "totalized" or illusory solid. Although this technique is used to sell coffee, petrol or cigarettes, it also aims at widening our metaphysical concept of the world.

[2] A comic cartoon version of Gogol's story has been made in the States by Mordi Gerstein (*The Nose,* 1966). There is none of the original power or eerie quality, but it is a very funny parody.

From Alexandre Alexeieff's LE NEZ

Bergère et le ramoneur, finished in 1953. This, like many cartoons before and since, was a failure financially, although as art and entertainment it is outstanding, and since then Grimault has only made one film, *La Faim du monde* in 1958. Recently however he was producer of a remarkable first work *La Demoiselle et le violoncelliste* by Jean-François Laguionie and his influence goes on.

Grimault's first work was a film on *Electricité* for an Exposition in Paris in 1937. Then came two films featuring a little boy, called *Go: Go chez -les oiseaux* and *Les Passagers de la grande ourse* (1941). *Le Marchand de notes* (1942), is an amusing film, full of invention although Lo Duca finds it "compromise par des trouvailles laborieuses" and trying too hard to be original. Grimault found his true style with *L'Epouvantail,* rich in colour and full of witty incident. In this also, typical of Grimault's work, there is an underlying sadness, the sense that the best characters are not necessarily the strongest. In 1946 came two films, *Le Voleur de paratonnerres* and *The Magic Flute* from a scenario by Grimault and Roger Leenhardt, based on the story of the

LA BERGERE ET LE RAMONEUR

opera. In 1947 appeared *Le petit soldat,* perhaps Grimault's most delightful film. All the characters in the film are toys, the little soldier himself being a slim marionette who returns wounded from the war. His rival is a grotesque Jack-in-the-Box who has profited by his absence to woo his sweetheart, a graceful dancing doll. To complete the soldier's discomfiture the Jack-in-the-Box seizes the soldier's heart, the red key that winds him up. The soldier, doomed and dying, is left drifting on an icefloe down the river. But the dancer steals the key and with it brings the soldier back to life while the monstrous Jack-in-the-Box comes to grief in the snow. As in all Grimault's films the hero and heroine are gentle creatures who only ask to be allowed to live their own lives. The wicked are punished but principally by the foiling of their own plots. In these days when the fashion is for heroes and heroines as brutal and sadistic as the villains, looking at it now in a period of violence, Grimault's gentleness has all the beauty of a sunset.

La Bergère et le ramoneur, from a script by Jacques Prévert, is similar in style. The characters in the title are taken from Hans Andersen,

102

and in spirit are brother and sister to the little soldier and his girl. But added to the Andersen story is another one of a fantastic dictatorship by a wicked king living in a castle as huge as a city, with secret police, trap-doors, dungeons, radar, helicopters, electronic devices of all kinds. The shepherdess and the chimney-sweep are tracked down, imprisoned, threatened, but they escape with the help of a benevolent bird and its fellows. Again virtue triumphs but the victory is an innocent one. *Faim du monde,* made in 1958, with a stone-age setting, came as a coda to his work.

Grimault's method of presentation is conventional, and does not break radically with the Disney tradition, but his handling of cel animation is artistically superior, and there is a lyrical delicacy about his style which makes other cartoons seem coarse. One cannot sum up his work better than by quoting two French critics: "He created a new world in the cartoon. For the first time human beings were neither gauche nor ridiculous, but presented quite simply without false realism or over-stylisation, as if good qualities of heart and soul were enough to bring these dream creatures to life. Grimault's films are neither philosophic theses nor revolutionary experiments; but he is the only cartoonist who can be compared with Renoir in his deep feeling for reality, for humanity, for the joy and sadness of our existence."

OTHER FRENCH ANIMATORS

The commercial film factory in France is represented by **Jean Image,** another Hungarian who worked with Halas in the Thirties. His earliest films were *Rhapsodie de Saturne* (1947), *Ballade atomique* and two feature cartoons, *Jeannot l'intrepide* (1950), and *Bonjour Paris* (1953). *Rhapsodie de Saturne* shows one of the rings of Saturn turned into a circular keyboard and a pianist playing on it. Then the notes of the music comes alive. *Bonjour Paris* shows the Eiffel Tower sailing across to America. *L'Aventure du Père Noël* (1957) attempts to re-create the New York of Steinberg. Some of Jean Image's early work has a certain vigour but it signally lacks taste, and by now the volume of his production has so far outrun his resources that nearly everything he makes today is trite and facile to the point of being virtually unwatchable. He has recently made a cartoon feature, *Aladdin and his Wonderful Lamp* (1969).

Omer Boucquey has done most of his work in the publicity field, but he is known for two short films, *Choupinet* (1946) and *Le Troubadour de la joie* (1949). Choupinet is a Puck-like figure of some originality. *Le Troubadour de la joie* is a medieval fable with modern themes introduced. There is a struggle between Choupinet and the Devil to build a cathedral. It even contains spiritual gags such as a machine to make people good, a mixture of *Modern Times* and the *New Testament*. Boucquey also made *Les Dessins s'animent* (1952), and *Drôles de croches* which showed musical notes brought to life; not a new idea, but effectively treated.

Jean Jabely has made a few pleasant films: *Teuf-Teuf* in 1955 then in 1957 *Ballade chromo* based on a collage by Jacques Prévert. The collage is composed of dozens and dozens of the glossy, coloured, embossed figures which are stamped out and used to decorate Christmas crackers: animals, flowers, human beings. Tiny ink-drawn figures wander about this simple but enchanting background, living in a world of childhood loveliness. Another of Jabely's films strikes an effective contrast between magazine illustration and sketches, *Elle et lui, elle* being a big, busty magazine cut-out-and-pin-up and *lui* a grinning, unromantic, scribbled lecher.

Henri Lacam has made a number of cartoons, principally *Les deux plumes* (1958), *Jeux de cartes* and *Les Nuages fous*. A disciple of Grimault, he works in a painted style with rather sombre colours and stories to match. His latest film, *L'Oiseau de la sagesse,* has a confused script and amateurish drawing and is altogether a disappointment. Between 1959 and 1963, **Robert Lapoujade** made a number of unusual films: *Enquête sur un corps, Foules, Chastel, Noir et blanc, Prison, Vélodrame. Prison* shows a man endlessly looking at a prison wall on which there are subliminal images of his tragic past. His best film is probably *Trois Portraits d'un oiseau qui n'existe pas,* three exercises on a central theme.

René Laloux made an odd film in 1960 with the assistance of patients at a mental home—*Les Dents du singe,* the story of a wicked dentist wizard who stole poor people's teeth and a monkey magician who outwitted him. The animation was crude and the story vague, and though it had some atmosphere, it was no more than an interesting experiment. Then came *Les Temps morts,* a shocker on the theme of man's inhumanity to man. Laloux's next film *Les Escargots* (1965), from Ronald Topor's work, uses pen-and-ink drawing, a water-colour wash, and jointed figures. A farmer grows giant lettuces by watering them with his tears and they develop giant snails who destroy the countryside, crushing buildings, killing people and finally exterminating each other. Back to the farmer, now growing giant carrots which attract giant rabbits . . . The style is unusual and the film succeeds in engendering a *frisson*.

André Martin is well-known as a writer and an authority on

Drawing from LES ESCARGOTS

animation, but he has made several films too. *Demain Paris* (1959),
Patamorphose (1960), the best perhaps being *Mais où sont les
nègres d'antan?* on which Michel Boschet was co-director. A white
hunter on safari records a native singer and his tune becomes a
hit. But the native sues the hunter for breach of copyright and
wins his case. The hunter become poor street musician is recorded
by a visiting African, and rushes off in turn to the copyright office.
The style is effective, the Negroes drawn in long, dislocated brush
strokes very reminiscent of Hubley.

Julien Pappé made the delightful *Sophie et les gammes* (1964).
A little girl goes off for her music-lesson. She is a real picturebook
little girl with flaxen plaits and a wide-brimmed hat, and the music-
teacher is a splendid figure, bosomy, impetuous, temperamental.
Sophie's playing drives the teacher demented, and she chases Sophie
all over her flat, gradually tearing the place to pieces. Whenever
Sophie has distracted the teacher's attentions or has got her in some
dreadful plight, she bursts into virtuoso jazz, playing nonchalantly
upside down or with her feet. Then back to the one-two-three, one-

105

two-three, nicely interlarded with discords. Finally Sophie leaves the flat a shambles and returns home. The film uses "pixillated" live actors, and is shot in vivid, staring colours which give it a circus swing. Pappé has also made *Histoire des baladins de France, Château de cartes* and *Oiseau en papier journal*. The last is a story of a little boy's dart which becomes a paper bird, agreeably drawn rather in the fashion of Peynet's magazine cartoons. Pappé's style is warm and rich and his films are achieved with unpretentiousness and mastery of the medium.

Jacques Vausseur made several films for Cinéastes Associés; best known is *Le Cadeau,* a bright little film about a clown who buys his girl a present of a hooter, only to find that all the sounds have got mixed so that the hooter moos, a cow honks, and a baby makes the sound of an orchestra. The little clown bustles about swapping noises, trying to sort things out, but the film ends with an animal ensemble producing Beethoven's fifth symphony. The style is gay as tinsel with wall-paper backgrounds.

Manuel Otero and **Jacques Leroux** have made several films together; *Maître* (1963), a satire on the esoteric of painting coteries in Paris, *Atom-Tilt, Les Deux Uranium, Autant qu'il y a de l'inquiétude, Ares contre Atlas,* and *Univers*. It seems that Otero is the more talented of the two, since, singly, Jacques Leroux has made the rather feeble *Pierrot* (1965), whereas Otero has made *Contrepied,* a witty cartoon in an unusual drawing style about a man whose squeaky boots wipe out everything around them including finally the man himself. Otero has since made *Le Balade d'Emile,* a homage to Cohl, *Tour de force* which dramatised a geometrical impossibility, a "straightline" circle, and *Patchwork* (1971), the latter an episodic piece made in collaboration with four Swiss artists.

Jacques Colombat is best known for a short *Marcel ta mère t'appelle,* drawn with real charm in a modern rococo style reminiscent of Rex Whistler. His latest film is *Calaveras* based on the painting of the Mexican artist, Posada, using crude cut-out animation, and with a powerful theme of death and life after death. **Jean Charles Meunier** has made two short cartoons, *Bahing,* about a car accident, and *Jetons: le Western* in which he uses differently-coloured circles for characters—an ingenious idea, but the result is rather dull.

Albert Champeaux and **Pierre Watrin** produced a farcical cartoon, *Villa mon rêve,* wildly satirising an estate-agent of the sell-refrigerators-to-Eskimos school, which had pace and zest. **Marc Andrieux** and **Bernard Brevent** are responsible for *Oeuf à la coque,* animating an egg in a desert of sand with a lot of squeaking and sinister laughter on the soundtrack. It has been much shown because object-animation is becoming increasingly fashionable but it is an empty exercise with over-fussy décor. **Bruno** and **Guido Bettiol** are Italians working in France and are well-known for their publicity films. In addition they have made *Un Touriste en France, Berthe aux grands pieds* and *Acte sans paroles* (1964), the last on a script by Samuel Beckett.

Henri Gruel first worked for Arcady where he had the idea of using children's drawings in cartoons, and using their ideas in the film script. In 1950 he showed his first film made on this basis, *Martin et Gaston*. Later came *Gitanes et papillons* and in 1956 *Le Voyage de Badabou*. The stories were conceived and the original drawings made by school children, but Gruel adapted and elaborated them into an acceptable whole. He hit the jackpot, however, with quite a different film. *La Joconde* (1958) is a series of hilarious variations on the theme of Da Vinci's Mona Lisa. It effectively mixes live-action and animation and makes extensive use of crude but (in the context of parody) effective movement. The Mona Lisa appears in every possible guise as a deep-sea diver, a football team, a skeleton, an x-ray photo, an electric pin-table game, with whiskers, glasses, wig and in military uniform. It was wildly acclaimed, is still popular with film societies, and had some influence on the British School of zany humour. In 1959 Gruel worked with Lenica on *Monsieur Tête* and in 1960 made *La Lutte contre le froid*.

Jean François Laguionie made a most interesting first film, *La Demoiselle et le violoncelliste* (1964), produced by Paul Grimault. The cartoon opens with the cellist playing, on scrolled cliffs, the rich music by Edouard Lalo which dominates the film. His music raises a storm which carries the demoiselle and her shrimp net out to sea, and when he tries to rescue her in a boat, both sink to the bottom, there to live through strange adventures with a giant crab and a swordfish. They escape and walk out of the water again at a crowded seaside resort, but retreat from the crowd to the seclusion of the wild cliffs. The film is made from flat, painted, cardboard cut-outs which gives the animation a charming period simplicity and it is painted in a style to match, not unlike Douanier Rousseau. Laguionie's second cartoon, *L'Arche de Noë,* is in a similar style and opens with archeologists seeking the remains of the Ark among the mountains. They are watched by a centuries-old Noah from his well-hidden, battered Ark, and when a Second Deluge comes, he repairs the vessel, kidnaps a lady archeologist to accompany him and his animals, and sails away. Laguionie's latest cartoon, *Une Bombe par hasard,* is on the theme of atomic disaster.

★   ★   ★

Another important cartoonist is the Hungarian, **Peter Foldes.** Born in 1924 he came to England when he was twenty-two and studied art at the Courtauld Institute. His first film, made with funds from the British Film Institute, was *Animated Genesis* (1952). It starts off with blue shapes, atoms, water rippling and reflecting, cell structures, branching growths, then a great spider (evil) chasing a moth (good). The spider enslaves tiny Egyptian human beings, the moth brings them scientific inventions (tractors, machines and so on) which the spider turns to destructive purposes. Finally the giant spider is blown up by his own bomb and the world becomes a modern utopia. It is an odd fantasy, but quite interesting. The patterns and colours are bold, the insects and people made of flat jointed shapes. Three years later came a better film, *A Short Vision,* an imaginative account of the world's destruction by an atomic bomb. Because of its subject and its clear, succinct treatment, the film was highly successful despite a certain prosiness in the commentary. Both these films were made with the collaboration of his wife, Joan Foldes. However the two films did not lead to further work, Peter Foldes moved to France and concentrated on painting for the next ten years. In 1965/66 he produced three new films: *Un Garçon plein d'avenir, Appétit d'oiseau,* and *Plus vite.* All three films are in a similar style, quite different from his earlier work: bold, flexible line-drawing against a white background, changing occasionally to pastel colours and other styles. All three films are violent, erotic, forceful. *Appetit d'oiseau* deals with the war of the sexes; woman turning into a snake, a gorgon, a bird; man turning into a fearsome lion or a tiger—but it is the woman who has the better of it. There is constant flow and invention in the images which are, moreover, invariably erotic and shocking. It is not a diet to be recommended for invalids, but there is no denying its force, and it is a difficult film to forget. *Un Garçon plein d'avenir (A Lad with a Future)* is similar but with a neater structure and a twist in the ending. A child suckling at his mother's breast grows to monstrous size and becomes a dictator, waging war, seducing, dominating, destroying, in the crudest, most brutal manner, literally red in tooth and claw. Then at the height of his triumphant power, as he stamps thousands under his feet, there appears a gigantic foot to crush the great dictator as if he were a fly. Less

Part sequence from UN GARCON PLEIN D'AVENIR,
by Peter Foldes

successful is *Plus vite*. A man and a woman are travelling in a
car that becomes an apartment by night, an office by day. On they
speed, eating, sleeping, working, but journeying incessantly at top
speed. The car becomes a speedboat, an aeroplane, a space-ship.
At the end the woman asks the man: "Where are we going?"—and
receives the reply: "I don't know." *Plus vite* seeks to make a
portentous statement and succeeds in cracking a stale joke. But
the other two make up for it. More recently in *Faces of Women*,
Foldes used electronic techniques and his *Meta Data* (1971), made
in Canada, is entirely computer animation. A French critic's opinion
is quoted in Chapter Thirteen. His most recent work is a feature
film, *Je tu elle,* combining live-action with animation. Unfortunately
it is arty and tedious.

★   ★   ★

Two cartoon features have been made recently from the popular
comic strip, Asterix the Gaul, by **Rene Goscinny** and **Albert Uderzo**
in Franco-Belgian productions. It has been reported that the first,
Asterix the Gaul, is not of great interest, but the second, *Asterix and
Cleopatra,* can be highly recommended. The characters are Asterix,
a scrawny, Gallic Popeye who is aided and abetted by Dogmatix
his faithful hound, Obelix a good-natured strong-man and Getafix,
a Merlin-type magician. In the Cleopatra adventure our friends are
summoned from Gaul to Egypt to help Edifice (a Good Architect
who has been ordered by Cleopatra on pain of death to build a
splendid temple in three weeks—Caesar having bet her she couldn't)
against his enemies—Artifice (a Wicked Architect who wanted the

job) and Caesar (in secret) who are putting obstacles in his way. Our friends of course defeat all enemies (including the Roman Army), escape from a sealed tomb, and triumph in the end. The old *clichés* are given a slightly new twist, the drawing is in a gay, colourful style, and the story moves at a lively pace. A point of appeal for English viewers is that a Lion who pops into the asses'-milk bath with Cleo and later does a belly-dance, is the spitting image of Frankie Howerd.

Another delightful French, feature-length picture, this time using puppets, is Serge Danot's *Pollux et le chat bleu* (1970), directed in an English version by Eric Thompson. It is taken from a popular television series *The Magic Roundabout*, and tells the adventures of a serious little dog, Pollux or Dougal, and his friends Zebedee, Florence, Brian (a snail), Dylan (a rabbit) and Ermintrude (an artistic cow), and follows their struggle against the wicked designs of Buxton, the Blue Cat. Though the characters are simple enough to appeal to children, the sophisticated and witty dialogue has an equal appeal to grown-ups.

20,000 ANS A LA FRANCAISE

Piotr Kamler's L'ARAIGNELEPHANT

A lot of very good work has been done in France for cinema and television commercials, and animation has also been used extensively in instructional films. Marc Cantagrel and Jean Painlevé have been prominent in technical and instructional animation. The French also claim the first use of animation in science with a cartoon by Bidet and Monier in 1920. In the publicity field, *La Comête, Cinéastes Associés* and *Arcady* are three of the largest groups and have employed excellent artists. Etienne Raik is a prolific director of advertising films and has worked extensively for Cinéastes. Jim Phabian, an American who had directed *Old Mill Pond* (1937), and *Peace on Earth* (1939), for M-G-M came to France in 1955 to set up an animated unit for Cinéastes. While there he made the cartoon *Bouli Bouli* (1957). Cinéastes' cartoon unit was taken over by another American, Frank Smith, who has since made *The Raisin Merchant* (1963). Borowczyk and Jacques Vausseur were also members of the Cinéastes team. Jacques Forgeot, the late head of Cinéastes, directed a long animated film, *20,000 Ans à la Française* which covers the whole history of France using photographs, prints and painting. For instance, fashion prints of the Louis XIV period are animated against actual shots of the Palace of Versailles.

Another organisation which has sponsored the production of many of the more experimental cartoons is the *Service de la Recherche de l'ORTF,* the French Television Service. One of their recent productions is **Piotr Kamler's** *Délicieuse Catastrophe* (1970). It is a strange film possibly symbolic of the reproductive process with a fat body in a striped jersey (an ovum?) pumping pink liquid, meeting a spiky burr (a seed?), and floating through vague caverns. Kamler is a Pole born in Warsaw, has been working in France since 1960 and in animation since 1966. His previous cartoons include *L'Araignée-Eléphant* and *Labyrinthe.*

★   ★   ★

So far as French animators are concerned the older generation still hold the laurels, and Grimault and Alexeïeff are the most important figures. Among the younger generation there are many varied talents, but no single artist who predominates. There has not been a *nouvelle vague* in animation. France deserves credit for its critical and theoretical discussion of animation, and for practical encouragement through the Cannes and more recently the Annecy Festivals. More than most countries it has also been a centre of international work and Alexeïeff, Starevitch, Peter Foldes, Jean Image and Piotr Kamler, are animators who have come from abroad. In addition there are two Poles, Lenica and Borowczyk, who have done some of their most important work in France and Germany. However, these two have been included in the next chapter.

7. Polish Animation at Home and Abroad

With Poland we move into a different world, a world of state enterprise, planning, security, control. Whatever we may think about it in general as an environment for the artist, it is arguable that in the field of animated film, Eastern Europe has produced more original, serious, finer, wittier work, more satiric work even, in the last twenty years, than the world of free enterprise in the last fifty. It may be simply a passing phase in the West, and due to conditions which are transient, that the animated film has been so neglected an art form. But certainly in the West it has been difficult to make the short or long entertainment cartoon of quality (series of television pot-boilers are another matter) a paying proposition. In the East it is easier. The planning authorities decide that the economy needs feature films, shorts, *and* animated films, and somehow or another they will provide the resources to produce them. Quality of course cannot be commanded. But, with art schools training those who have a natural bent, with instruction in film technique provided by the state, with the opportunity of working in a cartoon or puppet production studio, and with a broad-minded, liberal attitude towards the projects which are acceptable (there is a world of difference here between Russia and East Germany at one extreme of illiberality, and Poland, Yugoslavia and Czechoslovakia before Russian intervention, at the other extreme of considerable freedom)—given all these conditions, there is every chance that valuable work will be produced. Those with a political thesis to prove can point to the fact that artists migrate to the West from iron-curtain countries. But this may have more to do with a generally higher standard of living than anything directly related to their work. Borowczyk and Lenica have done just as good work in Poland as out of it. Vlado Kristl did better work in Yugoslavia than in Germany, perhaps because in Yugoslavia he was subject to an artistic discipline which he seems incapable of exercising on his own account. And Gene Deitch is a case to set on the other side, of an animator moving from West to East.

★　　★　　★

The two most brilliant Polish cartoonists are **Jan Lenica** and Walerian Borowczyk. Lenica was born in 1928 in Poznan, and first studied music, but later turned to architecture and then to art. In 1950 his first poster was issued and he took a leading part in the development of the Polish cinema posters which have since become

so famous. Besides his films he has written and illustrated children's books and worked as an exhibition designer. Borowczyk was born in 1923 at Kwilcz, studied painting at the Polish Academy of Fine Arts, and between 1951 and 1955 worked in all branches of graphic art. He exhibited in Poland and abroad, and in 1953 won a national prize for his lithography.

Their first three films: *Once upon a Time, Dom (House),* and *Love Requited,* were joint efforts. Lenica has since made: *Monsieur Tête, Janko the Musician, Labyrinth, Rhinoceros, A,* and *The Flower Woman.* Borowczyk has made *L'Ecole, Les Astronautes, Les Jeux des anges, L'Encyclopédie de Grand' Maman, Le Concert de Monsieur et Madame Kabal, Le Dictionnaire de Joachim,* and a feature-length film about the Kabals.

In their first films they seem to have achieved a perfect collaboration, and they show no dichotomy nor evidence of disparate styles. Their latter work also contains strong elements of similarity: the satiric power, bitter black humour and tragic irony born in Poland during the last war and other wars before it. At the same time both have strong individuality. Robert Benayoun characterises them thus: "There are enormous differences between Lenica and his old accomplice, the phlegmatic Boro. Lenica is the greater sculptor *(plasticien)* of the two and his work is stamped with his own peculiar graphic shorthand, an immediately recognisable style rivalling those of Steinberg or Miro in its subjective impact. Borowczyk, although an accomplished artist, is fundamentally a film-maker, an inventor of movements and phrases. He orchestrates objects as well as empty spaces, amusing himself by giving life to cyphers. One feels that he could construct a startling natural order from given quantities of absence, invisibility and negation."

Once upon a Time is a bit of a joke. A round, furry body with stick-like legs moves through a world of lithographs, old newspapers, famous paintings, postcards—changing its shape into a lamp, a chair, part yet not part of the scrap-book backgrounds. A bit of a joke but a sinister joke too. The "thing" has the metamorphic, indefinite, amorphous quality of the science fiction monster. One might compare it with McLaren's *Merle,* also made from sticks but definitely and reassuringly a real bird. The thing in *Once upon a Time* is far from reassuring. *Dom* has even more horrific chapters. It consists of

Opposite: the art of Jan Lenica. Above, LABYRINTH; below, MONSIEUR TETE

some five episodes describing the thoughts of a girl left alone in a house: thoughts of love; the monotony of everyday life represented by a man endlessly hanging up his hat; the violence of everyday life in a menacing little vignette in colour, showing a wig come alive, devouring and destroying all the things about it.

Lenica's next film, *Monsieur Tête* (1959), he made with Henri Gruel. In it he entered a world of his own creation. The sun rises golden over the town, the blue birds sing, Monsieur Tête at his window exercises gaily until he collapses and gets up, a vase of flowers on his head. Then just a glimpse of the devil at work below, before we join Monsieur Tête in the bathroom trying to shave a fly off his face. Before going out he is filled with noble thoughts. His head becomes Shakespeare, Napoleon, Charlie Chaplin. But in the office all movements are mechanical, the typist's eyes follow her carriage, and the chief clerk eats the documents. From our hero's head they take a dead mouse and a candle, he grows a flower halo, and with a heart-shaped head woos a girl in the park. Cold alas! Then food floats by, to a reception, and our hero follows to join the gourmands, eating jewellery and drinking wine, the incessant gossip drilling through his hearer's heads, the orator spouting posies, the letters swarming like bees until a listener swallows them. Monsieur Tête shoots the orator; black-out and riot; a struggle; cries; and figures in the dark. Monsieur Tête, thrown in prison, hammers his head and argues with it. Then he wins decorations, but as he does so he loses features. He ends loaded with honours, a faceless figure, with a guardian angel over his head.

Lenica explored his private world further in his next two films, *Janko the Musician* and *Labyrinth* (1961). *Labyrinth* is one of his richest works. It shows us a world of strange creatures and places through which a bowler-hatted man walks, polite, resigned, stoical. He rescues a woman from the clutches of a crocodile monster but is indignantly slapped for his pains. Flies swarm out of an empty refrigerator, a butterfly woman kisses her lover and leaves him a fleshless skeleton. In a vast building the man is measured, examined, recorded, his brain tapped and "readjusted" by filling it with a neutralising fluid. He escapes, straps on a pair of wings, and flies away, a modern Icarus, only in the end to be attacked and destroyed by hordes of black vultures. *Rhinoceros* borrows very little more than the name, and the spirit of lunatic despair, from Ionesco. A thunderous, black horned boss dominates the office, the clerk carefully locks away figures in the safe, men and women talk incessantly, producing piles of flowers and objects. In *A*, a neatly allegoric

116

film, the menace takes a more concentrated form. The man is secure and happy, alone in his own room. He dances about, prepares to eat. From out of the air there materialises a large letter *A*. At first it simply stays there and resists the man's vain efforts to get rid of it, to push it out of the way, to chip bits off it. Then it attacks him, crowds him into a corner, nips him, tortures him, renders his life a misery. Once or twice he thinks he has banished the incubus but his celebration is cut short by its reappearance. Finally, after he has been reduced to despair, the *A* disappears; he waits, wonders if he dare hope; seconds pass, and it seems clear his tormentor *A* has gone for ever. Suddenly there materialises an equally powerful, menacing letter *B*. Lenica's latest cartoon *Hell* (1971), gives similar glimpses of brains being filled, human beings on conveyor-belts, men attacked by strange missiles. Dante appears briefly and there is a laughable shot of top naval brass going up, then down, on an aircraft-carrier's lift.

In actual viewing Lenica's work is less pessimistic than it sounds. For a start the cartoon form takes the edge off the agony. Again one feels that his heroes are characters strong enough to meet their fate. The alphabet of woes which assail them represent the slings and arrows of outrageous fortune but they are maturely faced, and there is no massacre of the innocents to wring our hearts. Borowczyk's characters are more cutting, and there is more hidden violence in his dead-pan ferocity.

Lenica's style is varied, but generally favours heavy black lines, rather in the manner of Rouault, which are very effective on the screen. He occasionally uses colour, avoiding the obvious "paint-box" effects of the traditional cartoon, and so that it intensifies the strength of his line composition. His animation is often simplified to the extent of making his characters move like machines. He uses cut-out figures, engraved backgrounds and all sorts of collage.

★　　★　　★

The first film **Borowczyk** made by himself was *L'Ecole* produced in 1958 and given an award by the British Film Institute. It is an exercise in the absurd, the central figure a soldier against a wall who goes through ridiculous manoeuvres. In 1959 came *Les Astronautes,* surely the strangest science-fiction short ever created. The chief character is a live actor, Michel Boschet, who sits hunched at the controls of his space-ship. Various projectiles manipulate and jockey for position; the hero in his gim-crack machine torpedoes one of them only to be brought down by a sinister, droning, wasp-like object that explodes with atomic force. He descends in a parody of a hundred screen comedies, smut-faced and de-bagged, landing surely in the canal between the gas-works and the railway. The style is a wild mixture of collage, objects, pixillation, the lot.

L'Encyclopédie de Grand-Maman is a grave parody of the Victorian instructional book, arranged alphabetically (*A comme automobile, B comme ballon, C comme chemin-de-fer . . .*) though the film never gets any further than C. Again disasters and absurdity. The style is less mixed than *Les Astronautes,* and effectively echoes the engraved illustrations of early periodicals. *L'Encyclopédie* was followed by *Renaissance,* completely different from any of Borowczyk's or anybody else's films, unique, inimitable. *Renaissance* is a study in animated still-life and builds up to a set-piece. It is brilliantly constructed, makes effective use of suspense, has the sort of inverted logic Lewis Carroll delighted in, conveys a tragic, symbolic meaning, and does it all in ten minutes. To the sound of trumpet music a strange group of objects gradually integrate themselves, slowly,

From Borowczyk's LES JEUX DES ANGES

painfully emerging—a hamper, some books, a doll, a cornet, a stuffed owl. Gradually they take shape, climb out of chaos, become whole and perfect, until at last creation is complete and the little group, *the world,* stands for a moment like the first Paradise—then comes a blinding flash and Night and Chaos reign once more. The film was made by gradually destroying and disarranging the group, photographing it frame-by-frame and then reversing the film—childishly simple, supremely effective.

Le Dictionnaire de Joachim and *Le Théâtre de Monsieur et Madame Kabal* are two cartoons in fine line-drawing. Joachim with a dead-pan expression takes us through twenty-six words, one for each letter of the alphabet, giving a satirical definition in the style of Ambrose Bierce's *Devil's Dictionary* for each word. *Le Théâtre de Monsieur et Madame Kabal* is a feature-length cartoon and its principal characters, the hook-nosed Madame Kabal and her wooden-headed husband, are figures of cruelty and fear. Borowczyk sets them in landscapes arid and harsh, and the effect is not so much of human beings as of great insects hating and torturing one another.

Les Jeux des Anges is a film in which the tragedy and horror of the modern world—the concentration camp, the torture chamber, the experimental cell—are symbolised and suggested, rather than exposed by individual instances. It has the sort of abstraction which Resnais achieved in *Marienbad.* It has been described as being "like the unfathomable memories of an exotic journey." Again, though the mood is something different, it is the effect which De Quincy obtains in describing his opium dreams in terms which are the more terrifying because of their indefiniteness: "Then came sudden alarms; hurryings to and fro; trepidation of innumerable fugitives I knew not whether from the good cause or the bad; darkness and lights; tempest and human faces . . ." The film opens with a journey: the sound of travelling, the sight of a landscape which can be seen to move, yet whose details are indistinguishable. Then from darkness to light we arrive in a series of cells, bare, clean, waiting, enigmatic, pitiless. There is the sound of a struggle off-stage, a sound of wings yet with something metallic in it—a wing falls, hard, cold blue, made of steel or ice. Inside a box we hear a body thumping about as if trying to escape; a press is set to work; blood gushes out. Two headless, limbless torsos wrestle, entwined in an obscene death-struggle, their fighting accompanied by agonised sounds. To swelling music, organ pipes turn into horizontal gun-muzzles belching death at unseen victims. Then at the climax a naked woman sits enthroned, a prisoner, her head shaved, expressionless, her legs ominously encased in thigh-length, metal boots. At the end comes the journey again—the long journey back. The film is achieved in an unusual painting style reminiscent at some points of artists like Max Ernst or Edward Burra.

Between them Lenica and Borowczyk have done more than any other cartoonists, not only in Poland but anywhere, to raise the status of the cartoon to a serious art, one that can move us to pity and terror, one that can match in range and depth the tragi-comedy of the human condition.

★   ★   ★

At the same time, though these two are outstanding, other Polish animators are by no means negligible, and there are half-a-dozen other cartoonists and puppet film-makers who are in the top rank.

Witold Giersz is probably the best known, because of the great popularity of his *Little Western* (1960). This clever, good-humoured cartoon is painted in water-colour without hard outlines, a pleasant change from the usual cartoon composition. A good cowboy strikes it rich by lifting up the water of a river and scooping fistfuls of diamonds from the bed. He is set upon by two bad cowboys and robbed, but with the help of his faithful horse he turns the tables on them. The story is amazingly simple but fast-moving, mildly satiric, and neatly fitted to the technique. For instance one blue bad-man bangs into one yellow bad-man with the classic cartoon collision—result one green bad-man twice the size of the other two! The red hero retaliates by diving into a pool of red paint and growing in size to match them, finally battering them back into a series of little blue and yellow bad-men who run away. This use of the nature of the medium is quite suitable in comic vein, though it has its limitations. For instance in one sequence of a recent cartoon, *The Melomaniac* by a Rumanian, Horia Stefanescu, an elephant is disposed of very neatly. As he squirts water his body gradually drains of colour, then the outline shape is simply crumpled up and thrown away. This could be obtrusive in serious work but it does mean that the film-maker is aware of the possibilities of his medium, and it is far better than the cartoons, all too common, which are made without any heed to the properties of graphic materials or to the values inherent in graphic composition.

Giersz's film *The Red and the Black* is about bull-fighting, in the same style and with the same comic originality as *The Little Western*. However, at the end when we cut to a shot of Giersz actually filming the bull, the humour is overstrained. In 1964 he made *Ladies and Gentlemen,* also full of inventive humour. In Giersz's usual fluid

120

From Borowczyk's feature, LE THEATRE DE MONSIEUR ET MADAME KABAL

style it pictures two rivals for the same girl each struggling to get the better of the other, an ironical theme because they are fighting for nothing—the girl does not care a button for either of them. A little film, *Waiting* (1962), tells the story of two figures made by a lover waiting at a rendezvous, of twisted spills of paper. Giersz himself has said: "The fact that I used paper puppets determined the experiences they went through, just as the properties of painting determined the action of the *Little Western* and *The Red and the Black*." Giersz has also made two popular science films, *Dinosaurs* and *Was My Face Red* (1966), the latter an unusual film about the control of body temperature in cold-blooded fish and reptiles and warm-blooded mammals. *Portrait of a Horse* (1968), is a free-flowing CinemaScope picture of the taming of a wild stallion with dramatic graphics and action.

More prolific is **Jerzy Zitzman** who has made fifteen films including *Bulandra and the Devil, Mr. Trumpet, A General and a Fly, Don Juan,* and *The Coffee Grinder*. Elaborate stories most of them, with naïve but quite fetching plots. In *A General and a Fly,* the

General goes to fantastic lengths to destroy a fly which eludes all assaults by him or his entourage. *Don Juan* spends most of the film galloping away from outraged husbands or duelling with rivals. At one point he takes refuge in a coach with a beautiful Senora to leave the lady seconds later with the present of a bouncing baby. Zitzman's latest film, *New Year's Eve,* unravels the tangled tale of a house in which the lodgers get mixed up with each other, with an amorous postman, a hunter, a goose and a haunch of venison. Zitzman's work is very light, but he has a style of his own.

Daniel Szczechura is fertile in bright ideas which lend themselves to animation: *Stadium, Conflict, Machine, The Letter, First Second Third, The Seat* and most recently *Diagram.* He is particularly fond of pulling the spectator's leg. *Machine* for instance shows a gang of little men handling scaffolding which gradually builds up to a mighty machine with all the important parts that look like turbines, driving wheels, etc. A high-up party member comes to declare it open. Then, when we see the business end of it, we find it is designed as a super-mechanised pencil-sharpener. *The Letter* again builds up to a climax. A devoted band of toilers are hauling a huge letter N through thick and thin; through traffic jams, over obstructions, round corners. We wonder what new slogan it represents, what world-shaking "ism"; we think of *Two Men and a Wardrobe.* Finally they get it up on top of a building where it simply turns out to be the middle letter of End—E-N-D. *The Seat* shows a big political meeting with the bosses (coloured blue as opposed to the pink of the *hoi polloi*) sitting on the dais. One of the bosses' seats is vacant but as one after another of the audience tries to come up and fill it, he is held back, tripped up, prevented by his comrades. Then one darts out through the entrance doors at the opposite end to the dais, runs along a back passage, and gets on to the stage before anyone can stop him. As he sits down he turns a nice aristocratic blue. The whole of this cartoon is drawn looking vertically down from above, not very beautiful pictorially, but clear and effective for this particular theme. Szczechura's *Diagram* (1966), described as "a man in pursuit of everything," is well up to the standard of the others. The screen shows a little man and a black ball. He tries to catch it, but the ball evades him making a black line as it does so. Again he chases it and again and again, and again, until the screen is a tangle of lines and finally blacks out entirely. The brilliant economy of this film is satisfying logically; it makes a fascinating line of composition and movement, and at the same time neatly conveys a satiric meaning. In *Hobby* a woman in a

Magritte landscape lassoos men, pulls them down from the sky and puts them in cages.

Miroslaw Kijowicz has produced some outstanding work. Born in Russia, he studied art at Warsaw and has been working as a cartoon film director since 1960. He describes his aim as "short aphoristic films addressed to mental activity," a description which applies very well to other Polish animators. He has made nine films in Poland and also worked in Yugoslavia with Branko Ranitović. *Harlequin, The Town, Portraits, Cabaret* are early films. *Cages* and *Science Fiction* (1971), more recent. Perhaps his best work is *The Banner,* made in 1965. A group of little men are lining up for some sort of rally, a veterans' parade, Armistice Day, what have you. They are all dressed alike in civvies; they all carry identical little flags; they all take their places at spots marked on the pavement; the clock approaches the hour. But one place remains empty. The little men shuffle about trying to hide the gap; one of them holds the clock back. At last the missing comrade turns up looking cheerfully unconscious and is seized upon and lined up. But where is his flag? They search him all over, lift up the top of his head like a lid, and take a look inside. This turns out to be a dreadful mistake, because the inside of our friend's head is stuffed as full as a conjurer's hat with all kinds of frivolous irrelevancies. A bird in a cage, yards of ribbon, bunches of flowers, a gramophone and some records, a game of chess. The comrades pass the things round and little by little anarchy sets in. Two start playing chess, one puts on a record, another admires the bird. The place begins to look more like a social club than a serious Armistice day parade. Then at the bottom of all the junk someone finds the missing flag. Just in time, for important military music is approaching. Just in time all the toys are put away. Just in time the pathetic little band stand at attention. In its simple truth mixed with fantasy, in its wry humanity, *The Banner* is a present day fable with the charm and imperishability of the best of Andersen or Grimm.

Stefan Janik is another animator with an attractive style shown in *Attention, The Balloons, The Enemy in the Bottle,* the last a very funny anti-drinking film. His latest film *Pyramid* shows black-suited, black-hatted acrobats against a blue-grey background or a Douanier Rousseau forest. In the climax a beautiful woman throws them a rose and the pyramid collapses. She is sad and so are they, and both have a grave, faded grace. Another of Janik's recent films is *Fiddle-Faddle,* dazzling patterns of movement and colour made of folk

123

PYRAMIDS, directed by Stefan Janik

cut-outs from various regions of Poland, and accompanied by lively folk dances.

Among the earliest Polish animators were **Wladyslaw Nehrbecki,** Waiser, and Haupe and Bielinska. Nehrbecki originated a well-known Polish cartoon character, Professor Filutek, and created delightful cartoon animals in his *Zoo*. Best known of his films in this country is *Mouse & Cat (Myszka i Kotek),* made in 1958. From the very credits whose letters turn into tangled lines of string, this is a film which (like those of Giersz) brilliantly integrates the qualities of the medium into the action. A little toy mouse first comes on the scene: solid, opaque, perhaps a rubber toy. He goes up to a picture-book cat, much bigger, but drawn in outline only so that the coloured backgrounds show through his string-like body. The mouse gives the cat's tail a tweak and breaks it through, so that when pussy comes alive and tries to catch him, she unravels into a tangled mass. She manages to pull herself together again, tie a knot in her tail, and the chase goes on, puss getting tangled up in a globe and soaked in red ink. At the end the mouse jumps right into the cat's mouth and through its hollow body into his hole. The film is a little gem of visual wit. Nehrbecki also made an earlier film, *Among the Bushes*

(1961), based like Janik's *Fiddle Faddle* on traditional Polish cut-out patterns and figures.

Waclaw Waiser is best known for a cartoon, *Bicycle Race,* with strange characters looking something like those in *The Little Island.* **Wlodzimierz Haupe** and **Halina Bielinska** made one of the earliest and most famous films with animated objects, *Changing the Guard,* which uses match-boxes for soldiers and matches for their rifles. *The Circus under the Stars* is another of their puppet films, about a little black boy. Another leading puppet film-maker is **Edward Sturlis:** *The Boastful Knight, Damon, King Midas.* Two of his recent films are *Status,* a satire on sycophants, and *A Little Quartet,* animating the statuettes from an old-fashioned piano. Sturlis's puppet technique is excellent, but his scripts are inclined to be dull. **Kazimierz Urbanski** has made a good many cartoons, two recent examples being *The Fascination of Two Wheels,* a film about speed, and *The Robber's Dirge* (1969). **Stefan Schabenbeck** made his *début* in 1967 with *Everything Is a Number* which shows a human being lost in a world of figures, while his next film *Exclamation Mark* presented a tragedy in the world of geometry. *The Steps* was symbolic of human progress, and *Invasion* (1970) showed mysterious intruders in the human skull. **Jerzy Kotowski** works in both two and three dimensions. His latest film *Shadows of Time* brings to life two skeleton hands who come out of Nazi helmets, and try to destroy a household, but are electrocuted. The film has some macabre effects but as a whole is crude and unconvincing. More recently he has made *Horizont* using object animation to show a world of steel and iron.

★   ★   ★

The Polish studios—Miniatur, Se-Ma-For, Cracow Short Film etc.—produce fifty or more animated shorts a year, many of them for children, but others involved in contemporary issues, probing deeply into human feeling and experience, films not for children but for adults.

125

8. Puppets and Cartoons in Czechoslovakia

By far the most important figure in Czechoslovakia was Jiri Trnka, famous for his puppets and puppet films, but no less of an artist in the field of book-illustration and cartoons. Robert Benayoun makes some interesting comments on the development of marionettes, and points out that in many cases they form a focus for popular discontent and revolt: Punch, Guignol, Hanesgen, Kharagos (fomenting Greek resistance to the Ottomans) and Kasparek "who helped destroy the Austro-Hungarian empire."[1] In Czechoslovakia puppet shows were particularly popular from the Seventeenth and Eighteenth centuries onwards. They belonged to the people for they were the kind of entertainment to be given in the Czech language, and the creations of Josef Skupa—Speijbl and Hurvinek—were national heros. The first Czech puppet film, *Speijbl on the Spree,* was made in 1931, and Trnka had a long tradition behind him when he founded his puppet theatre in Prague in 1935.

Trnka was born in Pilsen in 1912, the son of a plumber, and remembered a Holiday Camp Puppet Theatre when he was four years old. After studying at Art School he started a puppet theatre in 1935 when he was twenty-three. It was after the war he turned to the cinema, and his first films were cartoons: *Grandpa Plants Beetroot* (1945), *The Animals and the Brigands, The Present, The Devil on Springs* (1946). Most are rich in colour, based on fairytale stories and with Czech traditional backgrounds. But *The Devil on Springs* (also called *The Chimney Sweep* or *The Springer and the SS*) is a savage anti-Hitler film which has never ceased to be popular and now has almost the status of a legend. The setting is in a modern town occupied by the Nazis where a little cartoon "everyman," a chimney-sweep, puts springs on his feet and a black hood over his head, and becomes a Czech version of the Australian, Spring-heel Jack. He makes a furious assault on the Nazis, on Hitler their chief, bashes them, smashes them, finally pile-driving them nose-first into the ground. The violence is similar in some ways to that of American cartoons, but there is more grim feeling behind it; the characters are human not animal, and the film is in hard outline and stark black-and-white as opposed to colour. This is the harsh anger of

---

[1] According to the inscription on a commemorative statue in Pizen. Surely the only monument put up in memory of a puppet.

adults, not the light hearted cruelty of adolescents. It is not a pleasant film to watch, but at least it expresses real emotion.

Trnka turned from cartoons to puppet films "because [he said] cartoons are limiting, their characters have to be constantly in movement. Marionettes have more *presence.*" One can see what he meant. It is related to the distinction made in the introduction to this book, that the camera is of less importance in cartoons. Puppets are *there* and they can be filmed like real actors. Kleist spoke of the lightness of marionettes compared with dancers: "They know nothing of weight or matter. The force which lifts them far outbalances that which keeps them on the ground"; but in the case of Trnka one of the qualities of his expressively-carved, wooden dolls is their solidity. He moves them with unhurried deliberation like a musician whose favourite tempo is *Andante.* "I never feel at home in towns," Trnka says. "I belong to the country," and his films refuse to conform to the bustle of the jet age.

All the same many audiences find his films slow-paced and most successful are his short early puppet films, on traditional historical themes, presenting a rural or burgher community, films too short for the audience to feel bored, too beautiful for them to feel impatient, and in which a deliberate pace is acceptable because it suits the setting: *The Czech Year* (1947), *The Emperor's Nightingale* (a Chinese setting after the Hans Andersen story, but certainly not modern), *The Devil's Mill, Song of the Prairie, Prince Bayaya, Old Czech Legends* (1953).

Trnka gives us with equal facility the little peasants with round heads, button noses and twinkling glances, and the heroes of chivalry with their haughty bearing and deep, sad eyes. His *Good Soldier Schweik* celebrates the unquenchable spirit of the peasant, the common man, eternally at war against the modern military machine, or for that matter any system which treats the individual as a number in a register. *Song of the Prairie,* an engaging send-up of the Western, is no exception, for a feature of the Western and one of the main reasons for its popularity, is that it represents an escape from our modern civilisation to a simple, rural way of life.

In 1959 came Trnka's most ambitious film, *A Midsummer Night's Dream,* in which his style is seen at its richest, but in which the ornate *décor,* the lavish costumes, the crowded scenes, finally become, like rich plum-cake, almost too much for our palate. Perhaps it is that the film gets lost in too much detail, exquisite as it all is, or that Trnka holds too faithfully to the intricacies of Shakespeare's plot and without dialogue it is difficult to follow (though a version

127

with words released in England was not successful). Something simpler, less pastoral, possibly something more tragic and piercing (*Macbeth* has been suggested) would have suited him better. Nevertheless the film has some lovely moments, scenes which in their miniature splendour are breathtaking, and it certainly deserves wider showing than it has had, for it has hardly been seen at all outside Central Europe.

For Trnka *A Midsummer Night's Dream* was a setback, and he made nothing more of interest until 1965, then surprisingly, five years before his death in 1970, he produced two puppet films, strong and bitter, and quite different from the rest of his work: *Archangel Gabriel and Mother Goose,* and *The Hand. Archangel Gabriel and Mother Goose* is a story taken from Boccaccio, of a lecherous monk who pretends to be Archangel Gabriel in order to seduce a foolish but pretty woman. The story seems harmless enough, but Trnka invests it with a bitter force. The monk is a loathsome-looking creature, bloated and gross with dissipation, Mother Goose a simpering idiot, and in the end the monk is betrayed and punished with pitiless savagery. Though not a very sweet film, it is a little masterpiece, and the miniature actors are handled and characterised with such skill that we almost forget they are not alive. *The Hand* shows an artist, a sculptor happy in his life and his work. There comes a giant hand which orders the sculptor to make a statue of it. He resists at first but the hand is all powerful, he is made to submit, and to produce the statue at the cost of his liberty and finally his life. A grim allegory, a long way from *The Czech Year,* but achieved with the same artistry.

★   ★   ★

Jiri Trnka was born in 1912, **Bretislav Pojar** in 1923. Pojar too has made cartoons, but his most important work is in puppet films. His first film was *Gingerbread Cottage* in 1951 but it was not until his second film, *A Drop Too Much* (1954), a puppet film about a motorcycle accident that he began to attract attention. Then came *Speijbl on the Track, The Little Umbrella,* and in 1958, *The Lion and the Song,* a puppet film about a troubadour threatened by a lion, regarded by some as his best work. After it came *Glory, Bombomania, How to Furnish a Flat* (a popular science film using marionettes, cartoon and paper figures), *Midnight Adventure,* and three films in paper sculpture about cats: *Cat Talk, Cat Painting* and *Cat School.*

French critics have called *The Lion and the Song* "unique, perfect, memorable, historic" and "the work of an exalted lyric poet whose vision attains the ineffable." Well—it is a conventional little puppet film with an ordinary plot of the boy-gets-girl variety, quite attractive and competently made. Nothing more. However Pojar has subsequently made three films: *Billiards, Orator* and *Romance*, which have more to offer. *Billiards* is a story of bad-temper passed from

Trnka's ARCHANGEL GABRIEL AND MOTHER GOOSE

the boss who has had a bad night to the office staff, to a boy in the street, to a dog, a replica of the one in the boss's nightmare. Then the boss meets the dog . . . The action comes full circle, having on the way given us some sharply etched portraits. *Orator* is made with a mixture of puppet figures and strange drawing. It starts with the orator trying his speech out on his wife, and imagining a great triumph. Then on the night, contrasting with the florid bla-bla-bla of the speaker, we see the thoughts inside the audience's head, a mass of irrelevant personal preoccupations—flirtation, food, sport. *Romance* shows a girl with a young chap on a motorbike, who transfers to an older man with a car, to a still older man with a bigger car . . . and so on. These films are not the ineffable work of an exalted lyric poet, but made by a talented young man who has something to say. His latest film, *It's Hard to Recognise a Princess,* about two little bears, is made for children, but so full of originality and wit as to appeal to any audience. I have never seen a puppet film with such pace and verve. Of its kind it is the best thing Pojar has done. Pojar is said to have been working in Canada recently, but to date no new films have appeared.

A new puppet film-maker regarded in Czechoslovakia as full of promise is **Jan Svankmajer.** His first film, *Messrs. Schwarzwalde and Edgar's Last Trick* shows two circus conjurers determined to outdo one another. The film has the bold simplicity in colour and form of peasant art with an added mechanical ingenuity. The characters are two giants, great wooden strong-men, pathetic yet formidable in their strength. They come to pieces, juggle with their heads and perform amazing tricks. Then a little beetle gets inside their brains, drives them into a demented rage, and they tear one another to pieces. His second film, *Bach's Fantasy in B Minor,* is an experimental synthesis of abstract form and music. His third film, *Coffin Factory,* is about a Punch and a Clown who beat each other to pieces in a fight over a live guinea-pig. Stones and numerals are animated in two other films made by Svankmajer in Austria. His latest animated movie, *Historia Naturae,* contains beautiful pictures of insects, birds, reptiles and mammals in museum arrangements as well as alive and is in a sense a comment on evolution.

Perhaps because of their strong puppet tradition, the Czechs have produced a large number of films using object animation. At the 1966 Mamaia Festival there were three good examples. **Garik Seko**'s *Stone and Life* peoples the screen with creatures made of smoothed river-stones: a man, an ostrich-like bird, little rabbit-like creatures, a kind of dog, a woman. They are startlingly lifelike, but the material is so strange and making animals of stones such a *tour-de-force,* that the technique dominates the film, and one is unable to forget the medium which remains too intrusive, too overpowering, too grotesque. A story would have been impossible and wisely none was attempted. It was an interesting experiment, but an isolated one.

More successful perhaps was **Hermina Tyrlova**'s *Snowman,* all the characters being made of wool, curled or bunched. This is a more flexible material, and lit so that the colours shone and sparkled, it gave the film a breathtaking, fragile beauty. Hermina Tyrlova is known for her children's puppet films, among them *Ferda, Revolt of the Toys, Golden Curls.*

Quite different from the other two was **Pavel Prochazka**'s *Figures* in which numbers of all kinds swarm and proliferate, jerking, jumping, constantly in motion, used for decoration in an endless, crazy, moving composition: numerals from badges, milometers, raffles, tickets, stamps, machines, serial numbers. They sing, they whistle, there is never a full moment, although (except for one inexplicable shot of nude pin-ups) only numerals are used. No doubt what makes the film so lively and amusing is the use of something with such strong associations as numerals in a completely different context. Again it is an experiment in technique which would hardly lend itself to repetition. Another of Prochazka's shorts, *The Crooked Chimney,* based on a folk opera, has been praised for the "impeccably controlled movement of its puppets and its design."

A veteran puppet film-maker is **Joseph Kluge** who has been working since 1950. *The Gossips* (1968), which uses grotesque cut-out figures is a story of true love wrecked by malicious gossip. Again with frightening cut-out figures, *The Helpers,* a satiric allegory of unconcerned bureaucracy, has superbly visual scenes. Most recent is *Playing Mama,* a puppet film, the amusing story of an egg and the chicken inside it. Czech puppet films continue to excel and *The Widow of Ephesus* (1971), directed by **Jaroslav Bocek,** is a delightful short tale taken from Petronius. A young wife falls in love with a soldier who catches a robber in her elderly husband's fine house. The husband dies, the robber is hanged, and the soldier set to guard his body. But when the soldier sneaks off at dead of night to visit the young widow, the robber's confederates steal his body. Her lover threatened with disgrace, the young widow helps the soldier to open her husband's coffin and allows him to "stand in" for the robber. The story is diverting, the action expertly handled, the puppet characters splendidly portrayed and the costumes and *décor* picturesque.

★   ★   ★

Though the Czechs are best known for their puppets, there are some excellent cartoonists. The pioneer was Dodal, a Czech painter, whose black-and-white cartoons were shown at the 1937 Paris Exhibition. One of the most prolific is **Jiri Brdecka.** His first cartoon—*Love and the Dirigible* (1947)—is an Edwardian period romance, drawn by Kamil Lhotak in a delicate, gentle style entirely appropriate to the story of a lover who elopes with his beloved in an airship. Then came a gap of ten years followed by *How Man Learned to Fly* (1957), a comic history of aviation, *Attention, Clementine,* and *Red Riding Hood.* In 1961 he made *Man under Water,* a comic account of early submarines and diving bells. It used early illustrations and prints to good effect. *Sentiment and Reason* (1962) pictured a contest between the romantic and the classical, a curious cartoon, drawn by Zdenek Seydl in hard ugly lines and with monochrome colouring. Brdecka had already used the same style in the cartoon *Attention* made in 1960. One has the feeling with these cartoons that the artist is trying to convey a protest against the ugliness, the rigidity of our modern, man-made, industrial and urban environment. One could hardly imagine them to be by the same director as *Love and the Dirigible.*

Gallina Vogelbirdae, one of Brdecka's most successful cartoons, is the story of a schoolboy's Picasso-like hen contemptuously thrown into the waste-paper basket by the drawing-master. At night the crumpled paper bird comes alive and finishes in glory at the zoo as a new specimen. Again in a hard, almost angry style, but with brighter colours, *Deserter,* is about a man who goes on a space ship to a new planet only to find all the things he hoped to escape from in this world identically present there. It is not up to the standard of his other work. *Why Do You Smile Mona Lisa?* is a rather feeble attempt to poke fun at the Giaconda, suggesting the lady's mysterious smile is due to a recent assignation with a lover. It is much inferior to Henri Gruel's cartoon on the same subject. *Hunting in the Forest* is great fun with lovely music from a Czech folk-song, a sad love-story but illustrated with gaily-coloured period hunting-pictures, half serious, half joking. *The Power of Fate* is a very curious fable about a fortune-teller and her client who wears a false hand! Finally *Metamorpheus* tells the story of Orpheus and Eurydice in the style of Pompeian wall paintings.

Zdenek Miler's cartoons are mostly for children, but he has made two outstanding films for adults: *The Millionaire Who Stole the Sun* (1948), and *The Red Stain* (1963). *The Millionaire Who Stole the Sun,* the story of a man who seeks to dominate everyone and everything, eventually meeting disaster, is a strange work, crude, powerful, ungainly, like one of Upton Sinclair's novels. *The Red Stain,* in heavy charcoal and red shading, evokes concentration camps and massacres, and a red stain, like a red flower, which cannot be wiped out but grows and spreads until it covers the screen.

Vladimir Lehky has successfully directed cartoons in a number of different styles, all with a sure sense of line and composition. His first film *The Goat and the Lion* was made in 1957 and up to 1965 he had made fourteen films. *The Parasite* (1960) is typical of a series featuring dynamic little figures with oval heads and sticks for arms and legs. In this particular film one character keeps battening on the other only to be discomfited in the end. His latest film *Odd Birds* (1965) is a delight. It is drawn by Jiri Toman with classic simplicity in the finest of lines, black on white, and there is masterly control of every movement. The story of two odd (very odd) birds is full of droll touches and quiet ironical invention. These cartoons of Lehky are outstanding and deserve to be better known, and he has also made some important puppet films.

In 1965 **Jan Karpas** made a film *The Lady and Her Luggage* after a poem by Samuel Marsak. The poem tells of a horrible lady with so much baggage that the railway staff are driven mad, and Karpas's cartoon recreates her in fine style in a Victorian setting. She meets her deserts when an enormous dog chases her down the railway line and out of the film. Karpas has made some half-dozen cartoons going back to *The Story of the Ghost Bear* in 1955 and including *The Enchanted Rock* and *Cecilia* 470.

From Lehky's ODD BIRDS

Eduard Hofman trained as an architect, and is currently professor of film graphics at an Art College in Prague. Since his first film *All Aboard,* in 1947, he has directed about twenty cartoons including a *Cat and Dog* series. His film *The Angel's Cloak* (1948) was one of the most successful. It tells the story of a magic cloak which has the power of changing its wearer's character from bad to good. His longest and most important film is *The Creation* (1956), a cartoon giving a humorous account of the Book of Genesis based on the drawings of the French illustrator, Jean Effel. In it Satan is shown as a saboteur who tries to spoil God's handiwork. Vaclav Bedrich should be mentioned for *The Last Shot,* a parody of the Western, *The Forty Grandfathers,* and *When I Am a Man,* an anti-war film.

Karel Zeman has made many straightforward cartoons and created Czechoslovakia's most popular cartoon character, the stoical *Mr. Prokouk.* In *Inspiration* (1949) he brought to life glass figures and in *The Treasure of Bird Island* (1952) he combined cartoon and puppets. His later films are a unique mixture of live action, cartoon, models, and trick effects of every kind imaginable. He has created a sort of combined film, as uniquely his own as Lotte Reiniger's silhouettes or Alexeïeff's pin-table engravings. The first of these strange films, all of feature length, was *Prehistoric Journey,* in which prehistoric monsters are brought vividly to life. *The Invention of Destruction* (1956) based on a Jules Verne story, featured underwater journeys and sea monsters, and was followed by a fantastic *Baron Munchhausen*—full of marvels and with a picturesque, period elegance. More recently he has made *A Jester's Tale,* a long story of the middle ages with plenty of fun and action, but in which some of the trick effects begin to pall.

Vaclav Bedrich has made a number of cartoons including *Unfinished Week-end* (1970), a parody of comic and horror-films.

Finally there are a number of single works which are particularly interesting for one reason or another: Frantisek Vytricl's *Start* (1964), Josef Kabrt's *Iron Helmet* (1962) and Macourek and Latal's *How to Have Good Children* (1966). *Start* is a satirical account of a race, in which none of the competitors want to run. They have to be bribed to consider such senseless activity, and then having engaged in it they all cheat ruthlessly. It is vivaciously drawn and with a sharp wit.

In Kabrt's *Iron Helmet* a hen lays its eggs in an iron helmet which is lying on the ground, but the owner, a soldier, comes in and wants his helmet back. There ensues a struggle between war and peace which ends, like Chaplin's *The Great Dictator,* with the weaker party (the hen in this case) crying out to the audience for help. The film is particularly interesting for its strong contrast of styles: the hen is cosy,

134

nursery drawing, a traditional cartoon hen; the soldier is tortured, jagged, dazzling lines, shattering on the screen into saw-toothed lightning flashes.

How to Have Good Children is a riotous essay on the insoluble problem of inculcating good behaviour. "Little girls may be angels," we are told, "but little boys are anti-social, destructive, selfish, disrespectful and lazy." Even the teacher in a steel-helmet cowering behind sandbags is not safe. The author's solution is a boy-factory where real children are turned into automata with a key to wind them. "It's the only way," we are told, "for the modern world, where proper conduct is so important." A grim thought—but it would find many echoes in the West.

9. Yugoslavia, The Rise and Shine of Zagreb

In Yugoslavia the cartoon has developed since the war as the product of a fairly closely integrated school—a closer group than any in Poland or Czechoslovakia. Although Yugoslav directors may have their own personal style, there are common characteristics: clever scriptwriting; satire or parody in subject and treatment; sophisticated drawing in modern styles. Also we find the same film-makers, working sometimes as scriptwriters, sometimes as directors, sometimes as artists, animators or designers. Collaboration and interchange of roles is as great, or greater than in the case of the National Film Board in Canada. These factors make for difficulty in writing about the work of the Yugoslav school briefly and with complete accuracy. Here as elsewhere in the book the director is regarded as the author of the film, but it should be recognised that this is to some extent a simplification.

The most prolific directors up to 1959 were Vukotić, Kostelac, Mimica, and Urbanić. Since then other directors such as Kolar, Bourek, Zaninović, Dovniković, have done more work. Then there are others such as Vlado Kristl who have directed only one or two films, but films of outstanding quality.

★　★　★

The leading figure is **Dusan Vukotic.** He has directed the largest number of films, and his work includes the most celebrated cartoon, *Concerto for Sub-Machine Gun,* a brilliant parody of the American gangster film, made in 1959. Vukotić was born in 1927 and first studied architecture, then worked as a newspaper cartoonist. He was in the group from the beginning though the first cartoon, a twenty-two minute political satire entitled *The Great Meeting* (1951), was directed by Norbert Neugebauer. The original impetus came from a group of writers and caricaturists on the newspaper "Kerempuh," and the first films were made on a more or less amateur basis. There were all sorts of difficulties and in the early years the venture nearly collapsed. However in 1954 the first colour film, *Little Red Riding Hood,* was made, in the same year cartoon work was taken over by Zagreb Films, and from then on production was put on a firmer footing and became fully professional. A new studio was set up in 1958, and by 1961 over thirty short films a year were being produced.

Vukotić had earlier made a parody of a Western, *Cowboy Jimmy* (1957), the story of a film-struck little boy and the cowboy he sees on the screen. *Concerto for Sub-Machine Gun* inherits generally from

UPA, but the keen edge of the satire was the product of sharp outside observation, and could probably not have been made in America. It is interesting to note how frequently westerns and gangster films have been a point of reference for film-makers in Europe since the war, in almost every form (from Trnka's *Song of The Prairie,* to Godard's *Alphaville*) and in almost every country. It has been suggested that the hardships of postwar Europe generated a nostalgia for prewar entertainment which included a high proportion of imported films, and this may well be a factor.

My Tail's My Ticket is the story of two deadbeats who disguise themselves as a horse in order to get bed and board in a home for animals. They are unmasked and kicked out "with the vague impression that they were better off as horses." *Piccolo* (1960) is about a musical feud. One man starts off playing the mouth-organ, his neighbour retaliates with a concertina, the first man gets a violin and so on. It is a situation anyone can appreciate, it is skilfully handled and works up to a stupendous climax. A memorable image is of one contestant on the roof of the maisonette curing a leak in his neighbour's roof while they are still friends, by cutting off the cartoon rain with a pair of scissors.

The Academy Award winning ERSATZ, made in Zagreb by Dusan Vukotić

Another outstanding film directed by Vukotić which has won many prizes, being the first non-American cartoon to win an Oscar, is *Ersatz*, made in 1961. It pictures a world of beach toys, rubber blown up with air, where passion, jealousy, revenge exist . . . but are exploded in an instant. The drawing style is unusual, reminiscent of Klee. *Play* (1962), about two children drawing and quarreling, a parable of war and aggression, is a mixture of live-action and cartoon; but it is not so successful as Vukotić's other films. Recent work includes *A Stain on His Conscience, Opera Cordis,* and *Ars Gratia Artis,* all three combining animation and live-action in a new, telling style. The first is a sinister allegory with fine colour and music, presenting the fate of a man sitting in a café who is attacked by a strange kind of matter, a sort of noxious vapour. Whatever he does he cannot evade it or dispel it, it grows round him and cuts off any way of escape. Finally he succeeds in shutting it up in a bottle; but in the final scene he is afraid to open the bottle of beer the waiter brings him. . . . *Opera Cordis* grafts an emotional story of jealousy on to the mechanics of a heart-transplant operation, combining strong feeling with precise technical details. *Ars Gratia Artis* is a study of artistic vanity, featuring a real-life glass-swallower and a cartoon magician, and suggests that human beings will do anything for applause—even swallow themselves.

★ ★ ★

Nikola Kostelac, born in 1920, is older than most of the group, and worked for thirteen years as an architect before starting in films as a designer. He has made *Nocturne, The Ring* (about prize fighting) and has specialised in *Inspector Mask* films: *The Case of the Eggless Hens* and so on, though several other directors have made cartoons featuring this Magoo-like detective, who in Vatroslav Mimica's *The Inspector Goes Home* finds a mysterious fingerprint only to trace it to his own finger. Kostelac's best film is perhaps *Opening Night* (1957), which satirises the haughty people who attend and perform in concerts.

Vatroslav Mimica was also one of the original group and has directed many cartoons. *At The Photographer's* (1959) depicts a serious little man having his photograph taken. The photographer tries everything he can think of to make him smile, but in vain. The smile always slips off his face at the crucial moment. But at the end he bursts out laughing when he sees his own finished photo. The cartoon is noteworthy for the dozens of horrid smiling faces which line the walls, and also for a splendid take-off of a cartoon explosion. The photographer's efforts to pose the little man work up to a great climax, when in despair he decides to press the shutter anyway, and then—CRASH, BOOM,

138

BANG, the dust and smoke take minutes to settle. *Mr. Marzipan's Marriage* (1963) is a brightly-coloured matrimonial farce as loud and lewd as a clown's red nose. On the other hand *A Little Story* makes a subdued tweed-coloured pattern out of the traffic of a big city. Among the tangled lanes is a blind man who loses his dog, and gets smudged out like a mosquito by the traffic. *Typhoid* (1963), an animated version of lino-cuts made by partisan artists during the war, evokes groaning monumental figures, agonised, stricken, toiling in an atmosphere of hallucination and death.

Aleksandar Marks, the artist responsible for all Mimica's pictures as well as those of other directors and master of a wide range of styles, has himself directed several pictures with **Vladimir Jutrisa** in recent years. *The Fly* (1967), is a terrifying science fiction miniature. A man stamps on a fly, but it escapes from his foot and grows . . . and grows . . . and grows. In the nightmare ending the man is helplessly trying to dodge the fly's great stamping feet, a midget in a forest of hairy, plunging pylons. *Sysiphus* and *A Small Mermaid* seem to have been less successful, but *The Spider* (1971), directed by Marks alone and in the same vein as *The Fly,* has been described "a tightly-woven, brilliant, macabre piece."

Boris Kolar, younger, born in 1933, was a newspaper caricaturist and illustrator before he turned to film-making in 1952. He directed his second film, *Boomerang,* in 1962. A butterfly on a radar-screen sets off an alarm which puts in motion the whole army of the defence. The drawing is brilliant, and the subject and treatment form a derisive satire on the ridiculous aspects of militarism. Kolar's latest film *Bow Wow* (1964) is also a *tour de force*. Cats and dogs, an old theme. The parents will have nothing to do with each other, cats are cats and dogs are dogs. But the children play together, the cats begin to bark and the dogs to miaou. Wow! What price the race problem? The greatest delight in this cartoon is the virtuosity and daring of the drawing, pushed right to the edge of meaning.

Zlatko Bourek made *The Blacksmith's Apprentice* (1966), a medieval story filled with all the crawling creatures of Bruegel and Hieronymus Bosch and with a fat Rabelaisian flavour. The blacksmith's wife is a witch; every night she turns the apprentice into a horse, and rides him to her sabbath meetings till he nearly drops. Then one night the apprentice turns the tables, so that *he* rides *her,* rowelling the luscious fat sow round the Milky Way and along the road to Capricorn and Taurus. *Fog and Mud* (1964), an evocation of the Thirty Years War, full of marching men, crosses, bones and gallows, in scarred red and black, is less successful, though impressive in its style. Bourek

139

has also directed a feature, *Circus Rex*. *Dancing Songs* is a *collage* cartoon in which the visuals of folk-dancers are closely integrated with the hypnotic music. *Schooling* is an original essay on the theme of new discordant, versus old harmonious music. *Captain Arbanas Marko* is a more powerful story in an impressive graphic style, about a character taken from Yugoslav folklore, a knight who pays court to three sisters and comes to a tragic end.

Besides films, **Borivoj Dovnikovic** makes designs for stamps, newspaper and TV advertisements, strips and illustrations. He has made the shortest, funniest cartoon since *The Critic,* called *No Credits (Bes Naslova)*. It is a film that never gets started. The only character in it, another little man, comes on to do his stuff, when the credits start interrupting. He dodges them, struggles with them, pushes at them as they sail across the screen from right to left, from top to bottom. He grows crosser and crosser, but finally, inevitably, defeated, he stamps off. Another of Dovniković's films, *The Fashion Show* (1965), runs for nearly half-an-hour but is not a minute too long. Period fashion-plates, from ancient to modern, are always fascinating to look at, and these are gently brought to life and treated with taste. The farcical, the graceful, the horrific: Dovniković has also made *The Ceremony*. Here is a row of earnest figures being arranged in the right order by the man-in-charge. Pathetically anxious to do his bidding they shuffle about as he carefully frames them, moves them an inch this way or that. Then having posed them just right, the man-in-charge turns with a gloating, sickly grin, the camera pulls back and instead of the photographer with his camera, there is a firing squad. . . . Of Dovniković's two latest films, one, *Curiosity,* is in a vein of quiet humour, the other, *Flower Lovers,* is about violence and about gentleness too. In *Flower Lovers* a horticulturist invents an explosive flower which becomes so widely popular that in the end an entire city is reduced to ruins. But from the rubble there grows a simple little flower.

One feels like speaking of "the mystery of" **Vlado Kristl** as though this animator was an enigma. Vlado Kristl was the artist for *The Great Jewel Robbery* (1961), directed by Mladen Feman, one of the most sharply drawn and successful of the Zagreb films. Then he co-directed a film with Ivo Urbanić, *La Peau de chagrin,* from Balzac's story of a gambler who makes a bargain with a croupier (the devil) for a skin which shrinks and at the same time shortens his life, for every wish it fulfills. Urbanić is not the best of the Zagreb directors and his *Love in the Cinema* is no more than a good average parody; so much of the credit for the style of *La Peau de chagrin* should go to Vlado Kristl. It is only a skeleton of the story, but the *décor* is quite, quite superb. It opens with carts going along a red street, Raphael gambling, Pauline, his sweetheart, bidding him farewell. The screen flames with red and gold, the furniture is made of newsprint, *la peau de chagrin* is a scarlet square. All the characters are magnificently decorative figures: Pauline in innocent white; the vermilion croupier with his mask hiding a death's-head skull, the glorious crimson young whore out of Toulouse-Lautrec, and Raphael himself in fencer's black, and bony, white, aging face.

Then Vlado Kristl made his own picture, drawing, animation, direction, everything, and he hit the screen with something extraordinary, *Don Quixote* (1962). Here is the romantic hero attacked by the regiments of the computer age, and he beats them, he beats them all. Don Quixote is a grasshopper arrangement of tin-can, tubes and stove-pipe, Sancho Panza a cross between a square sea-urchin and a meat-safe wearing spectacles. Against them are dots, shapes, creatures, bicycles, wheels; swarming, buzzing, stuttering; and in the background, lines of approach, contours, missiles. What are these strange shapes? We have really no doubt. They are guns, radar, tanks, planes, patrols, armies. It is a vision of chaos at once whimsical and terrifying. And in some amazing way the Don triumphs. The crack-pot individual wins the day. In sound, colour and design this is one of the most original things to come out of Zagreb. But it was Vlado Kristl's last cartoon. He went to Germany, has made various odd live-action shorts, including *Madeleine, Madeleine,* and *Autorennen,* and an incomprehensible live-action feature, *The Dam,* which is impossible to sit through. Yes, surely it is fair to call it the mystery of Vlado Kristl.

Zlatko Grgic directed *The Musical Pig* in 1965. A pig with a magnificent voice who wants to be listened to and appreciated. He goes to one person after another, but their ears are deaf, they see him as roast pork, utter a hunting cry and seize a knife. At last he meets a sympathetic soul, a fellow musician who accompanies him on the flute, and they go off arm in arm. Back comes the flute-player sucking the last knuckle-bone. It is interesting to speculate on the moral of this tale. Is it intended to illustrate the cynical saying: "I can escape my enemies but heaven save me from my friends"? Or is it intended to explode the artistic pretensions of the pig? Or the flute-player?

Zlatko Grgić has also made, with **Pavao Stalter,** a film to chuckle over, *The Fifth,* beautifully drawn in a shy, old-fashioned style. As the hand-out says it is "a humoresque of human stubbornness shown in the play of the indestructible pest—the trumpet player." A string quartet are playing a beautifully rounded phrase from Schubert. As they reach the end a tuba-player comes in and gives the wrong final note—*ouch*. They chase him away, but again and again he comes back with his

141

stubborn discord. Finally they *all* play the wrong note. There is a magnificent aplomb about this preposterous ending that makes it irresistible. Grgić also worked with Stalter to make *Scabies* in which a huge man scratches himself, dislodging swarms of little men until finally the giant crumbles to nothing. In his turn Stalter himself directed *Boxes,* and collaborated with Jutriša to make *The Masque of the Red Death,* perhaps the most impressive translation of Poe's ghostly world into the cartoon medium. Grgić worked with Branko Ranitović on *Tolerance* and himself directed *Little and Big* (a satire on pretentious movies as hilarious in its way as *No Credits*), *Twiddle Twaddle* and *The Inventor of Shoes.* The last film introduced a character, Professor Balthasar, who has become so popular (in Germany and America as well as Yugoslavia) that he now forms the basis of a regular series of cartoons for children and grown-ups.

Another director is Ante Zaninović: *The Trumpet, The Wall,* and *Crazy Story.* He was born in Belgrade in 1934 and studied painting at the Zagreb Academy of Art. *The Wall* (1965) is in an ugly style but

From Milan Blazeković's GORILLA'S DANCE

it has a sour, anti-heroic story which marks it out. It is about two individuals and a great wall that blocks their path. One of them, determined to get past the obstacle, sets about attacking it; the other simply sits and waits. The first one fails in all his attempts, but refusing to admit defeat he runs madly at the wall and smashes a hole in it with his head. The second one, casting his eyes up to heaven, gets up, steps over the first man's dead body and through the hole. In a similar satiric vein he has since directed *Result, A Pointless Story, Holes and Corks* (about a man sitting on a volcano) and *Feet*.

One can only mention briefly several new names, either animators who have recently begun to direct or who have recently joined the group. **Nedeljko Dragic** has directed *Tamer of Wild Horses, Diogenes Perhaps, Passing Days* and *Tup-Tup*. *Diogenes Perhaps* is full of visual fantasy—diners in a crowded room are arranged like a painting of the Last Supper, a stone pushed downhill rolls *up* again, darkness and stars pour like ink through an opened window. With *Per Aspera ad Astra* and *Striptiz*, Dragić started a series of one-minute mini-cartoons, pointed jokes which have become very popular. To date nearly sixty have been made by many directors. One who has contributed largely is **Milan Blazekovic,** who has also made a musical cartoon, *Gorilla's Dance* (1969), a co-production with Contemporary Films of New York, and *The Man Who Had to Sing*. Then there is Vladimir Tadej (*The World's Desires*), Zdenko Gasparović (*A Dog's Life*), Dragutin Vunak (*Between Cup and Lip*) and Nikola Majdak with a nonsense piece, *Time of the Vampire,* picturing ghosts and spectres larking about in a cemetery.

★   ★   ★

Quite recently an animator has started working in Belgrade outside the Zagreb organisation—**Borislav Sajtinac.** From 1966 he worked for Gloria-Linda Film Productions on the following: *Love with Three Cakes, Pardon,* and *Conference of the Animals* (a two-hour animated picture). In 1967 he made his first independent film, *The Analysis,* then *The Spring of Life,* working with Nikola Majdak, in which Bosch-like cripples move to plaintive music. He followed these with *Everything That Flies Is Not a Bird,* and *Temptation* and *The Bride,* the last showing "a sure sense of the scabrous and bizarre." Sajtinac claims that his pictures are "living stories about living men in living surroundings, and are transformed into cartoon characters in order to achieve a universal effect."

★   ★   ★

Another Yugoslav maestro: Borislav Sajtinac's
EVERYTHING THAT FLIES IS NOT A BIRD

From its early beginnings the Zagreb school has grown into perhaps the most important single centre of cartoon production in the world. It was reported recently that in a single year 857 copies of their films were screened in forty-five different countries. They have produced cartoons in a great variety of styles, and in subjects ranging from the most serious to the most comic. Their wit and invention seem inexhaustible and they are masters of the innocent story that has a twist in its tail or an underlying comment on human existence. Many of their cartoons are "literary" in the sense that the main interest is in the idea or story, but there are several which are mainly concerned with visual movement, and in all their work the graphics are always competent, frequently new and exciting. Their inspiration shows no sign of flagging and they are branching out into co-production and more extensive foreign distribution for their films.

10. Humour and Artistry in Italy

The cinema in Italy looks back to the golden age of *Cabiria* and the main early cartoon seems to be one made in 1916 by the director of *Cabiria*, Giovanni Pastrone, assisted by Segundo de Chomon, entitled *The War and Momi's Dream*. It featured puppets and staged a miniature war. Apart from a few isolated efforts, e.g. Domeneghini's *Harry and His Tiger Cubs* and Ugo Amadoro's *The Magic Writing* (1924), nothing more seems to have been achieved until 1940 after the Second World War had broken out, when the difficulty of getting American cartoons encouraged Italian producers to fill the gap. The first film was *Bravo Anselmo* (1940), a burlesque on medieval Italy by Gino Parenti, who also made *The Magic Bucket*. Several production companies were formed, one of which, Cartoni Animati Italiani (CAIF), produced an hour-long cartoon, *The Adventures of Pinocchio* (1940). Judging from the stills it appears less accomplished but possibly more genuine than Disney's film, and certainly closer to Collodi's original. Other films were Umberto Spano's *Barudda and the Fugitives; Punch and the Brigands* made by the brothers Corrio and the painter Luigi Giobbe; and Roberto Sgrilli's *Anacleto and the Polecat* (1942), the story of a hen protecting her chickens from the robber. In 1942 also, Antonio Rubino made *In the Land of the Frogs*. All these films derived to some extent from American examples, but the Italians infused into them a spirit of their own, gentler, more decorative in style, not depending to such an extent on the "gag." Certainly *The Last Street Boy* by Gibba was a cartoon that could hardly have been made in America. It told the story of a little boy and his dog Matteo, both poor and hungry. They come in after a bad day, the police having confiscated the boy's stock of cigarettes, and they go supperless to bed. In the freezing cold night the broken roof lets in the light of the stars and the little boy goes to a brighter world above to live there for ever with his faithful Matteo.

In 1942, **Anton Gino Domeneghini** made a feature cartoon, *The Rose of Bagdad*, about a little flute player, Amin, in love with an Arabian Nights princess. The wicked chamberlain, strangely called Burk, plots to destroy him, but Amin wins the day and love triumphs. The hero and heroine were just as sweet and pretty as Disney's princes and princesses, and in general there was nothing original in the style, but some of the scenes had a fragile, decorative quality. A brother and sister, Tony and Nino Pagot, made another long cartoon, *The Dynamite Brothers*, in 1947. The three Dynamite brothers, free and liberal spirits, dwell in an isolated desert until a well-wisher brings them to live in the company of other men. There is a profound gulf between the brothers and the people, brutish, vulgar and ill-disposed, and the experiment is not a success. Although the story sounds impossible, the film was in an accomplished style and as a result of its popularity the Pagots were able to make a career in cartoon commercials. They have also made a short cartoon, *The Wheel,* in a bold, decorative style.

Another team who have produced attractive work are the brothers **R. and G. Gavioli,** who have made *The Dandy,* a graceful little story of nursery toys, *The Magic Pot,* presented with success at the 1956 Venice Festival, and *Ugh, Me Hungry,* a cartoon with Red Indian characters. Perhaps Gavioli's most striking film is *The Long Green Stocking* (1962) made to celebrate the centenary of Italian Unification. First it shows the false, popular conception of Italy in a frenetic introduction with the whole of Europe gleefully dancing down for the tourist season to the tune of *Funiculi Funicula.* Then it turns to the true Italy and to an imaginative pictorial reconstruction of the *Risorgimento,* full of fire and movement, accompanied by some of Verdi's most stirring music, and done in a bold poster style reminiscent of Lautrec which has hardly been used by any cartoonist except Ivo Urbanić and Vlado Kristl in *La Peau de chagrin. The Long Green Stocking* is a splendid bravura piece which calls for prolonged applause. His latest cartoon is *Venetian Twilight* (1970), in which his style is said to have become over-refined.

Several distinctive films have been made by **Giulio Gianini** and **Emmanuele Luzzati.** All their work seems to have an historical setting. Their first film *Paladins of France* (1960), shows the Christian Knights of the West defeating the wiles of the Moors in Spain and repulsing the invaders. *House of Cards* brings to life the courtly characters of a pack of playing cards, but though they are vigorously active they never cease to be playing cards too. *The Thieving Magpie* (1964), is from Rossini's opera and fitted to the rattling pace of the overture. It tells the story of three kings who for an easy victory decided to make war on the birds, but who are outwitted and routed by an astute magpie. Gianini and Luzzati's films are tapestries, thick black lines and the deep glowing colours of stained glass or of a painter like Chagall. Again they have a style which is immediately recognisable. Together they have since made *Ali Baba* (1971), but Gianini has made two cartoons with other designers, *Swimmy* and *The Message,* from drawings by Folon.

Pino Zac is a sophisticated jester who has no illusions left, but is determined to enjoy himself all the same: *Man Superman Poor Man, Registered for Life, Postage Stamp.* The first is a sex comedy, women each glossier than the other, larger than life and twice as beautiful,

146

THE THIEVING MAGPIE

men tagging feebly along unable to help themselves but wishing that they could. The style is a paste-up of every kind of glossy illustration, picture postcard, and fashion plate. *Registered for Life* is similar, more romantic with vignettes of hearts and roses. *Postage Stamp* (1965), is a fast and furious game of decorative building, the camera following a crazy structure of coloured confetti that never reaches an end. In *Lo Iradiddio* (1963), every letter in the alphabet conforms and by one transformation or another becomes an I. Last to hold out is a tartan Z but even this stout individualist is turned to I by a bomb explosion.[1]

Giulio Cingoli is no more serious in *Canzonissima* (1962), a song illustrated with *bric-à-brac* of all kinds, and *The Woman of the Half Century,* a delirious vision of erotic postcards in the most serio-comic

[1] A feature cartoon *The Non-existent Cavalier* by Zac has just appeared and three feature cartoons are in the making—*A Marionette Called Pinocchio* (Cenci and Mussino), *Peynet's Lovers Round the World* (Manfredi and Severi) and *Robinson Crusoe* (Maria Guido). Two TV cartoons by Secondo Bignardi, *Ogni Regno* and *Corto Maltese,* should also be mentioned.

style of the Victorian era. **Elio Gagliardo** in *The Magic Laboratory* (1962), sets out to make an instructional film on the digestive system, but the whole thing almost turns into a joke; and a thing of beauty too, with the colours orchestrated in shades of yellow, blue and red. The human body is shown as an odd kind of factory where for example the bile is supplied by a Chinaman with a green complexion. If only all instructional films were like this. A recent work to be noted is *Sheep and Wolves* (1969), by Manfredo Manfredi, a cartoon depicting the oppression of black by white. **Osvaldo Cavandoli,** a new artist has made to date six little cartoons simply called *Line No. 1, No. 2, No. 3, No. 4, No. 5,* and *No. 6.* Their technique is simple but ingenious. From first to last there is only a single line across the screen shaped at the appropriate point to represent the characters—a man walking, a hen, a dog, a rocket etc. The hero talks to the artist, scolds him if he makes the going tough by drawing obstacles, praises him for any good things he puts in the hero's way. They are engaging little comedies, perfectly drawn, full of humour and in a unique style which should be capable of development.

★　　★　　★

More prolific than any of these, the leading animator in Italy now and perhaps for a long time, is **Bruno Bozzetto.** He studied for a period with Halas and Batchelor in London and now has his own flourishing cartoon studio in Milan. His first film, *Tapum,* the story of weapons, made in 1958, was an immediate success. It was followed in 1959 by *The Story of Inventions,* a light-hearted treatment of the most important human inventions, and in 1961 by *Alpha Omega. Alpha Omega* is a striking example of cartoon economy. It depicts the human condition from the cradle to the grave by the simplest means, a change of colour, a change of props, the turn of an eyelid. The little oblong central character stands midscreen from first to last, winding himself up for each new episode by turning an enormous key. Little figures appear round him, a schoolmaster, a wife, a mistress, an accountant, a priest. When a square, white doctor forbids him tobacco, wine and everything else, he first prepares to commit suicide, but on reflection placidly shoots the doctor instead. Bozzetto has also created a cartoon character, Mr. Rossi, the subject of half a dozen films: *An Award for Mr. Rossi, Mr. Rossi goes Skiing, Mr. Rossi on the Beach* etc., but these have not been shown much outside Italy. His other films, however, have brought him an international reputation. In 1963 he made another short skit, *The Two Castles,* a story of an extremely aggressive medieval lot in one castle who persist in attacking another oddly untenanted castle, usually with damage to themselves from their own missiles, and unhappily

Bruno Bozzetto's THE STORY OF INVENTIONS

finding in the end that the other castle is a giant's castle-shaped hat. The tiny figures which are a feature of Bozzetto's witty drawing and remind us of *The Juggler of Notre Dame* are both exasperating and endearing—in either case very funny.

In 1965 Bozzetto made a feature cartoon, *West and Soda,* a riotous take-off of the cowboy *genre.* The hollow-jawed hero, the burly bad-man, the wide-eyed, orphaned heroine down on the farm with her dear, dear cows and a faithful but peace-loving hound. It seems the whole thing has been done to death, but Bozzetto brings to it a fresh inventiveness that makes it impossible to be bored. The film is said to have recovered its cost in Italy alone, and in 1968 Bozzetto produced another feature, *VIP My Brother Superman,* a science-fiction adventure story about two heroic brothers who struggle against an attempt to control mankind by implanting brain missiles. Other short cartoons are *Man and His World, Life in a Box, Ego* and *Pickles. Pickles* (1971) is a series of short, witty comments on war, peace, drugs, religion, pollution. War is symbolised by a shouting, leaping, gesticulating little chap with a sword in one hand and a huge banner in the other. The device

149

on the banner changes from one cause to another but the man's behaviour remains exactly the same. Finally the banner settles for **PAX** in huge letters and the scene ends with our friend bestriding a heap of slaughtered bodies happily waving his peace flag.

★ ★ ★

Italy's contribution to the cartoon may seem a slender one. The neorealist movement which has given Italy a leading place in the cinema proper, has not touched the field of animation and by its nature could hardly do so. In the cartoon field, work comparable to Italian neorealism, in which one is moved because the artist is striving to express some deep emotion, has been achieved rather in Yugoslavia, Poland or Czechoslovakia. But there is something peculiarly Italian about their animation work, an airy elegance of form and lightness of content, making their cartoons things of beauty as well as entertainment.

11. Animation in the Balkans and Russia

BULGARIA, HUNGARY, ROMANIA

In central Europe, Yugoslavia, Czechoslovakia and Poland lead in the animated field. But the three countries mentioned above encourage the production of animated films, and have at least one or two animators with a more than national reputation.

★   ★   ★

In Bulgaria **Todor Dinov** is the leading director with several excellent films to his credit. His first film, *The Mighty Marko,* was made in 1955, and since then he has directed about fifteen cartoons. *Little Guardian Angel* (1956), inspired by the drawings of the French cartoonist Jean Effel, is about an angel who catches a bomb dropped from an enemy aeroplane over Paris and returns it to the pilot saying "Excuse me but you dropped something." He has also made *The Fox Outfoxed* (1957), *Cannibal Country* (1958), *Duo, Fledgling, Jealousy, The Apple* (1963). Best known are *The Lightning Conductor* and *The Daisy.*

The *Lightning Conductor* is afraid of lightning, and when a storm comes, it frantically dodges every flash and finally hides in the chimney. When the weather clears it proudly goes back to its place, though the house below it has been gutted. This apotheosis of the scrimshanker, made in 1962, outdoes most of the anti-heroic statements so popular in the West. *The Daisy* (1965), is a bible text. As it grows, it is in the way of an inexorable gardener, but none of his tools can pull it up or break its stem; shears, saw, bulldozer, explosives—all fail. Then a little girl comes, her heart goes out to its beauty, and she picks it easily with loving fingers.

Other Bulgarian animators are **Rada Batchvarova,** director of many children's cartoons, *The Snowman* (1960) being most successful. **Christo Topouzanov** has made puppet films and *The Little Boy with Scissors* (1966) from cut-out shapes. **Ivan Vesselinov** has directed *Rope Dancers* and two shorts with good acceptable Communist themes, *The Devil in Church* a satire on the unchristian behaviour of churchgoers and *The Heirs,* depicting a deadly feud among heirs to an estate. **Roman Meitzov** has made puppet and object-animation films including *The Kiss, Cosmos* and *Coloured Yarns.* His *Spinning Woman* is drawn direct on the film and shows the heroine overcoming war by entangling Mars in her thread.

★   ★   ★

In Hungary, the leading cartoonist has been **Gyula Macskassy,** best known for two films, *Duel* and *A Romantic Story. Duel* (1960) is a long struggle between war (in the person of Mars, a solid, bearded bruiser with a black beard, in Greek armour), and peace (in the character of a white-coated, dapper scientist). Mars pulls all the tricks he can, but the scientist pulls even more: imprisoning Mars inside brackets, and bombarding him with the differential calculus. He wins. *A Romantic Story* (1966), shows a young man with an umbrella sitting on a park-bench next to a girl who is immersed in a book. The screen is filled with the most hair-raising feats of derring-do, the product of the man's imagination, but the girl remains completely absorbed however hard he wills her attention. Then it starts to rain. She looks up eagerly, but he, this time, walks off under his umbrella. Macskassy's style is attractive but quite conventional, fairly heavy drawing and bright primary colours.

Josef Nepp has an unpretentious style of drawing and in his cartoons concentrates on the action. His films include *Till Tomorrow, Passion*

FIVE MINUTES OF MURDER

and *Five Minutes of Murder*. The last, a miniature black comedy, presents a series of murders, each new character murdering the murderer on the pattern—b murders a, c murders b, d murders c . . . and so on. Each time a new method is used and Nepp, with diabolical ingenuity, stays the course for five minutes and more than a dozen murders, without repeating himself.

Gyorgy Kovasznai is more of a stylist and his *Double Portrait* is an unusual film of outstanding quality. It simply shows in heavy oils the head of a man and a woman which do not move in the accepted sense, but change and develop as the artist paints and re-paints their features and their background. Although there are similarities it is quite different from *The Picasso Mystery,* but just as fascinating. It is not a presentation of action but an exploration of the painter's technique, and the idea could certainly be developed further. His *Darkness and Light, Waiting for a Train* (design by Josef Gemes) and *Gloria Mundi* (1970), a joke about the threat of atomic destruction, are also in interesting styles.

Recently **Josef Gemes** has himself made two outstanding cartoons, *Koncertissimo* and *Parade* (1970). *Koncertissimo* is a grim little drama showing ostentatious concert-goers (the art-conscious intelligentsia ?) so intent on themselves that they fail to observe until too late, that the orchestra assembling on the stage are carrying guns instead of instruments and are a firing-squad whose mission is to liquidate the audience. *Parade* shows a whole army assembled in dazzling array, marred only by a soldier with one leg longer than the other, whose limp spoils all the marching, until the puzzled generals hit on the solution of making the whole army limp. Not a new idea, but it is well executed with fine animation and in brilliantly-coloured acrylic painting.

Other work from Budapest includes Sandor Reisenbüchner's *Kidnapping of Sun and Moon* described as "one of the most original animated films ever made." It is based on Hungarian folk-art themes and is from a poem by Ferenc Juhasz. Bela Vajda's *On the Shooting Stage* is a joke about movies, Peter Szoboszlay's *Order for Ever* pillories narrow-minded bureaucrats, while *The Yeti's Song* (1971) (Zoltan Bacso) shows in a gay style, a bullying monkey tamed when he meets the superior force of a steam-roller. Another animator is Marcel Janković who has made *Gustav and the Season of Goodwill* and *SOS.*

★　　★　　★

In Romania there are records of cartoons made in the Twenties by **Aurel Petrescu** (*Man from Adam, Woman from Eve, Illustrated*

Proverbs, all 1926) and Marin Iorda (*Haplea,* 1927) and at the present time Romania produces more animated films than either Hungary or Bulgaria. The outstanding figure has been **Ion Popesco Gopo,** but in recent years he has been working much of the time on live-action feature films. Popesco-Gopo was born in 1923 and studied art at Bucharest. His father and an uncle were connected with the establishment of an animated film studio in 1950, and there Gopo made his first films for children: *The Naughty Duck, The Bee and the Dove, Two Rabbits.* He evolved his present distinctive style with *A Short History* in 1956 and this was followed by *The Seven Arts* (1958), *Homo Sapiens* (1960), and *Hullo Hullo* (1961). These films have only one character, a kind of archetypal Adam who appears, curiously nude, with an unathletic slouch, an enormous bald head, and (in repose) a dyspeptic expression. The films, like Kipling's *Just So Stories,* are mainly concerned with historical development, finding whimsical explanations of how things came about or introducing odd, joking bits of action. For instance *A Short History* presents a quaint, eight-minute history of mankind even going back to the origin of the earth itself, and presenting a final optimistic view of the naked little egg-head stepping off to explore the mysteries of the cosmos. *Hullo Hullo,* a history of communications, shows our friend discovering how to convey an imprint on a bit of stone and then bashing away on a stone-age typewriter. *Homo Sapiens* shows him being frightened by his reflection, imagining it a god and worshipping it.

★   ★   ★

In 1966 the Romanians inaugurated an animated Film Festival at Mamaia to alternate with the Festival at Annecy in France. Popesco-Gopo made a whole series of ten-second jokes to introduce every session of the Festival. One showed Columbus (our nude friend) putting down his egg and breaking it; another the homunculus smoking, growing progressively greyer with each puff and then collapsing in fragments; another the homunculus weighing his head against his body to see which was heavier; another the laurels he wears falling over his eyes and sending his arrow wide of the mark; another showed him standing on the globe at the edge of a rainbelt, holding an umbrella with one hand and with the other watering a plant in the dry zone; another, our friend standing on his head to reach the prize, a large silver cup, then putting it in the place of his head; and so on. The jokes are a little pedantic, almost professorial in humour (shades of *Carmen Silva*?), but are quite out of the ordinary, and in fact so simple that their appeal could be universal. Another film from Gopo in the same style is *Sancta*

Simplicitas (1969), in which he visualises, with earthy humour, the emergence of life on earth.

There are a number of other cartoonists and animated film-makers, but no one else of the same stature as Popesco-Gopo. Two interesting Romanian cartoons at the 1966 Mamaia festival were Virgil Mocanu's *Fairy Story* and Liviu Chigort's *Parallels*. *Fairy Story* was a Romanian folk-tale whose characters were figures cut out of cardboard, and whose colours were the rich variegated patterns of peasant art, typically Romanian, glowing and warm. *Parallels* worked up an atmosphere of menace which was then dissipated in humour. The characters were musical notes, roundheaded and making sweet harmonious sounds—until one note gets his head jammed and pushed square and his voice becomes harsh and discordant. He viciously attacks other notes, makes them square, and the "squareness" spreads frighteningly, although in some regions of sunshine the notes turn round and mellow again. The film ends when both sides are taken aback by the appearance of a triangular note!

Bob Calinescu has made a number of puppet films including *Rhapsody in Wood,* whose figures are based on popular traditional carving in willow. He has also made cartoons: *Antagonism* and *Old Iron New Humour. Old Iron New Humour* (1965), depicts a contest between nails and pincers; the iron "characters" are presented in menacing black against a red background. His latest cartoon, *The Thread of the Story,* is based on a graphically amusing idea presented simply and unpretentiously and telling a story in which the characters and their adventures are all outlined by an unrolled ball of wool. **Sabin Balasa** has made a number of painted cartoons with good graphics but marred by over-elaboration and obscure scripts—*The Drop, The Town, The Wave* and *Fascination.* His latest cartoon, *Return to the Future* (1971), shows strange creatures, lizards with money and bombs, and works up to a hopeful climax in which statues raise their head and the screen is flooded with light. Again the design and soundtrack are good in *The Lark* (Laurentio Sirbu), *The Field* (George Sibianu), *Fairy Story* (Virgil Mocanu) the last as mentioned above based on the colourful traditional folk art of the country. Sibianu's *The Champ* (1971) has for its hero a little mouse who climbs on a monster that has terrified a whole field of workers, and shows that it is nothing but straw. Folk art is also used with rich effect in Adrian Petrigeneru's *In the Forest of Yon.* There are perhaps half-a-dozen other cartoon or puppet animators, including Constantin Mustetea who has made *The Smile* and *The Whale.* The Mamaia Animation Festival seems well established and likely to continue, alternating now with Annecy and Zagreb. No doubt the stimulus of an international competition and the screening of films from other countries will improve the standard of work in Romania itself.

RUSSIA

The Russians were producing cartoons in the early Twenties and animation was apparently taught at the State Film School. *China in Flames,* made in 1925, was an early silent cartoon which showed the Chinese peasant enslaved by World Imperialism. Many of the subjects were propaganda caricatures: *Incident in Tokyo* (1924), *Political Skits (Humoresky), Windows of Satire* (made for the Russian GPO), *One of Many* (1927), a satire on the Hollywood star system. In 1925 a cartoon studio was established in Moscow which produced many films including the following: **Ivanov-Vano**'s *Senka the African,* a little boy's dream adventure; *The Adventures of Baron Munchhausen* by D. Cherkez, showing the hero riding on half a horse; *The Cockroach* (1927) by A. Ivanov and H. Voinov, an extraordinary cartoon showing a cockroach chasing and terrifying elephants who also bow down to him as he sits on a throne; and *The Young Samoyed* (1929), a story of Arctic adventures by the brother and sister, V. and Z. Broumberg.

One of the first sound cartoons was *The Postman* (1929) directed by M. Tsenkanovsky, and other early animated sound films included *Cross Roads* (1931) by V. Sutiev and Atamanov, and *Black and White* (1932) from a well-known poem by Mayakovsky, directed by L. Amalrik and Ivanov-Vano. Better-than-average productions were *The Music Box* made by H. Hodatyev in 1933, which satirised pre-revolutionary militarism, and *Quartet* (1935) by A. Ivanov and P. Sazonov, the story of a huge bear, a goat, a donkey and a monkey, who formed a musical group. In 1935 came a feature-length film using puppets and real actors, *The New Gulliver,* directed by **A. Ptushko.** The story is told in the form of a boy's dream, and the puppets are grotesque but effective caricatures. Swift's story was developed by the introduction of a workers' revolt against the effete monarch and military caste of Lilliput —young Gulliver aiding the under-dogs. There is a mad king whose speeches come from a hidden gramophone, parodies of crooners and jazz groups, bat-like secret police. *The New Gulliver* has been surpassed by later work, but at the time it was a remarkable achievement. In 1939 Ptushko made another film also using tiny puppets in contrast to life-sized live actors: *The Golden Key.*

By the end of the Thirties production was increasing and many cartoons were made in colour. The Soviet Mult-film Studio was founded in 1936. By 1938 production had risen to twenty-four films a year and the films themselves tended to be longer. The influence of Disney was strong. A version of *Puss in Boots,* by the Broumbergs, an Arab story *Little Muck,* directed by O. Hodatyev, and an animal cartoon *Dog and Cat* by Atamanov, all three made in 1938, show characters and scenes which are hardly different from those of American cartoonists. A version of *The Three Musketeers* (1938 also), made by Ivanov-Vano, "shamelessly copied the American pattern even to a Donald Duck." However another film made in 1938 still shows the fierce, satiric style of earlier caricatures—*How the Rhinoceros Got His Skin,* by V. Sutiev, based on Kipling's story. It was in colour, and possibly one of the best Russian cartoons.

The war was a set-back to production, but this quickly increased again and a number of postwar cartoons were shown at festivals abroad and won prizes: *Spring Song, A Winter's Tale* (Ivanov-Vano), *The Fox and the Thrush,* all made in 1945, and *Greyneck* (1947) a nature cartoon with attractive if unoriginal animal drawings. However, there seemed to be no new inspiration, and one has only to look at stills from Atamov's *Golden Antelope* (1954), Babchenko's *Recreation for Millions (Million v Mezke)* (1956), or L. Amalek's *Story of the Flying Arrow* to be depressed by the cheap colours and featureless drawing. Livelier, because at least the subject was different, was *The Wonderful Match* (1955), director M. Paschenko, about a football game.

Writing in "The Soviet Film" ("Der Sowietsche Film," Berlin, 1953), Ivanov-Vano boasted that the Moscow Animation Studios were the largest, the best equipped and staffed, not only in Russia but the whole of Europe. He also claimed that unlike the cheap stereotyped American entertainment film, each Russian film was in a personal and different style, that Russian animators were interested in ideas; and implied their work must be good because they were observing "the principles of social realism." In fact the work produced in the Fifties and Sixties has been inferior to the crude and cruel, but vigorous, political satire of the Twenties.

The Russian showing in recent animation Festivals has not been impressive. A critic wrote of one of the two Russian films sent to Annecy in 1962: "insipid, puerile drawing and a lame ending. We are really sorry that Russia disdains to send anything better to an international festival." Russian attempts to catch up with the style of Polish or Yugoslav films have not quite succeeded. *The Real Trouble* (1962), by the Broumbergs, is an ironic account of young Russian beatniks seduced by Western influences. Feodor Khitrouk's *Story of a Crime* (1963), shows a man driven distracted by the noise outside his apartment and finally killing one of his tormentors. *The Mystery of the Black King* (D. Tcherkassi, 1964), looks something like Inspector Mask; it starts off with the police investigating a mysterious fire, but ends with a heavy exhortation to all good citizens to be careful of electric plugs. Russia has been left behind by nearly all the satellite countries with fewer resources, simply because the latter have allowed the individual imagination free play. A curiosity is *The Bath House* (1962), by Sergei Yutkevitch and Anton Karanovitch, taken from a Mayakovsky play, and including cartoon, puppets and other techniques. The film is an attempt at novelty and up-to-date satire, but it never comes alive, not even the porcine figure of the English business man who is observed with regard as well as hostility.

There are some more hopeful signs. In 1964 Ivanov-Vano made a feature cartoon, *The Mechanical Flea,* using a cardboard puppet technique, whose décor successfully captured the Jane Austen period of the Napoleonic wars. His *Seasons* (1970) shows some superbly animated puppets and *Battle Under the Walls of Kerchenets,* a Grand Prix winner at Zagreb in 1972, is finely drawn in the style of old Russian icons.

Who said Meow?, directed by Degliarev and Voronov in 1962, was a charming enough children's story. And in 1966 at Mamaia, several Russian films for children were outstanding for the quality of their line and colour, although the same anodyne plots were in evidence. *Birthday Today,* director Lev Milsin, had delicate colour, intricate arabesque tracery and a fine villainous cat. In a children's puppet film, *Little Bear's Journey,* director Rasa Strautman, the colours and textures sparkle with light, and the movement has freshness and charm. In another puppet film, *Who Owns the Acorns?,* movement is clumsier but the characterisation of the animals, especially the dangerous wolf, is impressive. By far the finest film was *The Lion's Holiday* directed by **Feodor Khitrouk.** This showed a circus lion on holiday visiting his mother in her desert island home. The script was more personal, with many delightful touches, the drawing and colour were a constant pleasure, and nobody could help being taken by the film's warmth and unpretentiousness. More recently Khitrouk has scored another success with *Film Film Film* (1969), a light-hearted manual of film-making for film-makers. Lev Atamov has directed two fairly successful pictures recently based on the drawings of the Danish cartoonist, Herluf Bidstrup, *The Bench* and *We Can Do It* (1971). Noteworthy is *The Musicians from Bremen* (Ivan Kovalevskaia, 1971) because "it features as its hero a long-haired singer with a guitar who . . . who conquers a hip-looking princess." J. Nordstein's *The First Day* depicts the struggle of the Bolsheviks from the February to the October Revolutions in the bold style of early Russian posters.

In animation Russia still trails behind other countries, the few works produced being though technically accomplished of limited scope and limited interest. Her potential is as great in the animation field as in that of the cinema generally, but it is unlikely to be realised as long as bureaucratic controls and censorship deny the artist individual freedom or prevent the expression of any but the most anodyne or orthodox views.

12. Other Countries: Germany, Japan, Scandinavia

Some of the early German animators have already been mentioned in Chapter Two. Julius Pinschewer made *Die Suppe,* the first animated film in 1911, then *Der Nahkasten (The Sewing-Box)* and *Die Flasche* in 1912. In 1913 came Guido Seeber's *The Match Artist* and Herman's *How Plimps and Plumps Tricked the Detective.* There seems to have been little production during the 1914–18 War, but in 1918 there were not only films by Pfenninger, a Swiss, and Berthold Bartosch, whose work is discussed in Chapter Six, but also the first publicity short by Pinschewer, *The Writer and the Bees,* and two cartoons by Lotte Reiniger, one *The Ratcatcher of Hamlin,* in collaboration with Paul Wengener.

★　★　★

There were two influences which affected German animation in the Twenties and Thirties. First there was an important group of artists making abstract films, many of them animated. **Viking Eggeling,** Walter Ruttmann, Hans Richter and Oscar Fischinger were the leading exponents. Influenced by dada and surrealist theories in the world of painting and graphic arts, they made the first abstract animated films. Eggeling painted the figures of his *Horizontal Vertical Orchestra* (1920), and his *Diagonal Symphony* (1923), on scrolls or bands of paper from which they were transferred to film-stock. The line-drawings of the *Diagonal Symphony* were white on black and "the wing shapes and harp-like forms grow and mutate, sometimes two shapes in counterpoint, sometimes one alone turning on its axis." **Hans Richter** worked with Eggeling and in his own films manipulated cut-out paper squares under the camera making them "grow and disappear, jump and slide in well-controlled *tempi* and in a planned rhythm." His films include *Fugue* (1920), *Rhythm 21, Rhythm 23, Rhythm 25* and *Film Study,* and he went on to make live-action documentaries.

Walter Ruttmann, a litho and engraving artist, also began making abstract animated films at the beginning of the Twenties. He used a frame holding sticks on which plasticine shapes were mounted and lit to show only the top surfaces which could be easily moved between takes. *Opus 1,* a dynamic display of spots, was hand-coloured to enhance the effect. Other early films were *Opus II* to *Opus IV, Romance in the Night, Dream of Falcons* (an animated sequence for Lang's *Die Niebelungen*) and *Dream Play.* Ruttmann went on to make the documentary *Berlin, Symphony of a City.* Oscar Fischinger made his first films again from about 1920. They included *Gulliver's Travels* (with Louis Seel), *Study 1* to *Study 4* and *Spiralen* (1925). In the Thirties he made *Study 5* to *Study 12,* abstract animation set to music. In 1933 he produced *Circles* the first Gasparcolour film and *Composition in Blue.* As mentioned in Chapter Four, he later went to America and had considerable influence on abstract animation there.

The second factor affecting Germany was that a market for publicity films (Muratti, Eau de Cologne etc.) developed earlier than in most other countries and this enabled artists to find a living in animation work. Ruttmann began to make commercials from 1923; his *Composition in Blue* was used as publicity for Muratti cigarettes and in another Muratti advertisement he had lines of cigarettes marching like soldiers. In 1927 there was a vogue for *Kreuzworträtselfilms* (Crossword-puzzle Films) in which letters appeared spelling out the name of the product being advertised. Some of the animators were Kurt Wolf, W. Kaskeline and Hans Fischer-Kosen who produced *Das blaue Wonder,* the story of a cigarette dancing through the fields who meets a black cat and moves her to ecstasy with his vapours. By 1936 about 300 films a year were being made for publicity purposes.

Julius Pinschewer was active again after the war, mainly in publicity though he made two entertainment shorts, *The Chinese Nightingale* and *Carmen* in 1928. In 1934 he went to live in Switzerland and continued to produce animated films there. His later films included *Full Sail* (1946), *King Koal* (1948), and *Globi,* a cartoon based on a popular Swiss-German comic strip which was never released. *The Play of the Waves,* made in 1955 for Swiss Radio, shows him as a talented, inventive artist. The film starts with "Waves" spreading out from a radio-tower which then turn into chorus girls, singers, a pop group, ice-hockey, a military parade: every kind of radio or television programme. The figures are outlined against a black background in colour and done with some kind of luminous paint, so the effect is as if the drawing were done in neon light. The patterns are well designed, and the device suits the subject.

Another early animator, **Rudolf Pfenninger,** was a Swiss who had gone to live in Germany. His work included *Largo* (1922), *Sound Writing* (1929), *Serenade, Barcarole* and *Pitsch and Patsch.* Two cartoons made in 1928 are interesting because, though isolated efforts, they are by well-known artists: *The Sleeping Beauty* by George Lutz and *Adventures of the Good Soldier Schweik* by George Groz.

Most of this activity was brought to an end by the war and since then there are new names: in East Germany, Georg d'Bomba, Katja and Klaus Georgi, Heinz Steinbach, Bruno Boettige, Lothar Barke and

Stefan Zavrel; in the West, Boris Borresholm, Helmut Herbst, Wolfgang Urchs and Jochen Euscher.

★   ★   ★

In East Germany production is centred at DEFA's Animation Studios, many of the films being of a political or didactic nature. For instance Georg d'Bomba's *We Build a School* (1961), shows for our edification a model community of marionettes. *The Devil's Dirty Work* (1963) shows a soldier going down to hell to escape from a world in ruins. The devil takes him on to stoke the cauldrons in one of which is a major, in another a general, in another a king. Deaf to their pleas for help he claps on the lids and goes back to the world which without its rulers is now a happier place. This film, in a violent wrangling style, is a little too vehement to carry conviction.

Katia and Klaus Georgi have made a number of films: *Cigarette Charlie, The Statue in the Park, Matches, Henry and his Chickens.* The most effective is probably *Cigarette Charlie* (1962), an impassioned anti-smoking sermon, which has the incorrigible Charlie sitting up in his coffin asking for one last puff. Klaus Georgi and Heinrich Greif made *Respect Women* (1970), a feminist cartoon, and in 1971 Katia and Klaus Georgi, Feodor Khitrouk and Vadim Kurtschewski collaborated on a Germano-Russian co-production, *A Young Man Called Engels,* a twenty-minute cartoon based on the drawings of Friedrich Engels who was apparently a keen artist. Bruno Boettige has made children's cartoons, *The Hen and the Changelings* and *How to Tame Dragons,* the latter using cut-out silhouettes. Otto Sacher has made (curiously it seems) a Christian little film, *There Are More Things in Heaven and Earth (Dinge gibt's die gibt's gar nicht)* (1966), which shows how Guardian Angels look after mankind, even traffic on the roads, and when they take time off chaos results. Heinz Steinbach has made a series of puppet films for cinemas or television which are light, clever, and unpretentious, featuring two characters with wire bodies and round wooden heads: *Filopat* and *Patofil. Figaro* and *The Egg* are two of the titles. Other directors are Lothar Barke (*I Am Somebody*) and Werner Kraus—*Who Are You?,* a film about a dog seeking to find its identity.

★   ★   ★

In West Germany production is not concentrated in one large studio but scattered in several centres. Again subjects are often political. Helmut Herbst's cartoon, *Victory Celebration of a War Casualty (Überwindung eines Verlustes)* (1964), shows a man cut in two representing the present state of Germany. He keeps telling himself "I'm all right," but the truth, whenever we look at him or whenever he tries to do anything, is painfully evident. *Black White Red* shows a world in which a mechanical-helmeted Kriemhild shouts "Deutschland erwache!" and human beings are reduced to cyphers. However effective they may be politically, both films are ugly and not of any particular artistic value.

Wolfgang Urchs is of more general interest, and his two latest films are elegant and amusing. In 1962 he made *The Garden Gnomes,* a rather obvious allegory on the reconstruction of Germany ravaged by the war. Then *The Weed* is also symbolic, showing a village little by little overgrown by a creeping vegetation which nobody pulls out because everybody leaves it to somebody else. *The Pistol,* made in 1963, marks a big advance. The weapons themselves are finely engraved in black-and-white and the film has many witty touches. It is a comment of a sort on aggression but far from being an obvious one. *Contrast* is the story of a woman with a black-and-white flat who after much persuasion is brought to try a single touch of colour. But as soon as coloured ornaments are brought in, the old furnishings seems hopeless, soon the flat is a disarray of strident, clashing shades, and in the end she wishes the old order of black-and-white were back again. Urchs's latest cartoon is *Machine,* a Frankenstein story of man imprisoned by his own invention. France Winzentsen's *Windstill* (1969) is a Magritte-like surrealist journey through deserts, forests and buildings, evocative and haunting. Other West German animators are Jochen Euscher, Herbert Hunger (*Kaleidoscope*), Stephan Zavrel (*Via*) and Jan Habarta—*The World and Its People* (1969), and *Between Dreams* (1971).

JAPAN

In the past the Japanese animator whose work has been best known in the West is **Yoji Kuri.** He calls himself an anti-academist, the academic in the cartoon world being represented by Walt Disney. He is certainly that; his line drawing is reminiscent of Saul Steinberg's style with an added touch of distortion. There are affinities with some traditional schools of Japanese art in which a strong grotesque element appears—men with yard-long noses, huge ears, saucer-like eyes, and so on. The action in Yoji Kuri's films is strangely surrealistic, and he echoes Thurber in, for instance, his pictures showing women pursuing and tormenting men.

His longest film is *Here and There,* a mixture of cartoon animation, still photographs, newspaper cuttings and so on which lasts about half-an-hour. There are many brutal, shocking images: women chopped up;

a tree made of eyes; a helicopter leech; a penny-in-the-slot gallows; a television-set fitted into a human bottom. It is difficult to describe some of Yoji Kuri's films in detail, so crowded and unlikely is the action. In *Human Zoo* there are harrowing sounds accompanying the pictures which present a series of *tableaux* in an accelerating rhythm, each depicting males being tortured by females. In one the man is chained up with a collar round his neck, in another he is crouched in a tiny cage being poked by a stick. *Love* is similar except that both sides take turns to dominate, and the mood is more varied, though the cruel and gross are not far away. In one scene the woman swallows the man and excretes him, in another, tiny, she crawls into his mouth and out of his ear. On the soundtrack is the one word *Ai* (*Love*) endlessly repeated and sounding at times like a cry of agony.

The Button is a satire on the atomic bomb. It shows a big city being built, a modern Babylon; cranes pile the structure higher and higher. Then on the plain a solitary car drives up, with a man and woman, button-nosed bourgeoisie on solemn holiday or business. Quite unconsciously they approach an important-looking building, press a button

From Yoji Kuri's characteristic SAMURAI

by the door—and the whole lot blows up! Yoji Kuri writes: "The vanity of nuclear war is expressed in this film. Anyhow what is this atomic button that people talk about?" A good question. *The Window* shows an enormous building, a hotel or a block of flats at night which fills the screen throughout the entire picture, all eight minutes of it. Different tiny windows light up as the film goes on, and we can (more or less) follow a burglary, an alarm, the arrival of the police, a love-affair, and a fire which burns the place down.

Aos is Yoji Kuri's grimmest film. It is a series of tortures and distortions, like pepper rubbed in the spectator's eyes without humour or relief. Men's bowels on windlasses, tongues being pulled out endlessly, bodies squeezed to death. The style is different from his other films, the line harder and uglier.

On the film *Samurai* I can only offer a few notes: There are men in an aeroplane. Then tiny men and a huge woman. A man pokes the ground, then turns into a kind of animal aeroplane. The woman is placed in a vertical box, but horizontally so that her head and legs are outside. Her breasts stick through the top. The man kisses her. He gets inside her between her legs. Other men come; the men fight; they use the woman as a fort, coming out of tiny postern doors all over her body. Then they use the woman as a battering-ram. From tears flowers spring up. There is a flying box; the woman is in it. It flies over trees; there is a pagoda. A man cavorts on the woman. She holds a book between the cheeks of her backside. Lying in a pond her breasts spout water; a little man crawls on her nose; there are arrows through her hat. The woman takes a man in a cup to drink and kiss him. She kisses flowers. Men on the horizon. The men fight again. They poke holes in each other. One runs off with the woman. A zeppelin comes and steals the woman. The woman takes a hand, and tries to swat the men who are fighting. She holds them in her hand. She eats them. One hears the men fighting inside her. Then all is still. The woman cries. Her tears turn into flowers. . . .

Yoji Kuri wrote of *Samurai:* "People associate samurais with *Hara-kiri* but that is a mistake. Many samurais had a sense of humour and an old legend tells of Musashi Miamoto the mightiest of all who caught a fly with match-sticks, to everyone's amazement. Even today people give themselves the airs of samurais and I have tried to show them in this film. The music is authentic Japanese; *Sarashikaze Tegoto.*" *The Eggs* (1967) is a science-fiction disaster showing the world submerged by proliferating mountains of eggs. It could be a comment on overpopulation. *Au Fou* is a series of incidents in which great expectations lead constantly to violent disaster. Recently in *The Bathroom*

(1971), Yoji Kuri is back to a mixed style such as he used in his first film—pixillated live-action and big cut-outs against graphical and live-action backgrounds.

★   ★   ★

In recent years other directors have appeared working in similar personal styles, combining the grotesque, the absurd and the violent. There is **Taku Furukawa** who has made *Oxed Man* and *Catch Catch Yama* (1967). The latter has been described as an unusual blend of pop art, cartoon strip, *art nouveau,* plus Marilyn Monroe, Elizabeth Taylor, Richard Burton and Alain Delon (all in cartoon caricature), the whole forming a colourful comment on violence and bang-bang movies. Another director of animated shorts, **Sadao Tsukioka,** has made *Spotlight, A Man* and *Peace of Resistance. Spotlight* features a dragon breathing coloured flame, who eats something like railing and gradually expires. *Peace of Resistance* is a sort of cartoon *Rosemary's Baby* which shows a dove of peace sitting on an egg which eventually breaks open to reveal a grinning devil. Hal Fukushima's *The Door,* which through an open door showed worlds of fun and horror, was said to have been one of the best films at the 1971 Annecy Festival. Gentaro Nakajima has made thirteen animated films in twelve years including *Seshoseki* (1968), and *The Story of the Fox.* Taizo and Riyu-ichi Yokoyama, two brothers who are both well known for their political newspaper cartoons, have made some long, animated films, among them one called *Magic Journey* describing a trip round the world.

★   ★   ★

For popular audiences Japan produces both cartoon features and TV series. Perhaps the best-known cartoonist is **Osamu Tezuka** who was a doctor before he became a film-maker. His most popular TV series *Marine Boy* has been shown on BBC television. Another series by Tezuka is *Astro Boy* which features a Herculean youngster called Atom—the Japanese title of the series is *Iron-Armed Atom.* Feature cartoons have been produced in increasing numbers since the war. Ofuji made *The Magic Ship* in 1955. **Taiji Yabushita** has made *The Little Samurai, The Boy and The White Serpent* (1957), and *Arakazan the Great.* In 1961 Osamu Tezuka made a cartoon feature called *The Thirteen Labours of Hercules,* made for the Mushi Film Company, whose productions are on a lavish scale and with an appeal as much to adults as children. Their films include *Pictures at an Exhibition* (1966) (directed by Osamu Tezuka) and *The Orphan Brother* (1969) based on a Japanese fairy-tale about two kidnapped children and directed by Taiji Yabushita. Their most lavish production to date is *A*

Thousand and One Nights produced by Osamu Tezuka and directed by **Eiichi Yamamoto.** It is a long film crammed with colourful incident, a free rendering of the Sinbad story, about a scrawny opportunist called Aldin, who from being a poor water-carrier rises through many shifts of fortune, by amorous intrigue and dishonesty, to being Caliph of Baghdad. There is plenty of plotting and excitement including one erotic, supercharged scene, in which a bevy of voluptuous houris who welcome Aldin and his shipmates to their remote island with open arms, turn in the night into writhing snakes. The style is impressive throughout with masterly animation and brilliant colour and decor. Another company, the Toei Studio, has produced many features rather in the style of Disney. Their films include *Puss'n Boots* and *Fables from Hans Andersen,* both directed by **Kimio Yabuki** in 1969. In 1970 they made *Nobody's Boy,* directed by Yugo Serikawa, with animation by Akira Daikubara, and *30,000 Miles under the Sea* directed by Takeshi Tamiya, with animation by Makoro Yamazaki. Their latest feature is a cartoon version of *Treasure Island* made in 1971.

★   ★   ★

Japanese cartoon production is still too little known in Europe for full appreciation.[1] But as more becomes known, it is clear that the range and power of Japanese work in animation matches that of their live-action cinema. The Japanese are *inter alia* a nation of artists and their originality and graphic power seem to give them a natural mastery in this medium. The volume of their production is already impressive and seems to be expanding. As it does it will certainly offer richness and thought behind the pictures.

★   ★   ★

In **Denmark** before the war Jorgen Myller developed the cartoon character, *Columbus,* but the most ambitious film was *The Magic Lighter* (*Fyrtøjet*), made by Allan Johnsen. It was of feature length, appeared in 1946, and according to critics who have seen it merited a wider distribution than was in fact achieved. In recent years two young Danish animators, **Quist Moller and Jannik Hastrup,** have made *Concerto Erotica* and *Slambert,* cartoons which use unusual techniques and contain an unblushing measure of sex. They have recently made a vivacious forty-five minute children's cartoon, *Benny's Bathtub* (1971). A more serious artist is **Bent Barfod** who has been working since 1953 and has made about sixteen cartoons including *Somewhere in the North, Drums* (1958), *Apple of Discord* and *Ballet Ballade*

---

[1] A French writer, Claude Blouin, claims that many professional TV workers and artists make spare-time cartoons of merit which achieve only private showing, and cites the names of Riohei Yanigahara, Yoko Tanadori, Makoto Wada, Tatsuo Shima-mura, Akisa Uno etc., etc.

From the Danish animated film, BENNY'S BATHTUB

(1963). A Kafkaesque satire, *Don't Touch My Halo* (1960), did not quite succeed, but *An African Alphabet* (1962), a film for children, rich in humour and beautifully achieved in glowing colours, is delightful. Recently Ib Steinaa has made *Spirals* (1969), using linear monsters and doodles that fight each other.

★ ★ ★

In **Sweden** there were some early animators: Victor Bergdahl, M. R. Liljequist (*The Negro and His Dog* 1915) and Emil Åberg (*Little Charlie and the Snowman* and *Master Trick's Adventure* 1916). Bergdahl was the most successful; he worked with Winsor McCay in America, his character Captain Grog became popular, and he carried on making cartoons until well into the Twenties. Some of his pictures are *Captain Grog's Travels* (1916), *Captain Grog's Wedding* (1918), *Captain Grog Puts on Weight* (1922). Little more of interest seems to have been produced until recently. At the 1966 Mamaia Festival *Sleep Well* by **Lasse Lindberg,** in a daring torn-paper technique and with bright ideas, showed promise. Lindberg has used this style also in *Ole Dole Doff, Sleep Deep* and *Shadow*. A striking feature cartoon was made in 1968 by **Per Ahlin** and **Tage Danielsson,** *Out of an Old Man's Head*. The graphic style resembles that of Grimault but has more bite, and the theme of the picture, the reminiscences of an elderly man going over his past life, is not only entertaining in itself but can be viewed as an amusing parody of Ingmar Bergman's *Wild Strawberries* which has the same subject.

★   ★   ★

Finland has made a bow to the animation world recently with the work of Eino Ruutsalo (*ABC 123,* a bizarre exploration of a printer's note-book) and Seppo Suo Antilla—*Impression* (1970), which creates a drama out of empty bottles. An animation studio has also been opened in **Norway,** called Punktfilm headed by Trygve Rasmussen and Ivo Caprino who has made puppet films.

★   ★   ★

The early work of the Spaniard, Segundo de Chomon, has already been mentioned elsewhere. Another early animator was Fernando Marco, who made *El Toro Fenomeno* in 1917. However, it was not until the Forties that a centre of animation was established in **Spain.** The most important film was a feature cartoon, *The Little Knight* (*Garbancito de la Mancha,* 1946), by Arturo Moreno. Garbancito means "little pea," and the story is about a little boy (Garbancito) and a goat, Pelegrina, who outwit a wicked Wizard, Pelocha, and an ogre, Caramanca. Judging by stills it seems to have been very much in the style of Disney. At present in Spain a number of excellent publicity cartoons are made, principally by José Luis Moro and an American, Bob Balser, also director of an amusing short cartoon, *The Sombrero*. At present there are some five studios making children's cartoons and commercials.

★   ★   ★

Holland has been noted since the war for its short film production, but this has been mainly of live-action films, in particular documentaries. Animation is used for cinema and television commercials and the two best known firms have made entertainment films as well: *Holland Invites the World, Istamboul* and *The Dollywood Puppets* (made by Joop Geesink); *The Golden Fish* and *Moonglow* (made by Martin Toonder). The work of Georg Pal in the Thirties has been mentioned in the chapter on Great Britain. Two more Toonder films were praised at the Annecy Festival for their quick, well-timed well-animated jokes —*Rollo,* based on designs by Alan Aldridge, and *Man and Horse,* made in 1969 by Björn Frank Jensen, Per Lygum and Börge Ring.

Other Dutch animators are Rupert van der Linden who has made *Mr. X*, and the gifted Ronald Bijlsma—*The Duel* (1967) and *In the Void* (1969).

★   ★   ★

There were a few early cartoons from **Belgium,** for example Victor van Hamme's *Floods in the Saaftinge* (1926), but otherwise it is only recently that TV commercials and entertainment shorts have begun to appear. **Eddy Ryssack and Maurice Rosy** have made a good many animation shorts since 1960 and have created a cartoon couple, the Schtroumpfs: *The Schtroumpfs' Thief, Schtroumpf and the Dragon, The Flying Schtroumpf, Schtroumpf Plays False* etc. Perhaps their best films are *Teeth Is Money* (1962), and *The Great Big Crocodile,* which had a sardonic commentary by Charles Aznavour. Their style leans fairly heavily on that of UPA. Ray Goossens has made *Pinocchio in Outer Space, Clorophyll, Anthracite* and a TV series based on the French comic strip *Tin Tin.* There is an animation course at the Academy of Fine Arts Ghent taught by **Raoul Servais** who has made *Sirène* (about the love of a cabin-boy and a mermaid), *Harbour Lights, La Fausse Note, Chromophobia, To Speak or Not to Speak,* and *Operation X-70* (1972). *To Speak or Not to Speak,* done in an *art nouveau* style, is an interesting comment on the meaning—or lack of meaning—of modern slogans—FIGHT, LOVE, LOVE-BUY, WORK etc. Another animator Meissen has made a horrific little cartoon movie *1-2-3* which shows three robots dominating and destroying one another. An unusual recent cartoon is **Gerald Frydman**'s *Scarabus* which uses cut-out photo animation of a single person (an anonymous executive type) to form the population of a strange city, so that every citizen is identical. The action is surrealist and violent—a blind man breaks windows with his stick then breaks a man with the same sound of breaking glass; a man wipes his feet and legs away on a mat, a man is squeezed flat and played on a gramophone, a man's face is transferred like Saint Veronica's to a cloth, and so on. The lack of sound, the architectural style, the jerky movement, all add to the effect of inhumanity and alienation. In Belgium there are a few other animators including Louis van Maelder (*The Sleeping Bird, The Cage*) who draws direct on film.

★   ★   ★

Early **Swiss** animation was represented by Pfenninger and Pinschewer who have been mentioned in the chapter on Germany. There were also August Wyler and Werner Dressler who have been working in the commercial field since the Thirties, the latter in puppets and cut-out figures as well as cartoons. Recently Gisèle and Ernest Ansorge have

Raoul Servais's TO SPEAK OR NOT TO SPEAK

shown cartoons at a number of festivals. Their earlier efforts, *The Ravens* and *Fantasmatic,* had badly organised scripts, dull design and gloomy themes. However *Alunissons* (1971) is apparently lighter in tone and "less pretentious and arty." Urs Graf in *A Line Is a Line Is a Line* has experimented with linear forms somewhere between Emile Cohl and McLaren and there are said to be a number of young animators who show promise.

★ ★ ★

In the last few years several talented films have come from **Cuba** made by Jesus de Arma (*The Shark and the Sardines* and *The Cowboy*), Harry Reade (*The Thing*), Jorge Carruana and Luis Rodriguez (*Dreaming in the Park*). There is something individual about the style of these films; they are well made, and in several cases have something of interest to express. Harry Reade's *The Thing* shows us an anonymous object which attracts the attention of a number of important people. A gourmet tries to eat it, a soldier tries to fire it in a gun, a scientist tries to analyse it—but it baffles them all. Then a little girl

171

comes and plants it and it grows, covered with flowers. The parable may be slight, but it is neatly and wittily expressed in visual terms. Most recent is Leinaldo Alfonso's *I Want To Be a Sailor* (1970), in a gay, easy style.

★   ★   ★

Numerous animated films are made in **China,** but with stereotyped plots and stiff composition. For instance *The Spirit of Ginger, The Golden Shell,* and *Journey to the West* (Wan Ku Chan), *The Cleverest* (The Shanghai Students' Collective), *The Red Army Bridge* (Chien Yun Ta). Better are *Three Little Ducks* in cut-out paper (Yu Tse Kuang) and *Where's Mummy?* (Te Wei and Chien Chia Chun) in Chinese brush style. More recent are *The Cowboy and the Flute* (Li Keh Jan) in ink and water-colour brushwork, and *The Peacock Princess,* a feature-length puppet film with a traditional setting. Also Wan Chu Chen's *Golden Dream* and Tsien Kia Kun's *Why The Cow Went Black.* If the Chinese can loosen the stiff propaganda which binds them, their particular artistic heritage might well be the basis of new and valuable work in animation. From **India** have come a few films, but all either banal pastimes for children or mediocre sponsored or didactic films: *As You Like It, Let Us Sing, My Wise Daddy* (a film about birth control). During the Sixties a studio was set up in Bombay under Kantilal Rathod where animators could work and be free from commercial pressures. Recently several cartoons from **Iran** have been well received. There is Karimi's *Life,* Nooredin Zarrin-Kelk's *Duty First* (said to be outstanding), and Farshid Mesghali's *A Boy a Lute and a Bird* 1971, a lightly-coloured, decorative piece about a boy trying to tame a bird with music. At the 1972 Grenoble Festival two cartoons from **North Vietnam,** the collective work of the Hanoi Studios, were shown—*Caught in a Net* and *Brave Girl.* They were propaganda stories about the brave deeds of a boy and a girl, and the style of drawing, colour and animation was light, easy, unpretentious and typically oriental.

★   ★   ★

It was reported in *Funny World,* a new American animation periodical, that long cartoons had been made in **Australia** on the subjects of *A Christmas Carol* and *A Connecticut Yankee,* but the report added that they had been produced by "mechanics with pencils." More serious is the experimental work of Arthur and Corinne Cantrill some of which borders on animation. In *Earth Message* they use animated images of native flowers superimposed on Australian landscapes. *4000 Frames* in the style of Robert Breer is described as "a Single-frame, discontinuous film with no relation between the 4000 images which bombard the eye at the rate of 24 a second." Bruce Petty scored a resounding success at the 1972 Zagreb Festival with his witty and irreverent condensation of colonial mis-history in *Australian History* and is a promising talent for the future.

A puppet feature made in **Israel** in 1962 by Alina and Yoram Gross is said to have quality. There are abstract films from **Uruguay** (*Creation*) and **Brazil** (*Whirlwind* and *The Jungle*). In **Argentina** Jorge Martin made *The Wall* (1962), about a wall which is a barrier to paradise, mental as much as physical. One could go on listing titles, as a few animated films are now produced annually in almost every country, but most of them are derivative and only of marginal interest.

Chapter Thirteen deals with new trends in animation and below is a design from John Grunberger's INFLORESCENCE

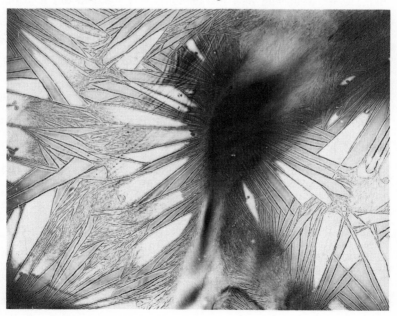

13. Present Trends, Abstract and Computer Animation

Previous chapters have traced the development of the animated film from its early beginnings in Europe and America, through its popular period as a programme-filler, to its present stage as a rich, multi-sided art form, widely dispersed in many different countries, being continually endowed with new means of expression, and finding new openings in television, teaching, science and art. This chapter discusses present-day trends and possible developments, both as regards the type of film presented and the technique of production, bearing in mind always that each of these two aspects will affect the other.

★　★　★

At the present time there are four main types of movie in which animation is used. First there is the specialised scientific or instructional short, dealt with only marginally in this book. In this field the drawn and invented image as opposed to the photo of reality, has an essential part to play, particularly in abstract sciences such as mathematics, statistics, chemistry and the like. But it is important also in natural or practical sciences where abstraction is used as a method—charts in history, schematic diagrams (which can be moving diagrams) in geography, geology, surgery, engineering and so on. As regards instructional films, we have already remarked how well animation, with its entertainment tradition, can combine lively interest with clear exposition.

Second is the old, popular cartoon or puppet movie which continues particularly on television. Popeye and Mr. Magoo are given a new lease of life and to them are added dozens of fresh creations from countries all over the world: Filutek, Prokouk, Signor Rossi, Marine Boy, the Schtroumps, Dougal. If one includes TV commercials and takes these two groups together, the last few years have seen an animation explosion, an expansion all over the world far greater than could have been predicted even five years ago. In this television age there are cartoon studios in Tunis, Seoul, Helsinki, Lagos, Bombay, Istambul, Tashkent, Hanoi, Sao Paulo, Oslo—any centre where pictures are transmitted for the small screen.

Thirdly, the animated movie has made a faltering start in the realm of satire, of grown-up comedy, of tragedy. There are cartoons of savage humour, puppet films of tragic intensity, drawn or painted movement as affecting as serious drama in any other medium. There are also longer cartoons, mostly light comedy, but offering the possibility of larger-scale and more sustained drama. Bringing the possibility also of cinema rather than television exhibition with a larger financial return, and so justifying a larger investment of talent and resources.

★   ★   ★

The fourth type of animated movie is abstract or semi-abstract in character, pictures in which the film-maker brings inanimate objects to life, paints or draws on the film or otherwise creates moving patterns of form or colour, offering a predominantly visual experience, and seeking to be judged not as dramatic form but as mobile graphic or plastic composition. Both live-cinema and animation techniques have been used for this type of movie, and it has been called at different times *cineplastics* and *expanded cinema.* Its beginnings in Germany in the Twenties have been briefly noted in Chapter Twelve, and its subsequent development in America in Chapter Four.

Here too there has been expansion if not an explosion. As we have seen the cinema adopted the cartoon as a medium of comic entertainment. But it never adopted the abstract cartoon in which the graphic element predominates. Abstract animation has sometimes been used in commercials (Fischinger, Alexeïeff and others have worked in this field) where it forms a colourful easily-integrated background to the sales message, but it never found a place in the cinema programme itself. Neither in the past has abstract movement been accepted by academic opinion in the graphic-art world. As a result the handful of artists working in this medium have been, for four decades, without any means of reaching any except the most insignificant audience. Now however, traditional art gallery patterns are changing to include many new forms which lie between established painting, drawing etc., and cinema. There are many kinds of mobile sculpture (bas-relief, haut-relief, freely balanced in space) moved by gravity, clock-work, electricity, air currents. There are light machines, colour scopes and colour organs of all kinds, projecting patterns, shades, beams—all kinetic in one way or another. To take just one example, the *Cybernetic Serendipity* exhibition in London and New York offered many new forms including robots composing poetry and music and walking round the gallery. Film is now common in galleries both by itself and in combination with other elements, and used either for information, or as a background or even as the exhibit itself. There is the creation of rooms or environments, often using moving elements. There are devices which go through visual cycles affecting the spectators' senses and emotions by light and colour variations, after-images, complementary colour-effects, optical illusions and the like. Visual material may be combined with sound, from voices to computer music, again bringing the art-gallery closer to the theatre and graphic art nearer to motion pictures.

Something, *en passant,* should be said about sound in relation to animation particularly in abstract films. Sound is a vital element in any cartoon or puppet movie and dialogue or effects may *make* the picture. At the same time, as with live-action, music may be an added finery and may be overdone. In an abstract picture where there is no argument, no narrative, no plot, music can play a more important part, it is free to predominate or combine with the visuals in an audio-visual harmony. Some abstract film-makers talk about "the music" of their designs, and it is perhaps easier to combine two elements which are both abstract of meaning since they are more homogeneous. There is also the view that modern music being less structured, less formally shaped, will better combine with abstract visuals. Furthermore the sounds of modern music are powerful, astringent, even explosive and may well introduce a dramatic element in vocal form either with meaning, with half-meaning, or simply in the form of wordless voices exclaiming, rejoicing, lamenting.

While the art gallery is becoming more theatrical, the theatre is becoming more abstract and diversified by the use of less realistic scenery, lighting, unusual stage effects, psychedelic patterns, film backgrounds, different kinds of audience involvement. Mixtures of mime, puppet, ballet, drama, cinema, may throw up new forms. An interesting example is an act staged by one of the living-theatre groups, which presented to the audience a hand-drawn "movie" copied larger-than-life on a huge roll of white cloth or paper which two of the actors unrolled like a great tapestry, while others supplied dialogue and sound effects for the various incidents. Hilarious and surprisingly effective, the method was by no means exhausted in a single performance. But is this cinema? Animation? Graphic art? Theatre? Or a reversion to Emile Reynaud? Nothing could illustrate better how new work refuses to conform to conventional definitions. The important fact here is that both developments in art gallery and theatre offer opportunities for animation, in the former case to present an artistic rather than a dramatic work, in the latter as a contributory element in a multi-media show.

Another factor, affecting particularly abstract animated movies, is a general growth and expansion of off-beat, underground, personal cinema. This derives some encouragement no doubt from the present fashionable trend away from the conventional towards newer, freer ways, but it is also on the production side, an offshoot of a more affluent, leisured society working with more-easily-handled, cheaper equipment, and on the viewing side encouraged by the growth of small audiences in cine-clubs and art-groups looking for something new.

★ ★ ★

Of the four types of animation (instructional, popular, serious, abstract) that have been discussed only the second has been intensively cultivated and the others offer every opportunity to the future artist. In considering future possibilities it is important to remember that boundaries are becoming more fluid, and new work may fall outside present definitions or consist of new combinations inside the animation field (mixing abstract and representational) or combinations of animation with live-action, or animation with other arts. Cartoons themselves have followed the *collage* of the artist in combining all kinds of objects, cut-outs, printed matter, illustrations, materials, textures, patterns, substances, arrangements—with or without their clashing or converging associations of meaning. This style is given unity by being put on celluloid and filtered through the camera's lens. More striking is the combination of animation with actors in the flesh. *Gertie the Dinosaur* (1917) was an early but isolated experiment. Recent examples are a *Living Screen* presentation in New York in 1964 with animated backgrounds by Halas and Batchelor, Dick Williams's work for *The Apple Tree* and Dunning's *Canada Is My Piano*. The Czech *Magic Lantern* used live-action film with actors on the stage, and slides and projected photos are now common in many shows from Brecht to Arden.

A particularly important mixture is the use of animation in live-action pictures. Animation has in the past been frequently used in movies like *King Kong* to extend the action to the fantastic or the miraculous but disguising the animation so that the movie seems to be in a single medium. Cartoon figures have also been used openly in live-action movies as a comic device or to give a magic touch from *Koko the Clown* in the Twenties to *Mary Poppins* and *Bedknobs and Broomsticks* in the Sixties. Again there is the now common use of animation in the introductory credits where the hand of the graphic artist has proved so effective, that critics have sometimes found the credits the best part of the film. Live-action and animation seems a combination that might be further developed. The use of puppets could be highly effective, not only for comic, but for dramatic and macabre effects. Animation could be used quite openly in serious drama to reinforce a dramatic or emotional scene, to obtain a striking contrast, to comment at another level, to affect the audience differently or more

177

strongly than would be possible in a single medium. At the climax of Disney's *Sleeping Beauty* the hero's battle with the wicked fairy has great dramatic power, because of the cartoon's ability to transcend the human scale. Given the colour and imagination of a Turner, a Van Gogh or a Vlaminck, the most wonderful effects, far beyond ordinary photography might blossom on the screen. One might object that the relatively simple style typical of cartoons made up to the present time, would not blend with live photography, but it seems that modern automation is changing this, and cartoon styles are likely to become richer and richer. When Kubrick's *2001: A Space Odyssey* reaches its stupendous climax the screen becomes a narrow way with sides of millenic dimensions, pressing together, turning, dazzling, exploding with light, and through it the spectator rushes, rushes, rushes at dizzying speed. The effect obtained by techniques akin to animation, is almost traumatic, quite unforgettable and quite unlike anything that could be obtained by live shooting. No doubt mixtures of this kind should be used with discrimination and restraint, but the cinema is not a "pure" medium in any case, and the contribution of the graphic artist could be just as effective on occasion as the use of music.

★   ★   ★

Before going on to discuss new techniques, there is another changing feature of the modern art scene to be mentioned—that is the relationship between artist and audience, and beyond it, ideas about the nature of art itself. More and more artists are experimenting with all kinds of audience involvement even to the point of physical contact. The "feelies" are in fact with us and it is not inconceivable that some time in the future artistic experience may be extended to include kinds of formalised or ritual activity, speech, singing, even drug-taking. A feature of this change, though perhaps not an essential part of it, is that the artist is less remote, nearer his audience, a cheer-leader rather than a dim figure in an ivory tower. Nowadays the underground film-maker attacks his audience presenting deliberately shocking, confusing, disappointing or insulting images. One might draw a parallel with the horse-play of the fun-fair in which one of the participants becomes a butt to amuse the others, or the heckling of a member of the audience by a music-hall comedian. The insistent presentation of nudity and fornication is aimed at breaking down acquired inhibitions, attacking not only the public censor but the censor within the individual so releasing him (the artist would say) for a fuller life. In a number of *avant-garde* cartoons this kind of aggression is manifested in an image (often abstract) changing so rapidly that it strains the eye to follow it, or an image which strains the eyes by switching suddenly and repeatedly from almost black to blinding bursts of white or near white. It is not all that far from the methods used in a more extreme form by Nazis, Communists and others in brainwashing and torture, to extract confessions, to break down resistance. In a mild form it may serve to heighten perception or have therapeutic effects. However the limitation of all these developments in which the artist seeks to break down barriers, invade the spectators' privacy, play the role of ecologist, reformer, medicine-man (or simply an irritant), is that they depend on the consent and co-operation of the audience. In the end he must entertain and benefit them. So far at any rate, compulsion does not belong in art.

★   ★   ★

Both animation styles and techniques are changing rapidly at the present time. One should consider the two in relation to one another since technique will be affected by style and style by technique. Several influences are at work. First, there is the virtual liberation of animation from its long association with live cinema and its place as a subordinate in Hollywood's big-business, international, entertainment industry. Secondly there is the influence brought to bear by modern diversity of art forms, the greater informality of art and the readiness of the artist to come to terms with the machine and use it as an artistic tool. Thirdly, there is a general increase in experimental and personal film-making of all kinds, including animation. Fourthly there is the growth of television everywhere, creating a market more varied and local than the popular-cinema industry which preceded it. Television is localised in many different centres all over the world, and controlled both by public corporations and private enterprise, so that neither commercial considerations nor bureaucratic "policy decisions" will have exclusive influence, and it is more likely that diverse tastes will be allowed expression. It is true that at present standards of production for TV programmes are lower than for cinema movies, and there is also the fact that animation is not yet taken seriously as adult entertainment. But there is more chance for small, independent studios to get a foot in, and if they have the talent, to try and improve the audience's taste. TV has also been vital in expanding the market, and many of the new techniques, especially computer animation (the most elaborate and expensive, but at the same time the most revolutionary and promising), are only likely to be applied to meet a large or potentially large output, since though using a computer may not in the end be more expensive foot for foot than the present hand work, it requires a large initial capital outlay.

Already there are several studios as large as Disney—in Moscow there is a studio with 625 employees, in Japan the Toei Company has 550 working, and in the United States Hanna and Barbera employ some 400. All over the world animators are experimenting with new methods. These include experiments with new materials, new styles, efforts to achieve novelty in what appears on the screen. And just as much in evidence is the increasing appearance of labour-saving and work-improving devices—from a new type of pencil which can put the artist's drawing direct on to the film itself, to a computer especially built for animation. It is difficult to write briefly and with complete accuracy about these developments for three main reasons. First descriptions are scattered in conference reports, technical journals and film-magazine articles, and may be missed. Secondly, many of the developments are highly complex and for detailed understanding require not only a technically-trained writer but a technically-trained reader. Thirdly, in the early stages of any technical invention, much enthusiasm is generated, large claims are made, and one may be led to think of new machines which are only prototypes, or even models, or even on the drawing-board, as if they were fully-fledged, commercially-viable, workaday systems. All that is possible here is to mention some of the techniques available, describe them generally and assess their likely influence. Those who wish to know more are referred to books like "Expanded Cinema" (clearly written and excellently illustrated though partisan in its views) or articles in such journals as "American Cinematographer" and "British Kinematography Sound and TV."

★   ★   ★

First there are the non-computer devices. The use of *xerography* or chemical copying, makes it possible to transfer the most detailed shading, engraving or textural surfaces, to film without laborious hand-copying. Thus the simple outline of the traditional cartoon is no longer the only style dictated by production conditions—richer, more subtle, more varied styles are possible. In the United States Leon Maurer and Harry Wuest have developed the *animascope,* a system using the rotascope and integrating it into animation routines, so that live actors can be put more or less direct on to film as cartoon characters by stressing outlines, by flattening shading, and by adding suitable cartoon characteristics. Accepting that one loses elements of caricature and invention which talented hand-drawing can give, the system can still be made to give acceptable results, and perhaps with imaginative handling other qualities suitable to the method could be brought out. The *Oxberry Animation Camera* makes it possible to film at one and the same time, both animation cels (with say moving figures) and a live background (treated if desired to give it graphic-art qualities). *Fritz the Cat* is a recent cartoon whose backgrounds are taken from real-life slum locations. The same camera is also capable of being controlled by a computer. The *cathode-ray tube* (the tube in a TV set) is mentioned later in computer systems, but in itself it facilitates the sort of combinations (of figures and backgrounds) previously effected by the travelling matte process, since the masking and erasing which had to be done optically, can now be done electronically. The cathode-ray tube has also made possible moving pictures in new styles, TV creations both representational and abstract. The films use new techniques belonging to "cathode-ray-tube videotronics"—distortion, staggering, debeaming, chroma-keying. Examples from America—all made in the late Sixties— are Terry Riley's *Music with Balls,* James Seawright's *Capriccio for TV,* Aldo Tambellini's *Black TV* and Eric Siegel's *Psychedelevision.*

Another new system, *Technanimation,* uses polarised light in such a fashion that "one area after another changes in density or colour, and the illusion of movement is created." This gives broad effects comparable to those of Alexeïeff's pin-table. A French studio, Arcady, has developed *Le Traceur d'Ectoplasm,* a cathode-ray-tube oscillograph which results in moving light as in the previous system, but which can be combined with other elements—painting, kaleidoscopic images or drawn animation. The *animograph,* developed by J. Dejoux for French TV and the Society of Optics, uses 70mm punched, kodatrace film on which the animator can draw, record and control the image through polaroid mirrors. Only three or four drawings a second instead of twelve to twenty-four are necessary, though detail and precision are less and the advantage is lost if the visuals have to be matched to dialogue. Though not exactly systems, two special entertainments devised by the Czech, Josef Svoboda, may be mentioned here, since they could be repeated with fresh material. His *Polivision* used a montage of 8,000 slides, 8 films and 36 screens, sometimes imparting a pulse to the image by mobile cubes or spring wires. His *Diapolyecran* shown at the Montreal Expo, used 112 three-dimensional movable, cubic screens, housing slide projectors and 15,000 slides.

★　　★　　★

Many new systems use computers to control one or more stages of the animation process. They can be used for the actual creation of frame-by-frame changes in animation, in the organisation of the studio or in the operation of the rostrum camera. The following are some of the systems using computers for the first function creating frame-by-frame pictures. The *De Joux Process* developed in America uses the following equipment: 1) A special drawing-table with built-in play-back, 2) an editing and colour table, 3) a patented optical console and multi-level projector, 4) a computer programmed for animation, 5) a video-tape recorder and camera. This system, it is claimed, can reduce the hand-drawing needed to achieve continuity to six or eight drawings a second with the film-maker retaining creative control throughout.

The artist John Whitney, whose work has been mentioned in Chapter Four, has devised a system in which "the camera advance, the art-work, orbital and rotational movement and illumination—are all knit into a comprehensive automated process." The system has been designed to suit the animation Whitney is interested in, not representational images but abstract patterns in motion. *Permutations* (1967) is one of the first films made by Whitney's automated system. Another approach making use of the computer is known as *key animation,* which involves creation by the artist of isolated frames at key intervals, the in-between frames being computed by interpolation.

The computer is basically a machine for making thousands of calculations at lightning speed and, as one can understand in principle, it can be used to calculate the position of a line or the shade of a colour. Combined with a cathode-ray tube it can make a picture, combined with a camera it can make a movie. But before the computer can draw there has to be either a visual input (which the computer will translate into figures) or the picture has to be programmed i.e. translated into computer (mathematical) language. One can see that even simple drawings will require extremely complex formulae, and an important step therefore is to devise a suitable "language" for use in programming since what is suitable for accounts, air-traffic, or weather will not necessarily suit drawings or paintings. So far several specialised languages have been developed—Fortran, Beflix, Auto-Haba and Algol. The work of animation can then by one method proceed as follows: 1) write the programme that will compute the pictures using the chosen language, 2) feed the programme into a digital computer by punched cards, 3) use the computer to convert the programmed instructions into commands for an electron beam in a cathode-ray tube and the film-advance mechanism in the camera, 4) read these commands on to a magnetic tape, 5) play the tape into the cathode-ray-tube-and-camera assembly. Another system using a digital computer called the "off line" method has been used by an American studio, Animated Productions Incorporated, under the direction of Al Stahl, to control an automated animation stand.

★　　★　　★

Some animators who have used a digital computer have complained about its limitations. One complained that where camera control was concerned, pans and zooms were easier than fades. Also that while a character could be moved in relation to his background, he could not be fully animated. Ken Knowlton, writing some years ago about a computer-animated abstract cartoon *Man and His World* which he made with Stan Vanderbeek, said that it was constraining because he (Vanderbeek) could not create the kind of picture he wanted. He could only play with the various parameters (determinant of a point, line or figure) that each instruction had, and then only with a set of a dozen instructions. Commenting on key animation, Knowlton said that the intermediate steps could be computerised for a stick figure, but with a character it was more difficult. Also action was likely to be dull because "to make something unusual happen, you have to write a new programme and it may not be worthwhile." There was a danger that cartoons would only use characters with a "good mathematical description" i.e. based on circles or other simple shapes. Another critic complained that computers could make only mechanical changes—expand, contract, stretch, squeeze, turnover, reverse or change dimensions—and would not *animate* in the sense of moving a character as if it had a life of its own.

But all the time improvements are being made in the computers themselves. Herman Kahn declared: "By the year 2000 computers are likely to match . . . man's abilities including perhaps some of his aesthetic and creative capacities, in addition having new capabilities that human beings do not have. . . ." It has also been predicted that new electronic brains will have speeds a million times faster and capacities a million times greater than present-day digital computers. Without going in detail into the difference between analog and digital computers (the former deals with and compares measures and quantities, the latter deals with numbers) it seems that neither alone is ideally suited to animation work, and the latest advance has been to build special-purpose animation computers incorporating both analog and digital elements. So far four have been built in America—Scanimate, Caesar, Animac and Animac II. It is claimed that Caesar, who belong to the Computer Image Corporation of Denver USA, can produce "instantaneous, full-colour, character animation," and they have made a cartoon *Apteryx and the Easter Bunny* to prove it.

There the matter remains at present. It seems clear that computer animation has come to stay, and an impressive piece of evidence is *Meta Data,* a computer-cartoon made in Canada by Peter Foldes and shown at the 1971 Annecy Festival. A French critic described it as "elegant and simple, the tenderest and most personal of films. Evoking both Nadja's drawings (in the lovers' eyes) and the economy of late Matisse, it distilled a poetry which gives one confidence that *computer technique can be made unobtrusive with enough feeling and inspiration.*"

That is one possibility. But many modern artists do not want to make technique unobtrusive, and it has been suggested that rather than using the computer to make cartoons in styles more-or-less resembling those of hand animation, artists should seek to discover new computer effects. New tools should generate new images, it is said, and the computer opens up vast new realms of possible aesthetic investigation. Gene Youngblood sees the need for "a new aesthetic discipline" and "a new breed of artist who is competent in both technology and the arts," and predicts that "a new kind of art will result from the interaction of science and art. . . ." This is perhaps the aim of *Pixillation,* a recent movie by Lilian Schwarz and Ken Knowlton in which up-to-date painting is blended with "computer-generated abstract shapes." Jordan Belson has said "computers have incredible power and magnetism. They create a vortex . . . you can feel their sucking power." Alan Kitching compares the animation computer with the MOOG sound synthesiser which *can* perform Bach, but can do undreamt-of things as well. He goes on to suggest we should use the computer "as a means of discovering the essential nature of moving images." It has also been suggested that, though styles are varied, the underlying basis of the traditional cartoon is photographic realism, and as the computer can deal with the subjective creation of imagined actions, it will extend our perception of reality "into other ranges of space and time." John Whitney says, "I foresee new forms of abstract design and typography which will bring unfamiliar delights of music for the eye to enjoy. . . ." How sound many of these claims are only time will show. But the computer has certainly brought new, richer possibilities within reach, whether in conventional moving graphics or abstract design or in areas between the two.

★   ★   ★

The animation computer may also help to bring developments in the field of communication, artistic and otherwise. In 1971 a Visual Communication Congress was held in Vienna (Vis-Com 71) in which animators took a leading part and one of whose aims was "to co-ordinate technology with creativity." Speaking in this context Dusan Vukotić, the leader of the Zagreb School, saw greatly expanded possibilities in animation and gave four reasons for its present limited scope: 1) failure to understand the relationship between verbal and visual knowledge,

2) failure to eliminate superfluous associations, 3) failure to grasp the principle of redundancy and reinforcement, 4) failure to understand that movement contains a wealth of hidden associations. Over the last seven years a Japanese, Yukio Ota, has developed LOCOS, an international visual language using standard elements to build up picture words. Thus we may see animation used as a language and a new international literature in picture form on a moving screen.

★   ★   ★

These then are some of the possibilities which the brave, new future holds. Our panorama stretches from the three-second cycle of the little black boy juggling with his head in the zoetrope, to the super-animation epic of fifty or one hundred years hence. But it will take thousands of years longer than that for the basic human condition to change, and in the foreseeable future as in the past and now in the present, it is the spirit of man, the divine flame the artist tries to express whether he uses a lump of clay or a million-pound computer, that will give us the things that matter—amusement, affection, excitement, warmth and light and inspiration.

14. Bibliography

The Animated Cartoon by John Daborn (Cinefacts, Amateur Cineworld).
The Animated Film by Roger Manvell (Sylvan Press, London 1954).
Animated Film: concepts, methods, uses by Roy P. Madsen (Interland Press, New York, 1970).
The Art of Walt Disney by Robert D. Field (Collins, London, 1944).
Cartoon and Puppet Films (*Rijsovani i Kykolni Film*) by S. Ginsberg (Moscow 1957).
Le Cinéma d'Animation dans le Monde, by Philippe Collin and Michel Wyn (IDHEC Paris, 1956).
Il Cinema di Animazione by W. Alberti (Radio Italiana, Roma 1956.)
Cinéma 57, Number 14. January 1957.
Cinéma 65, Number 98. July/August 1965.
Design in Motion by John Halas and Roger Manvell (Studio, London 1962).
Le Dessin Animé by Lo Duca (Prisma, Paris 1948).
Le Dessin Animé après Walt Disney, by Robert Benayoun (J.-J. Pauvert, Paris 1961).
Dessin Animé Art Mondial by Marie Thérèse Poncet (Le Cercle du Livre, Paris 1956).

Ecran 73 No. 11 Jan. 1973 (animation special).
L'Esthétique du Dessin Animé by Marie Thérèse Poncet (Librarie Nizet, Paris 1952).
Expanded Cinema by Gene Youngblood (Studio Vista, 1970).
Film and TV Graphics by John Halas, Ed. Walter Herdeg (Graphis Press, Zurich 1967).
J'Aime le Dessin Animé by Denys Chevalier (Denöel, Paris 1962).
The Penguin Book of Comics by Perry and Aldridge (Penguin, London 1971).
Der Sowjetische Film (section on animation by Ivanov-Vano), in German (Dietzverlag, Berlin, 1953).
Storia del Cartone Animato by Enrico Gianen. (Omnia, Milan 1960).
The Technique of Film Animation by John Halas and Roger Manvell (Focal Press, London 1959).
Walt Disney by Richard Schickel (Weidenfeld and Nicholson, London, 1968).

15. Filmographies

The following filmographies are extensive but even so they do not cover all directors mentioned in the text and do not give complete lists of films directed. The limitations of assuming the director to be the author of a cartoon or puppet film have been discussed. However, it would be impossible to give complete credits.

MUSTAPHA ALASSANE (Nigeria). *Bon Voyage Sim* 1969.

ALEXANDRE ALEXEIEFF (France). *Une Nuit sur le Mont Chauve* 1933, *La Belle aux Bois Dormant* 1935 (puppet film), *En Passant* 1943, *Le Nez* 1963, *Pictures from an Exhibition* 1971. Many publicity films including: *Parade des Chapeaux* 1936, *Franck Aroma* 1937, *Les Gaines Roussel, Ceupa* 1939, *Pure Beauté* 1954, *Sève de la Terre* 1955. With Georges Violet: *Fumées, Masques, Nocturnes,* 1951–54. Credits: *Cocinor* 1957, *The Trial* 1962.

GISELE AND ERNEST ANSORGE (Switzerland). *Sunstar* 1964, *Disassociation and Structure* 1966, *The Crows* 1967, *Father, Fantasmic* 1969, *Tempus, Alunissons* 1970.

JEAN ARCADY (France). *Kaleïdoscope, Guitares, Mouvement Perpétuel, Kapok l'esquimeau, Prélude pour voix, orchestre et caméra, Ondomane* 1962.

L. ATAMANOV (Russia). *Cross Roads* 1931, *Dog and Cat* 1938,

The Magic Carpet 1948, *The Red Flower* 1952, *The Golden Antelope* 1954, *Dog and Cat* (No. 2) 1955.

TEX AVERY (USA). *Henpecked Hoboes* 1941, *Dumb-Hounded* 1943, *Happy-go-Nutty* 1944, *The Shooting of Dan MacGoo* 1945, *King Size Canary* 1947, *Slaphappy Lion* 1947, *Half-Pint Pigmy* 1947, *Lucky Ducky* 1948, *Bad Luck Blackie* (Tom and Jerry) 1949, *The Cat That Hated People* (1949), *Garden Gopher* 1950, *Droopy's Double Trouble, Car of Tomorrow* 1952, *Billy Boy, Flea Circus* 1953, *Deputy Droopy* 1954, *Polar Pests* 1958.

CARMEN D'AVINO (USA). *Theme and Transition, Motif* 1956, *The Big 0* 1959, *Room* 1960, *A Trip* 1961, *Stone Sonata* 1962, *Pianissimo* 1963, *A Finnish Fable* 1964.

ALAN BALL (England). *The Self-Rescue Breathing Apparatus, A Sense of Responsibility* 1970.

BARBERA (See HANNA)

BENT BARFOD (Denmark). *Somewhere Up North* 1953, *Drums, Boogie Woogie* 1958, *Apple of Discord* 1959, *Viking* 1962, *African Alphabet, Ballet Ballade* 1963, *Konti-Skan* 1965.

SAUL BASS (USA). Many film credits including: *Carmen Jones* 1954, *The Big Knife* 1955, *The Man with the Golden Arm* 1955, *The Seven Year Itch* 1955, *Around the World in 80 Days* 1956, *Saint Joan* 1957, *Bonjour Tristesse* 1957, *The Big Country* 1958, *Vertigo* 1958, *Anatomy of a Murder* 1959, *Psycho* 1960, *West Side Story* 1961, *Nine Hours to Rama* 1961, *Walk on the Wild Side* 1962, *Spartacus* 1961, *Advise and Consent* 1962, *Bunny Lake Is Missing* 1965, *Seconds* 1966.

BATCHELOR (See HALAS).

RADKA BATCHVAROVA (Bulgaria). *The Mouse and the Crayon* 1958, *The Snowman* 1960, *Fable* 1964, *The Little Star* 1965.

VACLAV BEDRICH (Czechoslovakia). *Smallpox, Man of Men, 40 Grandfathers, Unfinished Week-End* 1970.

JORDAN BELSON (U.S.A.). *Mambo, Caravan, Mandala Bop Scotch* 1952–53, *Flight* 1958, *Raga, Seance* 1959, *Allures* 1961, *Re-Entry* 1964, *Phenomena* 1965, *Samadhi* 1967, *Momentum* 1969, *World* 1970.

VICTOR BERGDAHL (Sweden). *The Demon Drink* 1915, *Circus Fjollinski, Captain Grog's Travels, Adventure of Master Trick* 1916, *Captain Grog at the North Pole* 1917, *Captain Grog's Wedding* 1918, *Captain Grog at Sea* 1920, *Captain Grog Puts on Weight* 1922.

BRUNO AND GUIDO BETTIOL (France). Many publicity films. *Un Touriste en France,* 1963, *Acte Sans Paroles* 1964, *Berthe aux Grands Pieds* 1962 (with Lonati).

187

MILAN BLAZEKOVIC (Yugoslavia). *Gorilla's Dance* 1969, *The Man Who Had to Sing* 1971.

JAROSLAV BOCEK (Czechoslovakia). *Mannequin* 1966, *Pilgrimage to Charles IV, Svatoplouk and Son* (puppet) 1968, *Cooing of Doves* 1969, *Memory and Reality, The Sculptor's Wife* 1970, *The Invisible Actor, The Widow of Ephesus* (puppet) 1971.

GEORG D'BOMBA (East Germany). *We Build a School* 1961 (puppets). *The Devil's Dirty Work* 1962.

WALTER P. BOOTH (England). *The Hand of the Artist* 1906, *Comedy Cartoons* 1907, *The Sorcerer's Scissors, Prehistoric Man* 1908, *Sooty Sketches* 1909.

WALERIAN BOROWCZYK (Poland, France). *Once upon a Time, Love Requited* 1957 and *Dom* 1958 with Lenica, *School* 1958, *The Astronauts* 1959, *L'Encyclopédie de Grand-Maman, Renaissance, Le Concert de M. and Mme Kabal* 1963, *Les Jeux de Anges* 1964, *Le Dictionnaire de Joachim, Rosalie* 1966, *Le Théâtre de M. and Mme Kabal* 1968.

BOSCHET (See MARTIN)

STEPHEN BOSUSTOW (U.S.A.). Worked for Ub Iwerks, Walter Lantz and Disney until 1941. Formed UPA 1945. *Sparks and Chips Get the Blitz, Keep the Fleet to Keep the Peace* 1941/2, *Brotherhood of Man* (with Bob Cannon) 1943, *Hell Bent for Election* (with Chuck Jones) 1944, *Swab Your Choppers* 1947. A producer from 1947, *Joshua in a Box* 1970.

BRUNO J. BOTTGE (East Germany). *The Hen and the Changelings, How to Tame Dragons* 1970.

OMER BOUCQUEY (France). *Choupinet* 1946, *Le Troubadour de la Joie* 1949, *Les Dessins s'animent* 1952, *Drôles de Croches*.

ZLATKO BOUREK (Yugoslavia). *The Blacksmith's Apprentice* 1961, *Fog and Mud* 1964, *Circus Rex* 1965, *Dancing Songs* 1966, *Captain Marko* 1968, *Schooling* 1971, *The Cat* 1972.

BRUNO BOZZETTO (Italy). *Tapum* 1958, *The Story of Inventions* 1958, *An Award for Mr. Rossi* 1960, *Alpha Omega* 1961, *The Two Castles, Mr. Rossi Goes Skiing* 1963, *Mr. Rossi on the Beach* 1964, *West and Soda* 1965, *Mr. Rossi Buys a Car* 1966, *VIP My Brother Superman* 1968, *Ego* 1969, *Pickles* 1971.

JIRI BRDECKA (Czechoslovakia). Author of *Lemonade Joe* 1940, Director: *Love and the Dirigible* 1947, *How Man Learned to Fly* 1957, *Attention, Clementine* 1959, *Our Red Riding Hood* 1960, *Man Under Water* 1961, *Sentiment and Reason* 1962, *Gallina Vogelbirdae* 1963, *Minstrel's Song (Slowcem)* 1964, *Deserter* 1966, *Felicity of Love, Why*

Do You Smile Mona Lisa? 1966, *Hunting in the Forest, The Power of Fate, Metamorpheus* 1971.

ROBERT BREER (U.S.A.). *Frame by Frame* 1952, *Form Phases* 1955/56, *Jamestown Baloos* 1957, *A Man and His Dog out for Air* 1958, *Blazes* 1961, *Horse over Tea Kettle* 1963, *BLP 3* 1970.

V. AND Z. BROUMBERG (U.S.S.R.). *The Young Samoyed* 1929, *Puss in Boots* 1938, *The Story of Tsar Saltan* 1943, *The Night Before Christmas* 1951, *Flight to the Moon* 1953, *Walking Stick for Sale (Palka-Virvchalka)* 1956.

LOU BUNIN (France). *Ziegfeld Follies* 1948, *Alice in Wonderland* 1948 (puppets).

PETE BURNESS (U.S.A.). Many Magoo films including: *Bungled Bungalow, Trouble Indemnity* 1950, *Sloppy Jalopy, Captains Outrageous* 1952, *Magoo Goes West* 1953, *When Magoo Flew* 1954, *Magoo Goes Skiing, Destination Magoo* 1954, *Stagedoor Magoo* 1955, *Magoo's Puddle Jumper* 1956, TV shows and commercials, the *Bullwinkle Show* 1960/66.

MARY ELLEN BUTE (U.S.A.). *Synchronisation* 1934, *Anitra's Dance* 1936, *Evening Star* 1937, *Parabola* 1938, *Toccata* and *Fugue* 1940, *Tarantella, Spook Sport* 1941, *Colour Rhapsody* 1958.

BOB CANNON (U.S.A.). *Fear* 1945, *Brotherhood of Man* 1947, *Gerald McBoing Boing* 1950, *Madeline, Willie the Kid, The Oompahs* 1952, *Gerald's Symphony, Christopher Crumpet's Playmate* 1953, *Fudget's Budget, How Now Boing Boing, Gerald's Birthday, Ballet Oop* 1954, *Gerald on Planet Moo, The Jaywalker, Christopher's Invisible Playmate* 1955, *Department of the Navy* 1958.

DALE CASE (See MITCHELL)

CATTANEO (See WYATT)

OSVALDO CAVANDOLI (Italy). *Linea N.1, Linea N.2, Linea N.3* 1971, *Linea N.4, Linea N.5, Linea N.6* 1972.

ALBERT CHAMPEAUX AND PIERRE WATRIN (France). *Paris Flash, Villa mon rêve* 1961, *Merci M. Schmoutz* 1963, *Paris-Nice en Voiture, Victor et Horace* (TV series), *Le Robot* 1971.

GIULIO CINGOLI (Italy). *Canzonissima, The Woman of the Half-Century* 1962, *Study on Julietta of the Spirits* 1966.

EMILE COHL (France). Over 200 short films between 1908 and 1918 including *Fantasmagorie, Le Cauchemar de Fantoche, Drame chez les Fantoches* 1909, *Transfigurations, La Lampe qui file, Une Dame vraiment bien* 1908, *The Pumpkin Race* 1907, *Joyeux Microbes* 1909, *Le tout petit Faust* 1910 (puppets), *Le Baron de Crac, Castro à New York, Le Subway, Wilson et les tarifs, Metamorphoses, Le Voisin* *trop Gourmand, Flambeau chien perdu, Bonne Année* 1916, *Flambeau au pays des surprises, Tour du monde en 80 minutes.*

JACQUES COLOMBAT (France). *Marcel ta mère t'appelle* 1960, *Les Filous* 1966, *Calaveras* 1969.

DOUGLAS CROCKETT (U.S.A.). *Fantasmagoria, The Chase, Glenn Falls, Sequence.*

GENE DEITCH (U.S.A. and Czechoslovakia). *Howdy Doody and his Magic Hat* 1952, *Pump Trouble* 1953, *The Juggler of Notre Dame* (with Al Kouzel), *Flebus* (with Pintoff) 1957, *Clint Clobber* 1957/8, *Sidney* 1958, *Anatole* 1959, *Munro* 1960, *Nudnik* 1965/6, *The Tom-and-Jerry Cartoon Kit* 1962, *Rosie's Walk* 1970.

TODOR DINOV (Bulgaria). *The Mighty Marko* 1955, *The Little Guardian Angel* 1956, *The Fisherman Poacher, The Fox Outfoxed, Cannibal Country* 1958, *Prometheus, The Golden Slippers* 1959, *Story of a Twig* 1960, *Duo* 1961, *The Lightning Conductor* 1962, *Jealousy, The Apple* 1963, *The Daisy* 1965.

WALT DISNEY (U.S.A.). (Many directors have worked for Disney including the following: Ub Iwerks, Jack Hannah, Ward Kimball, Jack King, Jack Kinney, and Charles Nichols). Many short cartoons including: *Steamboat Willie;* (Mickey Mouse), *Galloping Gaucho, The Barn Dance* 1928; *The Skeleton Dance, Carnival Kid, Mickey's Follies* 1929; *Summer, Autumn, The Picnic* 1930; *Mother Goose Melodies, Mickey Steps Out, The Ugly Duckling* 1931; *The Grocery Boy, The Mad Dog;* (Pluto), *Flowers and Trees* 1932; *Mickey's Melodrama, Three Little Pigs, Mickey's Gala Premiere* 1933; *The Grasshopper and the Ants, Gulliver Mickey* 1934; *The Tortoise and the Hare, Mickey's Man Friday, Music Land, Who Killed Cock Robin?* 1935; *Mickey's Circus;* (Donald Duck), *Donald and Pluto, Three Blind Mouseketeers* 1936; *Don Donald, The Old Mill* 1937; *Donald's Nephews, Winken Blinken and Nod, Ferdinand the Bull* 1938; *The Autograph Hound, Tugboat Mickey, Mother Goose Goes to Hollywood* 1939; *Pluto's Dream House* 1940; *Chicken Little* 1943; *Tiger Trouble* 1944; *Donald's Double Trouble* 1946; *Clown of the Jungle* 1947; *Toy Tinkers* 1949; *Home Made Home* 1950; *Father's Day Off* 1952; *Melody* 1953; *Toot Whistle Plunk and Boom* 1953; *Pigs is Pigs* 1954; *The Conquest of Space* 1954; *Atom the Good Genie* 1956; *The Truth About Mother Goose* 1957. FEATURE FILMS: *Snow White and the Seven Dwarfs* 1937, *Pinocchio* 1939, *Fantasia, Dumbo, The Reluctant Dragon* 1941, *Bambi, Saludos Amigos* 1942, *The Three Caballeros* 1945, *Make Mine Music, Song of the South* 1946, *Fun and Fancy Free* 1947, *Melody Time* 1948, *Cinderella* 1950, *So Dear to My Heart, Ichabod and Mr. Toad* 1949, *Alice in Wonderland* 1951, *Peter Pan* 1953, *Lady and the*

Tramp 1955, *Sleeping Beauty* 1958, *101 Dalmatians* 1960, *The Sword in the Stone* 1963, *Winnie the Pooh and the Honey Tree* 1965, *The Jungle Book, It's Tough to be a Bird, The Aristocats, Winnie the Pooh and the Blustery Day, Bed Knobs and Broomsticks* 1971.

ANTON GINO DOMENEGHINI (Italy). *The Rose of Bagdad* 1942.

DONIOU DONEV (Bulgaria). *The Three Simpletons* 1970.

BORIVOJ DOVNIKOVIC (Yugoslavia). *Marionette, The Case of the Missing Mouse* 1963, *No Credits* 1964, *The Fashion Show, The Ceremony* 1965, *Curiosity* 1966, *Krek* 1968.

NEDELJKO DRAGIC (Yugoslavia). *Tamer of Wild Horses* 1967, *Diogenes Perhaps, Passing Days* 1970, *Per Aspera ad Astra, Striptiz* 1971, *Tup-Tup* 1972.

JIM DUFFY (U.S.A. and England). *The Weight-Lifter* 1969, *Digging* 1971.

GEORGE DUNNING (Canada and England). *J'ai tant dansé, Auprès de ma blonde* (Chants Populaires) 1943, *Grim Pastures* 1944, *Three Blind Mice* 1945, *Cadet rousselle* 1946, *The Adventures of Baron Munchhausen, Family Tree* (with Evelyn Lambart) 1947, *The Wardrobe* 1959, *The Flying Man* 1962, *The Apple* 1962, *Charley, The Ladder, The Yellow Submarine* 1968, *Moon Rock* 1970. Many publicity and sponsored films including: *Discovery—Penicillin* 1964, *The Story of the Motor-Car Engine* 1958, *The Ever-Changing Motor-Car* 1962, *The Adventures of Thud and Blunder* (safety film for the Coal Board) 1962/5, *Beatles* TV Series (director Jack Stokes), *Canada is My Piano* (triple-screen cartoon) (with Bill Sewell) 1966.

ANSON DYER (England). *Dicky Dee's Cartoon* 1915, *John Bull's Animated Sketchbook* 1916, *Old King Koal, Agitated Adverts* 1917, *Britain's Effort, Foch the Man* 1918, *Othello, The Taming of the Shrew* 1920, *Boy Scout* 1921, *Little Red Riding Hood* 1922, *Carmen, Three Hapence a Foot*.

VIKING EGGELING (Germnay). *Horizontal Vertical Orchestra* 1920, *Diagonal Symphony* 1923.

MLADEN FEMAN (Yugoslavia). *The Great Jewel Robbery* 1961, *Low Midnight*.

HANS FISCHER (Germany). *Petrus's Journey* 1921, *The Hole in the West* 1923.

OSCAR FISCHINGER (Germany and U.S.A.). *Gulliver's Travels* (with Louis Seel), *Study I, Study II* 1922, *Study III* 1923, *Study IV* 1924, *Spiralen* 1925, *Brahms' Hungarian Dance* 1931, *Composition in Blue* 1937, *Optical Poem, Allegretto, An American March, Fantasia* 1941.

MAX FLEISCHER (U.S.A.). *Out of the Inkwell* 1921, *(Koko the*

Clown) Bubbles 1922, *Koko's Hypnotism* 1929, *Betty Boop,* including *Betty Boop's Rise to Fame, Betty Boop's Hallowe'en Party, Little Nobody*. Many Popeye films including: *Popeye the Sailor* 1933, *Popeye the Sailor Meets Sinbad the Sailor* 1936, *Popeye Meets Ali Baba's Forty Thieves* 1937, *Gulliver's Travels* 1939, *Mr. Bug Goes to Town* (in UK, *Hoppity Goes to Town*) 1941, *Popeye and the Pirates* 1947, *Popeye's Mirthday* 1953, *Popeye for President* 1956. (Director of later films I. Sparber)

PETER FOLDES (England and France). *Animated Genesis* 1952, *A Short Vision* 1955, *Un Garcon plein d'avenir, Appetit d'oiseau* 1965, *Plus Vite, Awakening* 1966, *Brainy Beauty* 1967, *Women's Faces* 1969, *Narcissus-Echo, Meta Data* 1971, *Je Tu Elle* 1972.

FRIZ FRELENG (U.S.A.). *Bugs Bunny and the Three Bears* 1944, *Tweety Pie and Sylvester* 1947, *Bugs Bunny Rides Again* 1948, *Dog Pounded* 1953, *By Word of Mouse* 1954, *Captain Hareblower, Bugs and Thugs* 1954, *Speedy Gonzales, Pizzicato Pussycat* 1955, *Rabbitson Crusoe, Tugboat Granny, Tweet and Sour* 1956, *Birds Anonymous* 1957, *Knightly Knight Bugs* 1958 etc.

GERALD FRYDMAN (Belgium). *Scarabus* 1971.

TAKU FURUKAWA (Japan). *Oxed Man, Catch Catch Yama* 1967, *Head Spoon, New York Trip* 1971.

ROBERTO AND G. GAVIOLI (Italy). *The Dandy* 1955, *The Magic Pot* 1956, *Ugh Me Hungry, The Long Green Stocking* 1962, *Venetian Twilight* 1970.

JOSEF GEMES (Hungary). *Koncertissimo, Parade* 1970, *Event, Funeral* 1971.

KATJA AND KLAUS GEORGI (East Germany). *The Pyramid* 1961, *Cigarette Charlie, Henry and His Chickens, Cloudiness (Das Wolkenschaft)* 1962, *Allumettes* 1963, *Musicians* 1963, *The Statue in the Park* 1964, *A Young Man Called Engels* (with Feodor Khitrouk) 1971.

GIULIO GIANINI AND EMMANUELE LUZZATI (Italy). *The Paladins of France* 1960, *House of Cards* 1963, *The Thieving Magpie* 1964, *The Message, Swimmy* 1970, *The Italian Girl in Algiers, Ali Baba* 1971.

WITOLD GIERSZ (Poland). *The Secret of the Old Castle* 1956, *In the Jungle* 1957, *Musical Adventures* 1958, *The Gnomes in Spring, Neon Harmony* 1959, *The Little Western* 1960, *The Treasure of Black Jack* 1961, *Waiting* 1962, *Dinosaurus* 1963, *The Red and the Black* 1964, *Ladies and Gentlemen* 1965, *The Root* 1965, *Heat and Confusion* 1966, *Portrait of a Horse* 1968.

BOB GODFREY (England). *Watch the Birdie* 1953, *Polygamous Polonius* 1960, *The Battle of New Orleans** 1960, *Do-it-Yourself Cartoon Kit* 1961, *The Plain Man's Guide to Advertising** 1961, *The Rise* *and Fall of Emily Sprod* 1962, *Productivity Primer, Alf Bill and Fred* 1964, *One Man Band*, L'Art Pour L'Art** 1965. (Films marked* are wholly or partly live-action). *Rope Trick, Whatever Happened to Uncle Fred* 1967, *Henry 9 till 5* 1969, *Kama Sutra Rides Again* 1971.

MORTON AND MILDRED GOLDSCHOLL (U.S.A.). *Night Driving* 1956, *Texoprint* 1957, *Mag* 1958, *Faces and Fortune* 1960, *Shaping the World* 1961, *Envelope Jive* 1962, *Dissent Illusion* 1963, *From A to Z* 1964, *First Impression, Intergalactic Zoo* 1965, *The Great Train Robbery* 1960, *Pitter Patterns* 1966, *Up Is Down.*

RENE GOSCINNY AND ALBERT UDERZO (France). *Asterix the Gaul* 1969, *Asterix and Cleopatra* 1970.

ZLATKO GRGIC (Yugoslavia). *Devil's Work, The Musical Pig, The Fifth* (with Pavao Stalter) 1965, *The Short and the Tall* 1967, *Inventor of Shoes* 1968, *Happiness for Two, Scabies* 1970, *Hot Stuff* 1971.

PAUL GRIMAULT (France). *Go Chez les Oiseaux* 1939, *Les Passagers de la Grande Ourse* 1941, *Le Marchand des Notes* 1942, *L'Epouvantail* 1943, *Le Voleur de Paratonnerres* 1945, *La Flute Magique* 1946, *Le Petit Soldat* 1947, *La Bergère et le Ramoneur* 1952, *La Faim du Monde* 1958.

HENRI GRUEL (France). *Martin et Gaston* 1954, *Gitanes et papillons* 1955, *Le Voyage de Badabou, La Joconde* 1958, *Un Atome qui vous veut du bien, Monsieur Tête* 1959, *La Lutte contre le Froid* 1960.

JOHN GRUNBERGER (U.S.A.). *Onset* 1967, *Free to One and All* 1968, *Burden of a Song* 1969, *Subliminal Graphics* 1970, *Crystal Vision, Inflorescence* 1971.

JOHN HALAS AND JOY BATCHELOR (England). *The Pocket Cartoon* 1941, *Dustbin Parade* 1942, *Handling Ships* 1945, *Robinson Charley* 1948, *As Old as the Hills* 1950, *Magic Canvas, Poet and Painter (Twa Corbies, Spring and Winter, The Pythoness, John Gilpin), Submarine Control* 1951, *The Figurehead* (puppets), *The Owl and the Pussycat, Coastal Navigation, The Moving Spirit* 1953, *Animal Farm, Power to Fly* 1954, *Speed the Plough* 1955, *History of the Cinema, The Candlemaker, The World of Little Ig, To Your Health* (director Philip Stapp) 1956, *All Lit Up* 1957, *The Christmas Visitor* 1958, *Habatales (The Cultured Ape, The Insolent Matador, The Widow and the Pig) Foo Foo* series (33 films), *Snip and Snap* series (26 films), *Dam the Delta* 1960. *The Colombo Plan, For Better for Worse* 1961, *Automania 2000,* Hoffnung series: *The Symphony Orchestra, Birds Bees and Storks, Professor Ya Ya's Memoirs, The Palm Court Orchestra* (directed by Harold Whitaker) 1965, *Ruddigore,* 1966, *The Question, Flurina* 1967, *Fairy Tale* Series 1969, *What is a Computer, Children and Cars* 1970.

WILLIAM HANNA AND JOSEPH BARBERA (U.S.A.). *Mouse*

Trouble 1944, *Quiet Please* 1945, *Mouse Cleaning* 1945, *The Cat Concerto* 1946, *Kitty Foiled*, *The Invisible Mouse* 1947, *Professor Tom* 1948, *The Cat and the Mermouse* 1949, *His Mouse Friday*, *The Two Mouseketeers* 1951, *Johann Mouse* 1952, *Mouse for Sale* 1955, *Muscle Beach Tom* 1956, *Life with Loopy* 1960, *Just a Wolf at Heart* 1962. TV Series: *Ruff and Reddy*, *Quickdraw McGraw*, *Huckleberry Hound*, *The Flintstones*.

HELMUT HERBST (West Germany). *How to Live a Happy Life*, *The Picture Robbery* 1962, *Black-White-Red*, *Victory Celebration of a War Casualty (Überwindung eines Verlustes)*, *The Hat* 1964.

GEORGE HERRIMAN, LEON SEARL AND FRANK MOSER (U.S.A.). *Krazy Kat Bugologist*, *Krazy Kat and Ignatz Mouse* 1916.

HY HIRSH (U.S.A.). *Divertissement Rococo*, *Autumn Spectrum*, *Djinn*, *Gyromorphosis* 1958, *Eneri*, *Post No Bills*, *Experiment*, *Change of Key*.

HITROUK (See KHITROUK)

EDWARD HOFMAN (Czechoslovakia). *All Aboard* 1947, *The Angel's Cloak* 1948, *Formulas*, *Animated Posters*, *Lenora* 1949, *Cat and Dog* series 1950–54. *ABC* 1950, *Golden Apples* 1952, *Where is Micha?* 1954, *The Fox* 1955, *Creation of the World* 1956, *Tale of the Dog* 1959, *My Twelve Papas* 1960, *The Postman's Story* 1961, *The Ladder* 1964.

JOHN HUBLEY (U.S.A.). Worked for Disney until 1941 on *Snow White*, *Pinocchio*, *Fantasia*, *Bambi*, *Dumbo*, *Flathatting* (UPA and US Navy) 1945, *Robin Hoodlum* 1948, *The Magic Fluke* 1949, *Punchy de Leon* 1949, *Ragtime Bear* (Magoo), *Fuddy Duddy Buddy* (Magoo) 1949, *Rooty Toot Toot* 1952. Left UPA in 1952. *Adventures of an Asterisk* 1956, *The Tender Game*, *Harlem Wednesday*, *A Date with Dizzy* 1958, *Seven Lively Arts* 1959, *Moonbird* 1960, *Children of the Sun* (UNICEF) 1961, *Of Stars and Men*, *The Hole* 1963, *The Hat* 1964, *Tijuana Brass Double Feature* 1966, *Urbanissimo* 1967, *Windy Day*, *Zuckerhandl* 1968, *Of Men and Demons* 1969, *Eggs* 1971.

JEAN HURTADO (Spain and France). *14th July* 1961, *Dante Would Have Turned in His Grave*, *Siren* 1962, *Long Live Sea-Bathing* 1971.

WILLIAM HURTZ (U.S.A.). *Hotsy Footsy*, *Bringing up Mother*, *The Unicorn in the Garden* 1954, *Man on the Land*, *Look Who's Driving*, *Great Rights* 1963, *The Unchained Goddess*.

JEAN IMAGE (France). *Rhapsodie de Saturne* 1947, *Ballade Atomique* 1948, *Jeannot l'Intrepide* 1950, *Bonjour Paris* 1953, *Monsieur Victor*, *L'Aventure du Père Noël* 1957, *Magie Moderne*, *La Petite reine* 1959, *Les Aventures de Joe* 1960, *Aladin and His Wonderful Lamp* 1969, *Potatomania* 1970.

A. IVANOV (Russia). *The Cockroach* 1927, *Quartet* 1935, *The Fox and the Thrush* 1946, *Grandpa Ivan* 1939.

IVANOV-VANO (Russia). *Senka the African* 1927, *Black and White* 1932, *Tales of Tsar Durandai* 1934, *The Three Musketeers* 1938, *A Winter's Tale* 1945, *The Hunchback Pony* 1947, *The Snow Maiden* 1952, *Woodland Concert* 1953, *The Mechanical Flea* 1964, *Seasons* 1970, *Battle Under the Walls of Kerchenetz* 1971.

JEAN JABELY (France). *Teuf Teuf* 1955, *Ballade Chromo* 1957, *Elle et Lui* 1959.

STEFAN JANIK (Poland). *Attention, The Ballons, The Enemy in the Bottle, Pyramid* 1966, *Fiddle Faddle*.

CHUCK JONES (U.S.A.). *Private Snafu, Hell Bent for Election* 1944, *Mississippi Hare* 1947, *Mouse Wreckers* 1947, *Frigid Hare* 1949, *Rabbit Seasoning* 1951, *Bully for Bugs* 1952, *Punch Trunk* 1955, *Nightmare Hare* 1955, *Gee Whiz-z-z* 1956, *Robin Hood Daffy* 1957, *Scrambled Aches* 1957, *The Abominable Snow Rabbit* 1961, *Tom-ic Energy* (Tom and Jerry) 1964, *The Cat above the Mouse Below* 1964, *The Dot and the Line* 1966.

PAUL JULIAN (U.S.A.). *The Fourposter* 1953, *The Telltale Heart* 1954, *Baby Boogie* 1955.

JOSEF KÁBRT (Czechoslovakia). *The Telegram* 1949, *The Tragedy of the Watersprite* 1960, *The Tin Helmet, Man is a Being* 1962, *Studies in Marriage* 1964.

PIOTR KAMLER (France). *Conte* 1960, *Composition, Etude, Structures* 1961, *Lignes et Points* 1962, *Meurtre* 1964, *Galaxie* 1965, *Prière Enfance* 1965, *Etude, La Planète Verte* 1966, *L'Araignée Elephant, Le Trou* 1968, *La Labyrinthe, Délicieuse Catastrophe* 1970.

FEODOR KHITROUK (Russia). *The Story of a Crime* 1963, *Toptychka* 1964, *The Lion's Holiday* 1966, *Film Film Film* 1969.

MIROSLAW KIJOWICZ (Poland). *Harlequin* 1960, *The Dragon* 1962, *Town* 1963, *Portraits, Cabaret* 1964, *The Banner, The Smile* 1965, *Rondo* 1966, *Prisoners, Science Fiction* 1970.

JOSEF KLUGE (Czechoslovakia). (Puppets) *The Combine* 1950, *The Magic Ski* 1959, *Xantippe and Socrates* 1961, *Wise Grandpa* 1963, *Lifes Ironies* 1964, *The Detective and the Choir* 1965, *The Gossips* 1968, *The Helpers* 1969, *Playing Mother* 1970.

BORIS KOLAR (Yugoslavia). *The Boy and the Ball* 1960, *Boomerang* 1962, *Citizen IM-5* (Inspector Mask), *The Monster and I, Bow-wow* 1964, *Discoverer* 1968, *Happiness Two* 1970.

NICOLA KOSTELAC (Yugoslavia). *Dream Encounter, Opening Night* 1957, *Nocturne* 1958, *The Ring* 1959, *The Case of the Eggless Hens* (Inspector Mask) 1960, *The Case of the Missing Matador* (Inspector Mask), *All-round Help, Cupid* 1961, *Rape of Miss Universe* (Inspector Mask) 1963.

JERZY KOTOWSKI (Poland). *Precaution, Abstract Art Exhibition, Round the World in Ten Minutes, Shadows of Time* 1964.

GABOR KOVASZNAI (Hungary). *Double Portrait* 1965, *Darkness and Light, Waiting for a Train, Gloria Mundi* 1970.

VLADO KRISTL (Yugoslavia and Germany). *La Peau de chagrin* (with Ivo Urbanic), *Don Quixote* 1960, *Prometheus* 1965.

YOJI KURI (Japan). Has made 80 films since 1958, including: *Human Zoo* 1960, *Fantasia of Stamps, Here and There* 1961, *Locus, Love, The Button, The Chair* 1963, *Man Woman and Dog, Aos* 1964, *The Man Next Door, The Window, Samurai* 1965, *Eggs, Au Fou, The Bathroom, Poissons Grillés* 1970, *Fantasy of Piano, Living on the Boughs* 1972.

BOB KURTZ (U.S.A.). *My Son the King* 1970.

HENRI LACAM (France). *Les Deux Plumes* 1958, *Jeux de Cartes,* 1959, *Les Nuages fous* 1962, *L'Oiseau de la sagesse* 1965.

JEAN-FRANÇOIS LAGUIONIE (France). *La Demoiselle et le violoncelliste* 1964, *L'Arche de Noë* 1966, *Une Bombe par hasard* 1968.

RENÉ LALOUX (France). *Les Dents du Singe* 1960, *Les Temps Morts* 1964, *Les Escargots* 1965. (In preparation) *Sur le planète Ygam* (with Roland Topor).

DEREK LAMB (Canada, England, U.S.A.). *I Know an Old Lady Who Swallowed a Fly* 1963, *The Hoffnung Vacuum-Cleaner* 1964.

WALTER LANTZ (U.S.A.). *Woody Woodpecker, Andy Panda, Oswald.*

ROBERT LAPOUJADE (France). *Enquête sur un corps, Foules* 1959, *Chastel* 1960, *L'Image et le moment, Noir et blanc,* 1961, *Prison* 1962, *Vélodrame* 1963, *Trois Portraits d'un oiseau qui n'existe pas* 1963, *Cataphote* 1964.

LARKINS (See BERYL STEVENS)

VLADIMIR LEHKY (Czechoslovakia). *The Goat and the Lion* 1957, *The Blue Cat, Three Men* 1959, *Shadow, Parasite* 1960, *Course for Husbands* (puppets) 1961, *Three Men Fishing, Susan and the Letters, Course for Wives* (puppets) 1962, *Museum of Oddments, Three Musicians* 1963, *The Duo* 1964, *The Door, Odd Birds* 1965.

JAN LENICA (Poland, France and Germany). *Once upon a Time, Love Requited* 1957, with Borowczyk, *Dom* (*House*) 1958, with Borowczyk; *Monsieur Tête* 1960, *Janko the Musician, Italia 61* (with Zamecznik) 1961, *Labyrinth, Rhinoceros* 1963, *A, The Flower-Woman* 1964, *Adam II* 1968, *Quadratures, The Automobile* 1970, *Hell* 1971.

JACQUES LEROUX (France). *Maître* 1961, *Atom Tilt* 1964, *Les Deux Uranium* (all with Manuel Otero), 1965, *Pierrot* 1965.

196

COLIN LOW (Canada). *Cadet Rousselle 1947, Baron Munchhausen, Time and Terraine, Science against Cancer 1948, The Romance of Transportation 1952, It's a Crime 1957, Universe 1960.*
LUZZATI (See GIANINI)
LEN LYE (Great Britain). *Tusalava 1928, Experimental Animation 1933, Colour Box, Birth of a Robot (puppets) 1935, Rainbow Dance 1936, Trade Tattoo 1937, Musical Poster 1941, Bells of Atlantis 1952, Colour Cry 1955, Free Radicals 1957.*
ROBERT McKIMSON (U.S.A.). *The Mousemerised Cat 1946, Hop Look and Listen 1947, Mixed Bastard, Slap-hoppy Mouse 1956, No Parking Hare 1953, Dime to Retire 1954, Honey Mousers 1956, Mousetaken Identity 1957, Tabasco Road 1957, The Mouse That Jack Built 1958, Cannery Woe 1960, etc.*
GYULA MACSKASSY (Hungary). *Races in the Forest 1952, Magic Oxen 1955, The Greedy Bee 1958, Pencil and Rubber 1959, Duel 1960, Romantic Story 1966, 100 Grams of Immortality 1969, Behind Bars 1970.*
WINSOR McCAY (U.S.A.). *Gertie the Dinosaur 1909, Little Nemo 1911, Jersey Skeeters 1916, The Sinking of the Lusitania 1918.*
NORMAN McLAREN (Scotland and Canada). *Seven Till Five 1933, Camera Makes Whoopee, Colour Cocktail 1935, Book Bargain, News For the Navy, Many a Pickle, Love on the Wing* (for GPO Unit) 1937, *The Obedient Flame* (Film Centre) 1939. (In U.S.A.) *Stars and Stripes, Dots, Loops, Boogie Doodle, Spook Sport 1940,* (NFBC) *Mail Early for Christmas, V for Victory 1941, Hen Hop, Five for Four 1942, Dollar Dance 1943, Alouette, Keep Your Mouth Shut 1944, C'est l'aviron 1945, Là haut sur ces montagnes, A Little Phantasy on a 19th. Century Painting, Hoppity Hop 1946, Fiddle-de-dee, La Poulette grise 1947, Begone Dull Care,* Trip to China and 8 films on health rules 1949, *Around Is Around, Now Is the Time 1951, Phantasy, Neighbours, Two Bagatelles 1952, Blinkity Blank 1954, Rythmetic 1956, Chairy Tale 1957, Le Merle 1958, Serenal, Short and Suite, Mail Early for Christmas 1959, Lines Vertical, Opening Speech, New York Lightboard 1960, Lines Horizontal 1962, Canon 1964, Mosaic 1965, Pas de Deux 1968.*
ALEKSANDAR MARKS (Yugoslavia). (with Vladimir Jutrisa) *The Fly 1967, Sysiphus, A Small Mermaid, The Spider 1971.*
ANDRE MARTIN AND MICHEL BOSCHET (France). *Demain Paris 1959, Patamorphose 1960, Mais où sont les nègres d'antan? 1963.*
ROMAN MEITZOV (Bulgaria). *The Kiss, Cosmos, Coloured Yarns, Spinning Woman 1971.*
BILL MELENDEZ (U.S.A.). *Babar the Elephant, Peanuts* (TV

Series) 1968, *A Boy Named Charlie Brown* (feature) 1970, *Rainbow Bear* 1970, *Snoopy Come Home.*

ZDENEK MILER (Czechoslovakia). *Red Riding Hood, The Millionaire Who Stole the Sun* 1948, *The Red Stain* 1963, Children's films including *Who Is Strongest?* 1952, *How the Mole Got his Trousers* 1957, *The Mole and the Motorcar* 1963.

VATROSLAV MIMICA (Yugoslavia). *The Storm* 1955, *The Scarecrow* 1957, *Happy End* 1958, *At the Photographer's,* 1959, *The Egg, The Inspector Goes Home* 1960, *Little Story, Typhoid (Tifusari), Perpetual Motion, Mr. Marzipan's Marriage* 1963.

CHARLES MINTZ (U.S.A.). *Krazy's Newsreel, Krazy's Magic* 1936–39.

ROBERT MITCHELL and DALE CASE (U.S.A.). *The Further Adventures of Uncle Sam* 1970.

TERU MURAKAMI and FRED WOLF (U.S.A.). *The Insects* 1963, *The Top* 1965, *Charley* 1965, *Breath, The Bird, The Box* 1968, *The Point* 1971.

WLADYSLAW NEHREBECKI (Poland) *Cat & Mouse* 1958, *The Clown the Puppet & the Flame* 1959, *The Chimney Sweep* 1960.

JOSEF NEPP (Hungary). *Till Tomorrow, Passion, Five Minutes of Murder* 1967.

MANUEL OTERO (France). (See also Leroux). *Contre-pied, Arès Contre Atlas, Univers, Sec et Debout, Papiers S.V.P., Patch Work* (collaboration) 1970.

GEORG PAL (Holland, England, U.S.A.). *Aladdin, Sinbad, On Parade* 1936, *What Ho She Bumps* 1937, *Sky Pirates* 1938, *Love on the Range* 1939, *Jasper Goes Hunting* 1944, *Jasper's Minstrels* 1944, *Jasper's Close Shave* 1945.

JULIEN PAPPE (France). *Un Oiseau en papier journal* 1962, *La Mare aux garçons, Genèse d'un buste* 1963, *Sophie et les gammes* 1964.

TED PARMELEE (U.S.A.). *The Emperor's New Clothes, The Telltale Heart, The Man on the Flying Trapeze* 1954.

RUDOLF PFENNINGER (Germany). *Largo* 1922, *Sound Writing* 1929, *Serenade, Barcarole, Pitsch and Patsch.*

JULIUS PINSCHEWER (Germany and Switzerland). *Die Suppe* 1911, *The Sewing Box, The Bottle* 1912, *The Tale of a Shirt* 1926, *The Chinese Nightingale, Carmen* 1928, *Full Sail* 1946, *King Koal* 1948, *Globi, Play of the Waves* 1955.

ERNEST PINTOFF (U.S.A.). *The Wounded Bird* 1956, *Aquarium, Good Ole Country Music, Fight on for Old, Martians Come Back, Performing Painter, Blues Pattern* 1956, *The Haunted Night, Flebus* 1957,

The Violinist 1960, *The Interview* 1961, *The Critic* 1962, *The Old Man and the Flower* 1962.

BRETISLAV POJAR (Czechoslovakia). *The Gingerbread Cottage* 1951, *A Drop Too Much* 1954, *Speibl on the Trail* 1956, *The Little Umbrella* 1957, *The Lion and the Song* 1958, *Bomb Mania, How to Furnish a Flat* 1959, *Midnight Adventure, Cat Talk, Cat Painting, Cat School* 1960, *The Orator, Billiards* 1962, *Romance* 1963, *It's Hard to Recognise a Princess* 1966.

ION POPESCO-GOPO (Rumania). *The Naughty Duck, The Bee and The Dove* 1951, *Two Rabbits, Marinica, Marinica's Bodkin* 195, *A Short History* 1956, *The Seven Arts* 1958, *Homo Sapiens* 1960, *Hullo Hullo* 1961, *Sancta Simplicitas* 1969.

GERALD POTTERTON (Canada). *Huff and Puff* (with Grant Munro), *Fish Spoilage Control* 1956, *My Financial Career, Yes Yes, The Ride* 1962, *Christmas Cracker* 1964, *The Railrodder* 1965, *Cool McCool, The Quiet Racket* 1966, *Pinter People* 1968, *Superbus* 1970, *Last to Go, The Charge of the Light Brigade* 1971.

A. PTUSHKO (Russia). *The New Gulliver* (puppets) 1935, *The Fishmonger and the Fish* 1937, *The Golden Key* (puppets) 1939.

LOTTE REINIGER (Germany and England). *The Flying Coffer, Star of Bethlehem* 1921, *Cinderella, Sleeping Beauty* 1922, *The Adventures of Prince Achmed* 1926, *The Adventures of Dr. Dolittle* 1928, *Carmen* 1933, *Puss in Boots, The Stolen Heart* 1934, *Papageno, Galatea* 1935, *The King's Breakfast* (A. A. Milne) 1937, *The Daughter* (GPO Unit, Music, Benjamin Britten), *Mary's Birthday* 1949, *Snow White and Rose-red, Aladdin, Puss in Boots* 1953, *The Star of Bethlehem* 1956, *Jack the Giantkiller* 1957, *La Belle Hélène, The Seraglio* 1958.

HANS RICHTER (Germany). *Fugue* 1920, *Rhythm 21, Rhythm 23, Rhythm 25* (1925), *Film Studie*.

WALTER RUTTMANN (Germany). *Opus I, Opus II* (1918–1921), *Opus III* 1923, *Romance in the Night, The Falcon's Dream* 1924, *Opus IV* 1925, *Dream Play* 1926.

EDDY RYSSACK (Belgium). *Petit Noël, Le Voleur de Schtroumpf, Le Schtroumpf et l'Oeuf* 1960, *Les Schtroumpfs Noirs* 1961, *Teeth Is Money* (with Jean Delire) 1962, *Schtroumpf et le Dragon, Le Schtroumpf volant* 1963, *Flute, Le Faux Schtroumpf, Histoire des Schtroumpfs, Le Crocodile majuscule* 1964.

BORISLAV SAJTINAC (Yugoslavia). *Analysis* 1967, *The Spring of Life* 1969, *All Fliers Aren't Birds, The Young Bride, Temptation* 1971.

AL SENS (Canada). *The Puppet's Dream* 1958, *The Pedlar of Poesy* 1959, *The Sorcerer* 1960, *Once or Twice upon a Time and Thrice upon* *a Space, The See Hear Talk Dream and Act Film* 1965, *The Playground* 1966, *New World* 1970.

RAOUL SERVAIS (Belgium). *Ghost Story, The Sand Man* 1951, *Harbour Lights* 1960, *Chromophobia* 1966, *Siren* 1968, *Goldfinger, To Speak or Not to Speak, Operation X-70* 1971.

ZEDENEK SEYDL (Czechoslovakia). *ABC* 1970, *Rebus* 1971.

GEORGE SIBIANU (Romania). *Negro Island, The Magic Footprint* 1957, *Telephone* 1958, *Bull and Calf* 1968, *Human Folly* 1969, *The Champ* 1971.

LAURENTIN SIRBU (Romania). *Let's Go to the Circus* 1967, *The Adventure* 1968, *The Kite, The Lark* 1969.

PHILIP STAPP (U.S.A.). *Boundary Lines, Picture In Your Mind, Transatlantic, To Your Health* 1956, *From Generation to Generation, Water, The Gift, Homage to François Couperin* 1964.

LADISLAS STAREVITCH (France) (puppets). *Dans les griffes de l'araignée, L'Epouvantail* 1921, *Le Mariage de Babylas, La petite Chanteuse des rues* 1922, *La Voix du rossignol* 1923, *La Reine des papillons* 1924, *Le Sang du dragon* 1925, *La Cigale et le fourmi* 1927, *La Petite parade* 1928, *Le Roman de Renart* 1938, *Zonzabelle in Paris, Flower of the Fern, Comme chien et chat* 1965 (unfinished).

BERYL STEVENS (England). *Put Una Money for There* 1956, *Man of No Account, The Banking Game, The Bargain, The Curious History of Money* 1969, *Refining* 1970, *The Square Deal* (Dir. Douglas Jensen) 1971.

PAT SULLIVAN (U.S.A.). Many Felix titles from 1925 including *Felix the Cat on the Farm, Felix the Cat Trips through Toyland* 1925, *Felix the Cat Braves the Briny* 1926, *Felix the Cat Switches Witches* 1927, *Felix the Cat in Sure-Locked Homes, Felix the Cat in Ohm Sweet Ohm* 1928.

V. SUTIEV (Russia). *Cross Roads* 1931, *How the Rhino Got His Skin* 1938.

JAN SVANKMAJER (Czechoslovakia). *Messrs Schwarzwalde and Edgar's Last Trick* 1967, *Bach's Fantasy in B Minor, Coffin Factory, Historia Naturae.*

DANIEL SZCZECHURA (Poland). *Stadium* 1957, *Conflict* 1960, *Machine* 1961, *The Letter* 1962, *First Second Third* 1963, *The Seat* 1963, *Diagram* 1966, *Hobby* 1970.

PAUL TERRY (U.S.A.). *Aesop's Fables* in Twenties, *Mighty Mouse* from 1944, *Heckle and Jeckle* from 1946, *Little Roquefort* from 1951 (Mannie Davis, Eddie Donnelly, Connie Rasinski and Dave Tendlar are the principal directors at Terrytoons).

OSAMU TEZUKA (Japan). *Marine Boy, Astro Boy* (TV Series), *13 Labours of Hercules* (feature) 1961, *Thousand and One Nights* (feature, dir. Eiichi Yamamoto) 1969.

JIRI TRNKA (Czechoslovakia). Cartoons: *Grandpa Planted a Beet* 1945, *The Gift, The Devil on Springs, The Animals and the Brigands* 1946, *The Golden Fish, The Happy Circus* 1951, *How Grandpa Changed till Nothing was Left (Jak starecek menil az vymenil)* 1952, *The Two Frosts* 1954. Puppet films: *The Czech Year* 1947, *The Emperor's Nightingale* 1948, *The Song of the Prairie, The Story of the Double-Bass* 1949, *Bayaya* 1950, *The Devil's Mill* 1951, *Old Czech Legends* 1953, *A Drop Too Much, The Good Soldier Schweik* 1954, *Circus Hurvinek* 1955, *A Midsummer Night's Dream* 1959, *Passion* 1962, *Cybernetic Grandma* 1963, *Archangel Gabriel and Mother Goose, The Hand* 1965.

SADAO TSUKIOKA (Japan). *Spotlight, A Man, Peace of Resistance.*

HERMINA TYRLOVA (Czechoslovakia). *Revolt of the Toys* 1947, *Berceuse* 1948, *Nine Chicks* 1952, *Goldilocks, Dragon Story* 1956, *The Knot* 1958, *Romeo and Juliet* 1958, *The Strange Letter* 1960, *Snowman* 1966.

ALBERT UDERZO (See RENE GOSCINNY)

IVO URBANIC (Yugoslavia). *The Order of the Cactus* (Inspector Mask) *Trapped by a Skeleton, Dance on the Roof, Adam and Eve, The White Mouse, The Rivals, Love in the Cinema, Back to the Twist.*

WOLFGANG URCHS (West Germany). *The Garden Gnomes, The Weed* 1962, *The Pistol* 1963, *Contrast* 1964, *Machine.*

STAN VANDERBEEK (U.S.A.). *Wheeeels, Science Friction* 1960, *Breathdeath, Patterns for the Walls of the World, Man and His World* 1967.

JACQUES VAUSSEUR (France). *Atome et Fission Nucléaire* 1957, *Le Cadeau* 1961, *Concours général* 1963, *La Porte* 1964, *L'Oiseau* 1965.

DUSAN VUKOTIC (Yugoslavia). *Kico* 1951, *The Playful Robot* 1956, *Cowboy Jimmy, Abracadabra* 1957, *Great Fear* 1958, *Concerto for Sub-Machine Gun, Cow on the Moon, My Tail's My Ticket* 1959, *Piccolo* 1960, *Ersatz* 1961, *Play* 1962, *A Stain on his Conscience* 1969, *Opera Cordis* 1970, *Ars Gratia Artis* 1971.

WATRIN (See CHAMPEAUX)

JOHN AND JAMES WHITNEY (U.S.A.). *Exercises, Yantra* 1960, *Catalogue* 1961, *Lapis* 1966, *Permutations* 1967.

RICHARD WILLIAMS (England). *The Little Island* 1958, *Story of the Motor-Car Engine* 1958, *A Lecture on Man* 1962, *Love Me, Love*

Me, Love Me 1962, *A Christmas Carol* 1971. Films in production: *I. Vor Pittfalks, Circus Clowns, Mulla Nasrudin, Diary of a Madman*. Many publicity films including: *Guinness at the Albert Hall*.

PINO ZAC (Italy). *A Man in Grey* 1960, *Man, Superman, Poor Man* 1961, *Lo Iradiddio, Registered for Life* 1963, *Postage Stamp* 1965.

ANTE ZANINOVIC (Yugoslavia). *Trumpet* 1963, *The Wall* 1965, *Crazy Story* 1966, *Result, A Pointless Story* 1967, *Corks and Holes, Feet* 1968, *Happiness for Two* 1970.

KAREL ZEMAN (Czechoslovakia). *Christmas Dream* (Puppets), *The Horseshoe* 1946,·*Prokouk the Bureaucrat, Prokouk the Brigand, Prokouk the Cineast* (All Puppets) 1947, *Inspiration* 1949, *King Lavra* (Puppets) 1951, *The Treasure of Bird Island* (Puppets and cartoon) 1952, *Prehistoric Journey* 1953, *The Invention of Destruction* 1957, *Mr. Prokouk Detective* 1958, *Baron Munchhausen* 1959, *The Jester's Tale* 1964.

JERZY ZITZMAN (Poland). *Bulandra and the Devil* 1959, *Mister Trumpet* 1960, *A General and a Fly* 1961, *Don Juan* 1963, *The Coffee Grinder* 1963, *New Year's Eve* 1964.

16. Index

This contains most of the film-makers mentioned in the book, but only those film titles which are considered representative, important, or are discussed in the text. Subjects listed are restricted to key topics. Generally the index complements the lay out of chapters (chronological and geographical) and the filmographies.